CLOSE ENCOUNTERS

A *Better* Explanation

Involving Trauma, Terror, and Tragedy

by

Clifford Wilson, Ph.D.

Author of *Crash Go the Chariots*,
The Passover Plot — Exposed!,
and *UFO's and Their Mission Impossible*, et al

and

John Weldon

Author of *UFO's: What On Earth Is Happening?*,
The Transcendental Explosion,
and *Is There Life After Death?*

MASTER BOOKS
A Division of CLP
San Diego, California

Foreword

Now, more than ever before in history, we are in the midst of religious warfare. Although it comes in various disguises in order to conceal the fact of war, a wide variety of cults and all forms of humanism are at war with Biblical faith. We cannot begin to understand the world of our time apart from this fact of religious warfare.

As a result, very often what are seeming opposites must be recognized as members of the same family, however much in dispute.

This is clearly true of the usual pros and cons on the subject of UFO's. The usual critique of the subject is from the standpoint of "pure science." Only those things which conform to the naturalistic presuppositions of modern scientists are held to be facts. All such persons approach any and every subject with a naturalistic faith which determines in advance what can and what cannot be a fact. From such a perspective, it is a foregone conclusion that UFO's are hallucinations, nonsense, and undeserving of any intelligent consideration. Such a perspective is the mark of "scientific" humanism. The world is what man declares it to be, not what God ordains or declares.

On the other hand, we have another brand of humanism which is highly favorable to and pleased with any and every report on UFO's. It is for them "proof" that the universe is other than God declares it to be, that life has evolved universally, and that man is able to conquer time and space — and possibly disease and death. The motivation of all such is a romantic humanism and hence a receptivity to any and all reports which confirm that faith and negate Christianity.

The debate on UFO's has been largely confined to these two camps. The "scientific" humanists are unhappy with the nature of the evidences at hand; they do not conform to their presuppositions with regard to valid evidences. The romantic humanists are delighted with every report and regard each as a new kind of revelation, and they see UFO's as the prelude to some major advance in human life.

In this study, Weldon and Wilson approach the subject from a radically different presupposition, from the premise of Biblical faith. We can differ at points with their theological premises; I myself do not share their premillennial eschatology, and hence have very different reactions at points. However, the important point is this. From a Christian perspective, Weldon and Wilson analyze the data as no one else has, and their work constitutes a major approach to the subject — and a compelling one.

The occult orientation of much of the UFO data is carefully analyzed, and in detail. The contradictory nature of many of the sightings, their ability to appear and disappear on a radar screen, and much, much more, is fully discussed and assessed. The information gained from UFO contacts is treated with patience and skill. The authors conclude that the UFO phenomena are real; they are demonic, and they are totally anti-Christian.

It can be added that in every crisis in civilization marking the end of an era and the rise of another, such occultist phenomena have proliferated. In each case, they have been in conformity to the prevailing myths and expectations. Before the fall of Rome, at the end of the medieval era, and again in these final days of the modern age, we see a remarkable rise of occultist phenomena, which finds a responsive chord in the soul of modern man. In each era, the occult phenomena spoke to the longings of apostate man and his dreams of humanistic fulfillment and fantasy, and thus gained a wide and powerful following. In our so-called "space age," the occult phenomena speaks in terms of space age myths and hopes. Its product, however, is not a fulfillment of these hopes but a radical disintegration of those who look to the occult phenomena. Man, having been created in the image of God, cannot long function when he denies his Creator. The UFO mythology is a radical denial of God and of Scripture. We are given an alien view of man and the universe, and we find also that those who give themselves to this view and to the occult manifestations are marked by a disintegration of mind and even of body. Clearly, UFO's are not a harmless concern nor merely an amusing case of superstition.

For these reasons, this study is important. The wise man's life is marked by hedges and fences. He is not open to every absurdity, folly, and insanity that comes along. Weldon and Wilson have done some careful fence-building in a contemporary area of growing concern. Their purpose is to help define the boundaries of godly thought and exploration. We can differ with their eschatology, but we cannot underestimate the conscientious research nor the timeliness of their work.

Dr. Rousas John Rushdoony
Vallecito, California

Contents

*"The only thing left for UFO's to do is make overt
contact. This is the computer projection."*
Aerospace Engineer Bill Spaulding
New West, *Nov. 7, 1977, p. 24*

*"Generally speaking, I find it possible to hope that
we are entering a new era in which interventions
will be replaced by contacts: Then we will be part of
a galactic community."*
French Scientist Jacques Bergier
Extraterrestrial Visitations From Prehistoric
Times to the Present, *p. 170*

*"If we really were visited centuries ago, we may be
on the threshold of a 'second coming' of intelligent
beings from outer space."*
Dr. Vyacheslov Zaitzev
Addressing a Russian parapsychology meeting.
Psychic Discoveries Behind the Iron Curtain,
p. 99

*"In view of the recent increase in UFO landings,
sightings, and the new trend toward UFO abductions, we seem to be precariously near the realm of
forced communication with our cosmic visitors."*
Alan Landsburg
In Search of Extraterrestrials, *p. 97*

Preface

In this book we do not set out to "prove" the reality of the UFO (Unidentified Flying Object) phenomenon: that has already been established by various authors. Our own books, *UFO's and Their Mission Impossible* and *UFO's: What On Earth is Happening?* are two that could be mentioned (and obviously we do) as giving sufficient evidence for the unbiased reader to be satisfied that the UFO phenomena must be accepted as real.

We now take the subject further: in a sense we go on where we left off. Perhaps strangely, neither of us knew of the other at the time each of us wrote a "UFO book," but our conclusions were remarkably close. That is part of the reason for our coming together. John suggested a coauthored book, and Clifford already had a book on a similar subject matter in mind, so the research was intensified, and this book resulted.

If you are not yet convinced by the evidence, read the earlier two books. Thousands of others have done so and have been surprised at the extent to which the arguments make sense.

FACING CONFUSION
AND PARADOXES

Now we go on from there — analyzing the writings of leading UFO researchers, bringing together their coinciding views, as well as the confusions and paradoxes to which they point, and we come up with answers that are so obvious that on logical grounds they cannot be rejected.

Yet they will be rejected by most researchers, because the truth can be uncomfortable and can demand a course of action that is unexpected. It is far easier to bury one's head in the sand and hope the trouble will go away. Unfortunately it won't. For those who don't like the taste of sand anyway, this book is written. It might even change their lives.

Here and there you might notice a point of overlap in the chapters that follow. This is because some sections are basically by one author and some by the other. Usually we have eliminated the "crossovers," but occasionally that would have spoiled the "flow" and so at those places the material has been retained.

WHAT ARE "CLOSE ENCOUNTERS OF THE THIRD KIND"?

A brief explanation of some terms used in this book may be helpful to the reader. The three close encounter categories involve an encounter with a UFO in close proximity to the observer. The CE-I involves a close encounter with a UFO at a given distance. CE-II occurs when there is a UFO-induced physical impact on the environment. CE-III involves UFO occupants. The term "percipient" refers to the UFO observer, or the one involved in the UFO experience. A UFO "flap" is the occurrence of a large number of UFO sightings or events during a period of time. A UFO "contactee" is a person who claims to be in personal contact with UFO occupants on a continuing basis usually by telepathy. A UFO "abduction experience" is where a person claims he was involuntarily taken on board a UFO.

In an analysis of 1,276 close encounter events, Drs. Hynek and Vallee calculate that 60% involved landings, and 32% had occupants.[1] In that same volume, Dr. Hynek estimates that there are 100 sightings a night somewhere around the world.[2]

In this book we are dealing with those cases in the third category — those involving occupants (CE-III).* They include

---

* See footnote next page.

cases where the UFO and its occupants temporarily inhabit 3-dimensional space, and others of an apparitional type. These latter are *visibly* present (temporarily) in physical space, but are not necessarily "physically" present in space. Both categories are from the same source and share many of the same characteristics. It is not always possible to be dogmatic as to

---

Note: Dr. Hynek, who formulated the close encounter categories, largely rejects "contactee" phenomena. In defining close encounters of the third type, he states: ". . . in these cases the presence of 'occupants' in or about the UFO is reported. Here a sharp distinction must be made between (these) cases . . . and the so-called contactee cases." *(The UFO Experience,* p. 33.) Most researchers are in agreement but we feel this distinction is inadequate for reasons discussed in the appendix and elsewhere. To be sure, there are some differences between contactees and close encounters of the third kind. In contactee cases, there is usually long-term contact with the entities through occult methods. In close encounters of the third type, the experience is usually not sought out, is of short duration, and is not repeated. However, it may involve an abduction onboard the UFO. As we will show, the evidence points to an essential unity among all UFO categories — close encounters, abductions, and contactees. They cannot be arbitrarily divided into genuine and false (or signal and noise) simply because in one category the phenomenon is more fantastic and harder to believe than the other. Close encounters of the third type, including abductions, are contact cases and at times they even progress to contactee stature. Hence our use of the term contactee may at times involve more than the above limited definition.

which is which, for there is imitation by one of the other's characteristics. This sounds fantastic, but the evidence is convincing.

The UFO entities materialize and dematerialize in similar fashion to the UFO's themselves. In their messages they themselves claim to explain the process.

Riley Crabb, Director of the Borderland Sciences Research Associates writes:

> We are told time and again in the messages received that they [the extraterrestrials (ET's)] convert to pure energy . . . at the point of origin and reconvert into three dimensional structures again at their destination, in this instance our planet . . . using our physical matter for as long as they want to stay materialized here.[3]

They can also involve apparitions, and, so far as the witness is concerned, these are as real as though they were physical phenomena. The person who sees an apparition does not know it is such: his "close encounter of the third kind" is indistinguishable from the other two categories — those where either a being has assumed physical form, or when the experience itself was implanted in his mind.

In this book we do not always separate the three, for the end result is the same. It is this contact experience which is at the heart of the UFO mystery, and researchers are increasingly realizing this. As we have said, there is no longer any need to "prove" UFO's. For the unbiased, that has been done. The real question now is, "What is the purpose behind the contact?" To answer that question this book has been written.

Note: The authors do not vouch for the accuracy of every UFO incident reported herein. They have simply recorded information and events as claimed by the participants.

Footnotes: Preface

1. *The Edge of Reality*, p. 22.
2. Ibid., p. 254. Based on figures given by various researchers, several million living people have had "close encounters."
3. *Flying Saucers and the Coming Space Probe* n.d. p. 12.

Chapter 1
WHAT ARE UFO'S?

They stall engines and black-out power stations. They come in many shapes and sizes — little saucer-shaped vehicles, large cigar-shaped "mother-ships," and everything in between. They give messages that at times are remarkably accurate, while at other times their prophecies are patently false.

They fly unmolested over Russian airfields, and they have even buzzed the White House. They maneuver at right angles, reverse instantaneously while traveling at thousands of miles an hour, and disappear just as mysteriously as they appeared. Some have occupants, and some have none. They recognize no territory as "out of bounds," for the sighting reports come from Brazil and China, America and Australia, England and Russia. They are busy in jungle and city, over rivers and

---

Note to reader: A definition of unfamiliar terms has been provided in the Preface, i.e. CE-I, CE-II, and CE-III.

mountains. They "land" on farms and on public highways; their occupants appear to make repairs to their vehicles and converse with the local residents. They speak English and Spanish equally fluently, but also transmit their messages by telepathy, without opening their mouths.

NO MOUTHS . . .
BUT THEY COMMUNICATE

In fact, sometimes they *have* no mouths, no ears, no legs, no hands — just misshapen heads and bodies. At times they smell like rotten-egg gas; at other times they are the smartest dressed beings one could imagine.

What *are* these things? Are they real, or projections of the mind, or some primal force not yet understood? The answers are now clear, but the solution brings with it a frightening realization.

Flying Saucer Review Volume 15, No. 4, dated July-August 1969, has an article by Charles Bowen headed "UFO's and Psychic Phenomena." In it he gives some startling comments, following a lecture by British Air Marshall Sir Victor Goddard on May 3, 1969, at Caxton Hall, Westminster, England. In his retirement Sir Victor has developed a long-standing interest in psychic phenomena and extrasensory perception. So far as this book is concerned, the interesting point is that in all seriousness the Air Marshall was associating UFO's with psychic phenomena, and Charles Bowen also develops that theme. Their arguments are typical of many put forward in recent times. Bowen discusses some of the problems, such as the fact that many UFO's have been found to be solid and metallic sounding when struck, with bullets richocheting off their surface. Despite that, according to Bowen, "I would not be greatly surprised if one day it were demonstrated that certain types of psychic phenomena and certain types of UFO phenomena are one and the same thing, and that they are triggered off by a common cause."[1]

UFO'S IN ALL SHAPES AND SIZES

In this book we develop that theme. Bowen acknowledges that there is little evidence to support the view that UFO's could be interplanetary spaceships, though he suggests it is a possibility. He recognizes other arguments, such as that the UFO's are reflections from another unseen parallel world, or from a world that exists across from our world. According to this view they would be able to pass through gates or windows where the time streams of their civilization and ours impinged momentarily. However, Bowen admits that he has an uneasy feeling that much of what we hear about UFO's is hallucinatory in character.

Other researchers have the same sort of problem, and we shall especially consider the arguments of John A. Keel, a highly respected and competent investigator. He is a prolific writer in the areas of UFO research, and Bowen is not alone in such an assessment. In the same issue of *Flying Saucer Review* referred to above, John Keel has an article entitled, "The Principle of Transmogrification." He writes that, contrary to public opinion, there are many different shapes and sizes of UFO's, and that in 434 "unknown" cases "there was no single basic uniformity in all the reports." Therefore either every object was individually constructed and utilized only once, or *"none of the objects really existed at all."*[2] He makes the point that if by superior technology the occupants of some distant planet had manufactured a complex flying machine, they would not send it out for just one maneuver over a farmhouse in Georgia. It would be used many times in many places, and eventually there would be identical photographs of the same object. Instead of that, there are almost as many different descriptions as there are witnesses to the sightings. Even though the descriptions agreed as to time, a group of people 20 miles away from the first group to see the UFO would be describing a seemingly different object. This would be true even when each group agreed within the one geographic location as to what they saw.

UFO RESEARCHERS ARE MYSTIFIED

Clearly, UFO researchers are mystified, and that is true in various other ways beside the differing appearances of these strange phenomena. We have also pointed out that sometimes bullets richochet off them, and this means they are apparently solid. Yet the above evidence suggests they are psychic phenomena, and therefore NOT solid. They are solid . . . and they are not solid. Where does the truth lie?

Another highly respected UFO researcher is Dr. Allen Hynek. His book, *The UFO Experience,* is a best-seller among the UFO writings. He was the original astronomer associated with the United States' *Project Blue Book,* the official investigation of UFO's, sponsored by the United States Air Force. He makes no secret of his original skepticism about UFO's. He openly scoffed at the whole phenomena, considering witnesses as unreliable and their stories to be regarded only as huge jokes or deliberate hoaxes. However, as time went by Hynek realized there was a nucleus he could not explain to his own satisfaction. As a man of integrity he acknowledged this, and he has become a highly-respected writer for the UFO cause. As a top scientist his opinions and conclusions have necessarily carried considerable weight.

Dr. Hynek acknowledges the possibility that the explanation for UFO's is in the realm of paranormal phenomena, but then says, "Should those psychic claims be true, it opens up another can of worms."[3] He acknowledges that the problem then essentially would be solved, and this would explain why they can be dematerialized and violate numerous physical laws.

He then tells us, "But that's dangerous territory to tread." When Dr. Jacques Vallee asked Dr. Hynek to elaborate he commented, "Psychic projections aren't picked up on radars, that I know of." He went on to make the point that sometimes UFO's are picked up on radar and that at other times they are not.

VIOLATIONS OF LAWS OF PHYSICS?

Dr. Hynek referred to the apparent violation of laws of physics, which could be explained by the fact that if UFO's were psychic projections they probably did not have mass. In the discussion that followed between the authors, Dr. Hynek made the point that poltergeists ("noisy ghosts") do not have physical reality but can move physical objects.

Thus there is a phenomenon with physical effects, but having the attributes of the psychic world. Dr. Hynek draws the parallel to light, which sometimes is like a wave and at other times like a particle: sometimes light behaves like a bullet, but in other experiments like a wave, and in these latter the particle model does not explain its activities. According to Dr. Hynek, UFO's have a similar duality.[4]

This parallel to light can be taken further, for as light offers the opposing concepts of both a wave and a particle, so UFO's have both psychic and physical aspects. This can be well illustrated by the relationship of UFO's to electricity in that they both often demonstrate that they are psychical and non-physical, but in other cases they demonstrate equally convincingly that they are physical and, therefore, non-psychical. The fact is, "Phantom objects have been tracked electronically with radar and visually with theodolites* traveling at speeds far exceeding the speed of sound within the atmosphere, without producing sonic booms."[5]

This absence of a sonic boom is a strong pointer to the thorough psychical nature of

---

*A surveying device measuring horizontal and vertical angles.

UFO's. Because they are not solid constructions in the fullest sense, they do not displace air mass as they move at their fantastic speeds through the atmosphere. The tracking reports and visual sightings suggest they are physical: conversely, the absence of a sonic boom points to the psychic nature of the phenomenon. These are apparently violations of the laws of physics: or should we say that they are variations, not violations, of those laws? Is there a variable not taken into account by scientists with a physics bias?

We have seen some of the evidence pointing to the psychic nature of the phenomena, but there is also considerable evidence pointing to the physical nature. We shall illustrate that by referring to the way UFO's affect electrical installations, motor car engines, and even airplanes.

WHY ARE UFO'S INTERESTED IN ELECTRICAL SYSTEMS?

In one of a series of articles entitled "UFO's and the Fourth Dimension,"[6] Luis Schonherr comments on the often-discussed fact that UFO's seem to be interested mainly in motor vehicles that have electrical ignition systems. The purpose for such interference by UFO's is not clear, according to Schonherr. Some researchers believe that UFO's might be indicating that they want to stop traffic on some future occasion, but if this is so they have demonstrated their capabilities very often, and so they have given opportunities for counter-measures to be developed. Schonherr suggests that UFO's are really interested in another activity—perhaps the monitoring of the memories of people. That, once again, illustrates the uncertainty in the minds of researchers. What *is* the purpose of these "electrical" interventions? What danger is there to vehicles or to people? Are they electrical or is there some other force to be contended with?

There is clearly a mind behind the incidents. At times there is even something approaching a spirit of mischief. Sometimes the UFO entities become associated with apparently normal vehicles, and as such they are pursued and the registration numbers of the vehicles are taken. However, when checked, the numbers are found to be non-existent. At other times, the beings drive back to the UFO in another vehicle, such as a 1955 Buick, "which looked and even smelled like new."[7] In a footnote to that article John Keel makes the statement, "Old cars that look like new keep turning up in my investigations."[8]

Much more could be written about UFO's and electricity, including the report of an investigation by the Ford Motor Company. They carried out a series of tests to determine what magnetism would be needed to stall a motor car. They found that a field of 20,000 gauss was needed. The investigators also reported that such an intense field would have quite definite effects on the vehicles involved, such as motor cars; they "would bend and damage many of the delicate parts."[9] However, invariably we find in UFO literature that when cars have been affected, immediately after the incident they are driven quite normally. This is true of clocks, watches, radios, etc. Once the UFO has departed, these things resume their normal operations. All this is further thought-provoking evidence which leads to the conclusion that these are not true electromagnetic effects in the sense that we humans know them. The UFO phenomenon must be regarded as paraphysical.

INCIDENTS WITH AIRCRAFT

This is also true with regard to the effects on airplanes. David Brobeck, Junior, has an interesting article about the possibility of liability if there was an air crash caused by a UFO.[10] His article is relevant in a number of ways, but at this point we are interested because he has a summary of some of the properly recorded incidents where aircraft have been associated with the approach of UFO's. He tells of one case on July 8, 1947, when an Air Force pilot was flying a P-51 near Los Angeles, when he was approached by a flat round object which reflected the sunlight as it passed above his fighter.

On the 5th of October, 1959, a California Central Airlines plane saw a wing-shaped UFO without any fuselage, approaching them head-on. Captain Cecil Hardan and his first officer, Jack Conroy, watched as the object suddenly dipped, then passed below their plane. They saw bands of blue light across its width.

There have also been reports of near misses in other countries, beside the United States, one taking place over Essex, England, on October 4, 1954. A Royal Air Force pilot of the 604th Fighter Squadron, F/Lt. J.R. Saladan, was in his meteor jet when he had a near collision with a metallic object of tremendous size, shaped like two saucers pressed together. At the last possible moment it turned on one side and swooped past the fighter plane at tremendous speed.

On the 19th of October, 1953, an American Airlines DC-6 was 15 minutes out of Philadelphia on its way to Washington, D.C. when it encountered a shining object that moved in and out of the thin clouds ahead. The copilot called it to the attention of the pilot, Captain J.L. Kidd. The captain cut back his air speed and switched on his landing lights as a warning to the object that the object itself had no lights. The UFO approached him at high speed, and all he could do was jam the wheel forward, as he put the plane into a steep downward arc. Those passengers in the plane who did not have their seat belts fastened were thrown up and down as the plane leveled off. The National Airport informed the pilot there were no other planes in the area. Many of the passengers were taken to the hospital by ambulance, but fortunately, first aid was all that was required. The near miss was reported in the *Washington Post*. (There is even one factual case where a UFO was reported as actually landing on the wing of a commercial jetliner.)*

The impact on electrical apparatus has been reported from many places. One report comes from Buenos Aires.[11] It tells of radios, clocks, and other domestic electrical equipment being stopped and needles of compasses reversed. It also tells of a strange smell associated with the passage of a UFO in the vicinity. The report tells that the powerful odor was also associated with an unidentified flying object about the same period (May-June, 1968) in the vicinity of El Choro in Bolivia. We discuss this odor in our chapter dealing with another strange topic, "monsters."

---

*Related to the authors by a personal friend of the pilot.

POWER INSTALLATIONS IMMOBILIZED

According to some reports, even power installations have been immobilized at time of UFO sightings. In a four-state power failure on June 5, 1967, in the northeast of the United States, the personnel of the Kittatinny Power Plant in northern New Jersey claimed that their equipment did not actually shut down but simply stopped as if it had been frozen.[12] It is relevant to state that this particular power plant was in no way physically connected with other power plants that failed at the same time in other states of the U.S., but there were almost daily UFO sightings in the Kittatinny Mountains during that period of time.

There have been similar inexplicable failures associated with telephone installations. Throughout 1967 there were over 1,000 unexplained telephone failures in the United States, and they often involved whole counties. Keel[13] tells of interviews with telephone company personnel who were baffled because, as they put it, "The wires simply did not seem to conduct the current." There are many other peculiar UFO incidents associated with telephones, including strange messages, imitations of people's voices, and even manipulations of telephone accounting. Once again, researchers often express their confusion.

Are these things directed against the installations themselves, or against the persons concerned? That again highlights the paradox: psychical or physical?

That sort of paradox is carried over to the way camera batteries are affected. There have been many similar incidents where some sort of influence disturbed the function of electrically operated objects.[14] In the fall of 1967 Dan Drason, a New York television producer, tried to signal an unidentified flying object near Point Pleasant in West Virginia. His powerful flashlight had brand new batteries, but the flashlight went out immediately and would not operate again until the UFO had passed out of sight. Attempts to cause a similar flashlight to fail because of the influence of a powerful magnetic field were unsuccessful.

In the spring of 1967, with other witnesses, Keel attempted to photograph a UFO in West Virginia. He was using a battery-operated motion picture camera, but the camera would not work. The UFO was in view long enough for him to change his batteries, but still the camera would not work. Once again, as soon as the UFO had passed out of sight the camera functioned perfectly.

THE "BELL WITCH"

There are many such incidents recorded

in the literature of UFO research. Yet the apparently electrical effects are baffling, for at times the same effects are produced in an entirely different way. An illustration of that is related to a sinister influence that was present on the farm of John Bell in Robertson County, Tennessee. Flying lights, a voice from an apparently invisible source carrying on dialogues with visitors, and other strange activities were associated with the celebrated "Bell Witch."[15]

General Andrew Jackson was one who visited the Bell homestead at the time of this supposed haunting, and as his horse-drawn wagon approached the homestead the wheels froze into stillness. Though the horses strained, they could not budge these wheels. There was no apparent reason for the problem; the wheels simply would not go around. General Jackson himself dismounted and examined the wheels, but he could find no reason for the problem. He stood there, scratching his head in bewilderment, and then a sharp, metallic voice told him from the nearby bushes, "All right General, let the wagon move." Everybody was amazed to find that the wheels immediately began to turn again.

No electrical apparatus was involved, but the effect was very similar to what some ufologists (one with a professional interest in UFO's) refer to as the EM (electromagnetic) effect, along the lines of the above illustrations.

That "magnetic effect" is sometimes regarded as the explanation for burns, running sores, and even cancer that follow contact with a UFO. We shall see that though the effect is similar, the actual cause is different from magnetism as it is usually known to physicists.

In passing, it is relevant to note certain similarities to spiritists' phenomena. Before the spirit associated with the Bell homestead disappeared entirely, it is supposed to have declared in one of its many conversations, "I am a spirit from everywhere, heaven, hell, the earth; I am in the air, in houses, at any place at any time, have been created for millions of years; that is all I will tell you."[16] Such messages are often associated with the seance room, as well as with UFO's.

STRANGE UTILIZATIONS OF ENERGY

So also are some of the strange utilizations of energy. In the seance room ectoplasm is the explanation for materialization of beings in expected shapes and sometimes in shapes that are totally unexpected. A medium is available; their body and its physiological functions are made available for the being who possesses them. They go into a trance, and ectoplasm from their body is used as a form materializes: it is as though the medium is paralyzed.

UFO sightings are often accompanied by "paralysis" of electrical power. Keel suggests that possibly the same UFO power is utilized with humans who are paralyzed: "Perhaps the same device or technique is used on both animate and inanimate objects."[17] He conjectures that General Jackson's wheels might have been "frozen" in the same way that the Kittatinny generators were brought to a sudden halt — that a basic alteration of physical properties involved paralysis in both instances. He further conjectures that earthly matter is composed of energies from one end of the electromagnetic spectrum, and that perhaps there are beings at the other end of the spectrum that might have power to tamper with and even alter the physical properties of terrestrial substances.

> If the matter of our world can be manipulated freely by such entities, then we would have an explanation for many of the manifestations which have always been classified as supernatural. Such entities might conceivably be able to walk through the walls . . . and anyone seeing them doing so would automatically regard them as "ghosts."[18]

He suggests that because many compasses and magnetic instruments have reacted to the presence of UFO's, the utilization of the electromagnetic field has been widely accepted as an answer, but that, in fact, this might simply be an effect, not a cause. Perhaps the occupants of UFO's are somehow taking advantage of areas of magnetic deviation in some way not yet understood.

Keel's argument makes a lot of sense. He reminds us that these UFO's are able to move at fantastically high speeds through our atmosphere without displacing the air, and so they are not producing sonic booms. Some physical power, beyond that employed by physical objects, is being utilized. He argues that the objects are possibly composed in such a way that they can pass between the molecules of air, just as the entities themselves seem to pass through solid walls in many cases. Perhaps the objects take advantage of magnetic currents and deviations and ride those currents as a glider can ride in the updrafts of air that surround various hills.

"A BASIC PARALYSIS OF ELECTRONS"

He suggests that it is not simply the utilization of electromagnetic power, but that, in fact, "We seem to be dealing with a basic paralysis of electrons. It may even go deeper and involve a temporary alteration in the basic properties of matter."[19] As "burnouts" are not being reported, it does not seem that a force field of magnetic induction is being utilized, for that would overload the circuits and burn out the equipment.

Charles Bowen, in an article entitled "Thinking Aloud,"[20] summarizes some of the background to the UFO phenomenon and suggests the possibility that, "All UFO phenomena, psychic phenomena, poltergeists and ghosts, and even the legends of fairies and other elementals which have caused some of us to pause . . . are caused by the same thing . . . radiation."[21] He goes on to say that Maxwell Cade, a top specialist in radiation and medicine, has indicated that this could be done by means we are beginning to understand, and that we ourselves are capable of doing this. He then suggests the possibility that ghosts, bumps in the night, psychic healing, and clairvoyant seeing into the future will be explained in this way; and that possibly these intrusions could even take place while we humans are sleeping.[22]

Clearly, many researchers are pointing to a paradox. The beings appear to utilize electricity and physical properties, yet are not bound by physical laws. Whatever the cause, humans are involved. In the reports we constantly find mention of paralysis, dazzling lights which cause headaches and nausea, a loss of time which cannot be accounted for, various temporary physical effects, and longer nervous effects on those who have been contacted. This is especially frightening when young children are involved. There are a surprising number of UFO sightings (and even landings) in the areas of schools, and sometimes when a vehicle is stalled we read that a child in the back seat was paralyzed until the UFO disappeared.

There are many accounts of a human — often a child — being paralyzed while a UFO is present, but there are also accounts which suggest the possibility of other forms of "borrowed" energy being utilized. They are reported as digging up trees, stealing plants and shrubs, even kidnapping animals. Unless the UFO phenomenon is what we claim it to be in this book, these happenings make no sense. In fact, they are unbelievable; they are the reports of crackpots who cannot be taken seriously. If that is so, it is strange that there are so many similar stories, from highly credible witnesses. These UFO beings give the impression that they need an energy form associated with earth, and so they tap electrical power, paralyze a child, steal a dog, dig up a tree, or simply use a willing contactee as a medium.

ENTITIES REQUIRE A SOURCE OF ENERGY

John Keel discusses all this, and

suggests that:

> In order to materialize and take on definite form, those entities seem to require a source of energy; a fire or a living thing, a plant, a tree, a human medium (or contactee). Our sciences have not reached a point where they can offer us any kind of working hypothesis for this process. But we can speculate that these beings need living energy which they can restructure into a physical form. Perhaps that is why dogs and animals tend to vanish in flap areas. Perhaps the living cells of those animals are somehow used by the ultraterrestrials to create forms which we can see and sense with our limited perceptions. Perhaps human and animal blood is also essential for this purpose.[23]

Keel further elaborates this need for energy, and says that for these things to enter into a solid state, "They need some atoms from our world — parts of an airplane, an auto, or blood and matter from an animal or human being. Or, in some cases, they need to drain off energy from the human percipients, or from power lines and automobile engines."[24]

This idea of some strange mystic force is discussed in various books dealing with psychic phenomena and the occult. Idries

Shah[25] refers to "certain well-documented so-called miracles [which] are accounted for by the existence of an undiscovered force (akasa), which seems to have some connection with magnetism."

There is that "magnetism" again, and the similarities between the occult, spiritism, and the UFO phenomena are obvious. All this fits the concept of a superbeing, the Biblical Satan who has hordes of demon beings ready to obey him, and even to be manipulated like puppets. Keel suggests that if these UFO beings can manipulate energies which compose atomic structure, it is also possible that they can manipulate time and space, for these are measurements conceived by man within his own environmental frame of reference and are not absolutes.[26] We are suggesting that the possibilities of manipulations, at least to a limited degree, are very real. In fact they are to be expected. They are part of the pattern of signs and wonders of the "last days" as Satan takes on his prophesied role as an angel of light, seeking to deceive the elect (see Matthew 24:24).

In another article entitled "A New Approach to UFO Witnesses"[27] John Keel states:

> There may be a basic force at work which unites the UFO's with the occult . . . and deep interrelationships. The UFO buffs scoff at

the "occultists" and vice versa. The time has come for us to read all the occult literature and find the links . . . if they exist.

THE DANGER OF "PSYCHIC ATTACKS"

John Keel sees demon possession as somewhat different from the Christian teaching of the New Testament. He recognizes that those who practice witchcraft and black arts are likely to be controlled by the forces they themselves are trying to control, and they are likely to be the subjects of psychic attacks.

When the human mind is channelled in these directions, it literally attracts negative energy from what I call the super spectrum — the spectrum of energies that lies outside the normal electromagnetic spectrum.[28]

In *The Eighth Tower* John Keel talks about demons supposedly being allergic to loud sounds, especially in the ultrasonic range: right through history, high-pitched bells, musical instruments, and other sounds have been used to get rid of dragons and monsters. He points out that dogs, cats, and other animals have hearing far more sensitive than humans, and they are often terrified before a human knows that a UFO is in the vicinity. He goes on:

> Our funny ultraterrestrials are not only sensitive to sound, they seem very sensitive to light. Historically, psychic manifestations take place in complete darkness. If there is a light, the phenomenon somehow puts it out.[29]

He again refers to the fact (which has been noted in many books discussed above) that widespread power failures occur in UFO flap areas, radios and telephones becoming affected, with many other abnormal magnetic effects.

It is clear that our "demonic theory" is not so "way-out" after all. It makes sense of a special use of paraphysical and paranormal concepts as the solution to the UFO phenomena. We are seeking to give logical argument from properly researched evidence, and as we proceed, we shall give further consideration to physiological, theological, and other areas of knowledge.

Footnotes: Chapter One

Consult Bibliography for full information on references.

1. FSR, Vol. 15, No. 4, p. 23, "UFO's and Psychic Phenomena."
2. Ibid., p. 27.
3. *The Edge of Reality,* p. 259.
4. Ibid.
5. Keel, *The Eighth Tower,* p. 107.
6. FSR, Vol. 14, No. 6, p. 12, "UFO's and the Fourth Dimension, Part 4."
7. FSR, Vol. 15, No. 3, p. 9, "The Time Cycle Factor."
8. Ibid., p. 13.
9. Keel, *The Eighth Tower,* p. 123. Citing the Condon Report, *UFO's: Operation Trojan Horse,* p. 63; FSR, Vol. 14, No. 6, p. 16.
10. FSR, Vol. 14, No. 5, p. 17-20, "UFO's and Commercial Air Traffic."
11. FSR, Vol. 14, No. 5, p. 23.
12. FSR, Vol. 14, No. 6, p. 17, "Is the 'EM' effect a myth?".
13. Ibid.
14. Ibid., p. 16-18.
15. Ibid.
16. Ibid.
17. Ibid.
18. Ibid.
19. Ibid.
20. FSR, Vol. 15, No. 6, p. 26-8.
21. Ibid.

22. Ibid.
23. *UFO's: Operation Trojan Horse,* p. 233.
24. Ibid., p. 299.
25. Idries Shah, *Oriental Magic,* p. 6.
26. Note 9, p. 11.
27. FSR, Vol. 14, No. 3, p. 24.
28. Keel, *The Eighth Tower,* p. 26.
29. Ibid., p. 123.

"Also, UFO's are capable of doing things that do not exist in our technology. They can dematerialize, or two can simply merge into one. They can project a beam of light that will just stop dead after some feet. They violate the laws of motion as we know them making our concepts of space and time wrong — which is all right, except if they violate those principles, they could be from anywhere, any time. And mainly, they can exercise a physical and psychic control over objects and humans. We have nothing like that in our technology or physics. All we really know about flying saucers is that they are a tremendous amount of energy stored in a very small volume — the energy of a nuclear power plant, say, contained within something ten feet in diameter."

Dr. Jacques Vallee
Astrophysicist and computer scientist
New West, *Nov. 7, 1977, p. 26*

Chapter 2
FACTS THAT MUST BE FACED

The ostrich buries its head, but that does not alter the reality of the sandstorm. Some people ignore facts and hope they will therefore go away. The circumstances might change, and the facts might therefore become more tolerable, but facts are persistent.

Many people prefer to ignore UFO's — aren't they tied in with little green men from Mars? Or is it Venus? And now that we have learned that no one could live on Venus anyway (it's too hot), why bother about those absurd UFO stories?

It is just not that simple. The sandstorm is all around the ostrich, intensifying its attack against its helpless feathers. Only it is far worse than a sandstorm: the UFO phenomenon goes beyond the physical and brings mental torment of unbelievable intensity. It does not ignore the physical, and there are thoroughly investigated and documented cases of paralysis, insanity, and even death, following a UFO contact.

CONTACTEE PHENOMENA

The UFO occupants are looking for suitable contactees — persons with psychic potential — whose minds can be taken over to give a message (always "special") to the world. They are searching for hands that will be suitable for transmitting their "revelations" by means of automatic writing. They are roaming the world, on the lookout for suitable bodies whose energies they can utilize so that their grotesque manifestations can be exhibited at a time and place of their choosing.

Weird? Grotesque? Absurd? At first sight, yes. As objective investigation proceeds, however, the case is seen differently. This is no fantasy world of distorted, childish imagination. This is a deadly serious phantom world of living evil spirits. They have no permanent bodies, so they seduce humans, men and women. They have no hands, no tongues or vocal chords, so they "possess" those suitable humans. These, then, are what are called "contactee episodes." Many have taken place in association with UFO's, and there will be many more.

The fact of UFO's is established. Our

earlier books, *UFO's: What On Earth is Happening?* and *UFO's and Their Mission Impossible* analyzed the evidence, and other writers have also shown that these mysterious entities must be taken seriously. The credibility of the witnesses, the widespread consistency of the reports, and the nature of the effects on contactees are but three of the evidences that cannot be ignored.

Nor are they ignored. However, they are not reported objectively by many writers, and, in the main, researchers have been very biased, not facing the facts as they would with more usual phenomena. They are biased even though they accept the reality of UFO's: many of them already formed the judgment that UFO's are extraterrestrial in origin on the ground that they could not be anything else.

Such an approach is premature, and even unscholarly. At best, the extraterrestrial concept is a hypothesis, and the mounting evidence is that it is a hypothesis that must be discounted.

ONE THEORY SOLVES ALL PROBLEMS

Only one theory can satisfy all the evidence, and that is the demonic theory. This explains the interest of UFO "occupants" in Christian theology and prophecy, their fantastic numbers, the "nonphysical" nature of the evidence they leave behind, and the many close parallels to various forms of the occult. If all the evidence fitted any other hypothesis, it would be universally accepted that the problem was resolved. However, because demons are unacceptable for most modern men, the demonic theory is usually rejected. "We know *that* is not the explanation," is the attitude. What really is being said, is, "We don't *want* that to be the answer, and so we have rejected it without considering it."

Aimé Michel has said that Guerin's Law is "the only law known to Ufology that has proved resistant to time." Guerin's Law itself states, "In Ufology any law is immediately falsified by subsequent sightings just as soon as it is formulated."[1]

The demonic theory is the only exception to that law. When one understands the true nature of demonic activity, it is seen that at no point does UFO activity disprove the demonic source of that working. For example, they will sometimes give true messages, but only as a means of gaining credibility for a bigger lie that is to follow.

THINK THINGS WE HAVE NEVER DARED THINK BEFORE

As we analyze the writings of top

researchers, we find that in presenting this volume we are doing only what they have urged should be done. Thus, Drs. Hynek and Vallee state:

> The UFO phenomenon calls upon us to extend our imaginations as we never have before, to think things we have never dared think before — in short, to approach boldly the edge of our accepted reality, and by mentally battering at these forbidding boundaries, perhaps open up entirely new vistas.[2]

Those "entirely new vistas" include the Demonic Theory, and researchers are intimately aware of the relevance of such a theory. A number of top researchers (to our personal knowledge) have themselves witnessed demonic encounters in their UFO investigations, sometimes finding the experience to be frightening. Their awareness of the argument can also be seen by consulting the bibliographies they offer in their writings. References to demonology and the occult keep recurring. John Keel's writings have many such references, and so also do many of the articles in the high caliber publication *Flying Saucer Review*. Another is Lynn Catoe, who compiled a 400-page bibliography for the U.S. Air Force. She states:

> A large part of the available UFO literature is closely linked with

mysticism and the metaphysical. . . . Many of the UFO reports now being published in the popular press recount alleged incidents that are strikingly similar to demonic possession and psychic phenomena. . . .[3]

MANIFESTATIONS . . . SIMILAR IF NOT ENTIRELY IDENTICAL TO THE UFO PHENOMENON

John Keel states:

The manifestations and occurrences described in this imposing literature [of demonology] are similar if not entirely identical to The UFO phenomenon itself.[4]

Clearly, UFO's and demonology are very closely related: in fact, they are outworkings of the same phenomenon. Trevor James writes, "A working knowledge of occult science . . . is indispensable to UFO investigation."[5] Janet Gregory states, ". . . the features listed above as pertaining to demons crop up again and again in UFO reports."[6] Ivan Mackay, lifetime occult researcher, says, "These [occult] similarities are so remarkable . . . ."[7]

Jonathan Caplan comments:

. . . a strong body of opinion, to campaign for the terms of reference of UFO investigation — to include such subjects as occult religion, parapsychology, spiritualism, folklore, and demonology.[8]

Bryant Reeve is clear as to the relationship:

Is there any connection between psychic and the occult fields and flying saucers? Indeed there is. There is a psychic component to saucer research which simply cannot be ignored. It enters into a study of sightings, communications, and contacts.[9]

Charles Bowen writes in an FSR editorial:

[The] idea of the observation of, and contact with UFO entities, and of the possible interrelationship of psychic and UFO phenomena . . . [are] proving to be of the greatest significance and importance in the study.[10]

Again, Drs. Hynek and Vallee state, "If the facts seem to demand a paranormal explanation, then let us boldly examine that avenue."[11]

Many similar quotations could be added, but in this chapter we are simply establishing the premise that our hypothesis is close to what other researchers are saying. It is not logical or scholarly to reject the "demonic theory" simply because it is acceptable only to those Christians who believe that the Bible's teachings on this

subject are still relevant. Even a biased
reviewer of *UFO's: What On Earth Is Happening?* wrote, "Demonology is certainly
one of the logical possibilities."[12] This
present book should be considered on its
merits as a research work that considers
the evidence for the "logical possibility" of
"the demonic theory." Academic integrity
demands that it should not be prejudged
and rejected without consideration.

Robert Galley, the French Minister of
Defense, has stated regarding UFO's:

> . . . my own profound belief is
> that it is necessary to adopt an ex-
> tremely open-minded attitude
> toward these phenomena.[13]

IS THERE A HYPOTHESIS,
NO MATTER HOW STRANGE,
THAT EXPLAINS THE FACTS?

That is what we are doing. Dr. J. A.
Hynek states:

> We need to line up all the things
> that a viable theory needs to ex-
> plain; . . . is there a hypothesis, no
> matter how strange, that explains
> the facts?[14]

Later on, Dr. Hynek says:

> Should those psychic claims [re:
> UFO phenomena] be true, it opens
> up another can of worms. *Then
> the problem is essentially
> solved*; . . . ."[15] (Emphasis added.)

After stating this, the discussion in that book eventually concludes that UFO's represent a temporarily physical and occult reality, in the way poltergeists and other occult phenomena do. The authors conclude, "We stand at the edge of reality."

MANIPULATING HUMAN MINDS

We shall see that demonic powers vary in their capacities. Some are extremely intelligent entities that are nonphysical in nature but have a capacity to assume a physical shape and to undertake certain physical activities.

Whether or not they are physical, some entities can manipulate the human mind to the point that the contactees believe that an experience is "real." The "nonreal" experience is real so far as the contactee is concerned: physically, physiologically, and psychologically it is experienced as real. There are entities having a limited capacity to see the future, and they can "manipulate" time and space so far as the contactee is concerned: this again involves the control of their functions of perception.

There are entities who, though inherently evil, masquerade as benevolent, with the intention of deceiving man. They have an overriding plan, and their strategy includes the destruction of man whom they hate with an implacable hostility. They will reveal unknown facts, and correctly prophesy certain forthcoming events, with the sole purpose of insuring credibility and thus gaining converts to their cause. They are in the category of "false prophets," and their major prophecies consistently prove to be false.

To accept the demonic hypothesis, the "extraterrestrial" theory must be put aside. However, as Arthur C. Clark states, "One theory that can no longer be taken very seriously is that UFO's are interstellar spaceships."[16] Again, as Harvey Cox states on the dust jacket of M. Martin's *Hostage to the Devil,* a book about demon possession cases, "We are entering a world in which the classical Christian wisdom will have a lot to say to us again."

In *UFO's and Their Mission Impossible* Clifford Wilson systematically examined the various theories that have been taken seriously as to the nature and origin of UFO's. In reviewing that book Dr. Shildes Johnson wrote:

> . . . a very objective, comprehensive, unprejudiced analysis. . . . Only after he has exhausted all other explanations and has noted how none of them account for the total phenomenon does he present

the paraphysical (demonic) explanation."[17]

WHY DO UFO ENTITIES HAVE SUCH A GREAT INTEREST IN THEOLOGY?

The theory put forward in this book explains why there is so much evil associated with UFO's, so many cases of deception, and so many seemingly meaningless and pointless cases. It makes sense of there being so many parallels with the occult, including "possession" of humans. Why would extraterrestrial beings possess earthlings in the way some contactees are taken over? There is a high unnatural death rate and insanity among contactees and even with researchers. There are many cases of ruined lives of contactees and drastic effects on their wives/husbands and dependents.

Such a theory explains the preoccupation of the UFO entities with Biblical theology and eschatology, an interest that would be irrelevant to beings from another planet. There are, of course, many practical reasons why they cannot be from another planet — the impossibly great numbers of sightings by credible witnesses, the consistency of contactees' reports, the nonmaterial nature of evidence left behind, the fact of many "repairs" being

sighted despite their vastly superior
technology (but metal fragments are never
found at the site), the lack of suitable
places for the vehicles and their occupants
to exist on earth while performing their
assignments, and the utterly fantastic
nature of those assignments.

SOME OF THE MAJOR PROBLEMS

There are other problems, and it would
be of some value to list some characteristics of the UFO phenomena themselves:

a. They do not act normally — they
   play "games," buzz and follow
   cars, and perform other strange an-
   tics, which would be very unlikely
   for an advanced civilization.
b. No crashes of UFO's have ever been
   found. Crashes have been "seen,"
   but this is merely another "set up"
   in the same category as the UFO
   "repair operations" which people
   report.
c. They have never really "come out
   in the open."
d. The wide variety of craft and occupants, which indicates that few,
   if any, are exactly alike. It is impossible that each craft would be
   individually constructed and then
   used only once.

e. The occupants are liars and deceivers, and in other ways they demonstrate hostility to the human race. Sometimes people are even dead after a UFO close encounter.*

f. The occupants consistently deny the truths of the Bible.

g. The phenomena correlates with demonic phenomena perfectly in dozens of areas.

h. Their "selective" nature is a consistent characteristic. They can be seen but do not usually appear on film, and at other times can be photographed but not seen. The same is true for radar — sometimes they appear on radar and sometimes they do not.

i. How do the wide variety of beings reported as being seen outside their craft survive in our atmosphere?

Aside from the occult issue, there are several unsolved problems which also cast doubt on the "reality" of these UFO's being from another material civilization.

a. Tremendous recurring accelerations that violate the mechanical law of mass-ratios (or Newton's Second Law of Motion): the

---

*e.g., see Hynek and Vallee, *The Edge of Reality*, pp. 159-165.

amount of fuel needed for these craft is far greater than that which is possible for them to carry, if they use similar propulsion methods to ours. The law of mass-ratios is the ratio between the original mass of the vehicle and its mass at any subsequent moment due to fuel expenditure. The payload of a rocketship is almost nothing compared to its fuel requirements.

b. Their resistance to the tremendous amount of heat caused by air friction at great speeds.

c. Sometimes they are completely silent in flight. There are no sounds or supersonic booms that should result if they are physical craft. At other times, a crackling or buzzing noise is heard.

d. Their ability to change shape, size, or color, to disappear instantly, and to nullify their mass and gravity with only a small expenditure of energy.[18]

WHAT PHYSICAL LAWS OPERATE?

It is possible that an advanced civilization could work on different physical laws than ours, though unlikely. However, if that be true, more problems are raised than solved. They would still be operative under some type of *physical* laws, and how could we even begin to explain the cases of two UFO's merging to become one?

Another problem is the occupants of the UFO's — a good number of them, probably a majority, are humanoid. Yet *any* creature similar to us in constitution could not inure the tremendous accelerations these craft have. There are reports of craft traveling up to 18,000 miles per hour, fast enough to splatter its occupants against the walls with any quick turn and cause any structure of which we know (except a fully solid object) to be destroyed. If the craft were unoccupied (i.e. remote controlled) we should be able to pick up the control signals, but there never are any.

Other problems abound. Their physical maneuvers oppose physical laws as known on earth, but there are many strange peculiarities when thought of by earth's standards. In some cases the UFO's are fiery red, in other cases they are pitch black. Sometimes they change colors *in* mid-air. They have been seen linked together with "chains," merging together to form one UFO, growing and shrinking in size, splitting apart into two UFO's, etc. They have repeatedly changed shape, color, size, and mode of action. This is very similar to the powers of supernatural beings (i.e. demons) in the occult literature. There is also a UFO connection to just plain weird things, monsters, unearthly animals, mysterious fires and explosions reported by or near UFO sightings, etc. The fires have included forest fires, burned bridges, and melted steel girders.

DISCARDING THE "INTER-PLANETARY VISITORS" HYPOTHESIS

Clearly, conventional UFO theories about "extraterrestrial civilizations" have some very serious questions to answer. This has been recognized by many. Jerome Clark says the "interplanetary visitors" hypothesis is no longer so easy to accept. He says we now know that these forces are "infinitely more complex" and "infinitely less susceptible" to our theories than the interplanetary hypothesis once so readily believed.[19]

PROJECT BLUE BOOK AND THE PARAPHYSICAL EXPLANATION

Brad Steiger, an Iowa college professor who has spent a decade studying UFO's, recently had the opportunity to research first hand the entire Air Force Project Blue Book files. These constitute 94 reels of microfilm, each reel containing 1,000 to 14,000 pages of material. Some of his findings are reported in his *Project Blue Book* (Ballantine, 1976). In the Summer, 1977 *Canadian UFO Report*, Steiger discusses his personal findings as follows. While not entirely discounting the extraterrestrial view, he states:

I have to say with great earnestness and sincerity that examining *Project Blue Book* has fortified the hypothesis that I have set forth [in other books]. We are dealing with a multi-dimensional paraphysical phenomenon, which is largely indigenous to planet earth.

THE STAGE IS SET

This chapter has set the stage. In the pages that follow we analyze the phenomena in some detail. We bring together many incidents that have close relationship, and show the worldwide consistency in the reports and experiences of contactees.

We discuss theology and eschatology, psychology and parapsychology, and even weird and way-out things such as monsters, smells, and mini-men. Sometimes we have hesitated to include particular stories, and indeed have put many grotesque incidents aside. However, intellectual integrity demands that issues be faced. If at first you think some things are absurd, let us simply say, "so did we." As we kept researching we found that the demonic sphere was indeed weird, unreal, absurd, even grotesque. That will become clearer as you proceed through the following pages.

Footnotes: Chapter Two

1. FSR, Vol. 20, No. 3, p. 8, "The Mouse in the Maze."
2. *The Edge of Reality*, p. 1.
3. *UFO's and Related Subjects: An Annotated Bibliography*, p. IV.
4. *UFO's: Operation Trojan Horse*, p. 215.
5. FSR, Vol. 18, No. 1.
6. FSR, Vol. 17, No. 2.
7. FSR, Vol. 16, No. 4.
8. FSR, Vol. 20, No. 3.
9. *The Advent of the Cosmic Viewpoint*, p. 41.
10. FSR, Special Issue, No. 5, p. 1.
11. *The Edge of Reality*, p. 2.
12. *The APRO Bulletin*, Feb. 1976.
13. *The Edge of Reality*, p. 58.
14. Ibid., p. 240.
15. Ibid., p. 258.
16. *New York Times Book Review*, July 27, 1975.
17. Institute of Contemporary Christianity Newsletter, Box A, Oakland, New Jersey.
18. James McCampbell, "A Hypothesis Concerning the Origin of UFO's," AIAA (September 27, 1975), *Proceedings* p. 45.
19. FSR, Vol. 16, No. 5, p. 21.

Chapter 3

THE IMPACT OF UFO'S AND ATTEMPTS TO COMMUNICATE

Parapsychology is experiencing a tremendous upsurge today. The study of psychic abilities and occult methodology is increasing all over the world. For example, the dangerous practice of psychic healing has infiltrated the modern medical field.[1] The expanding field of "holistic medicine" incorporates numerous occult practices as legitimate "healing" methods. Scientists have put forth the idea of storing and utilizing psychic energy.[2] Yoga, mediums, astrology, Eastern meditation — all are currently being scientifically investigated, and it is doubtful if science as we know it can long survive. Uri Geller who is famous for his metal bending and other psychic exploits, is sponsored by parapsychology groups, and his space contacts

tell us we must move into the realm of
psychic research.[3] The problem with all this
is that the world of the occult is under the
control of a host of demonic beings.

How does all this relate to UFO's? The
connecting link between psychic
phenomena and UFO's could possibly be
the most important aspect of future UFO
research. Stanford Research Institute in
California receives hundreds of letters
every month from psychics who want to
have their abilities tested, and many of the
letters refer to UFO experiences.[4] The
research done on Uri Geller has caused
some scholars to believe that he is the link
which could bind together psychic and
UFO research. Both threaten the entire
structure of science as we know it. John
Keel says that UFO study should *rightly*
be a branch of psychic research.

C. S. LEWIS AND CLOSED HUMAN MINDS

On the whole matter of parapsychology,
C.S. Lewis made a brilliant statement. He
imagined one demon speaking to another:
"I have great hopes that we shall learn in
due time how to emotionalize and
mythologize their science to such an extent
that what is, in effect, a belief in us
(though not under that name) will creep in
while the human mind remains closed to
belief in the Enemy."[5] As we understand

the *nature* of parapsychological and UFO research, and their tie-in to occult study, and then consider the number of serious scientists who are advocating expanded research, we see that this analysis by C. S. Lewis is profound in its implications. It would not surprise us to find parapsychology and UFO research going hand in hand in the near future.

Researcher Charles Bowen, is another who believes that the mass of collected UFO data will be of "paramount importance" to psychical research, and that eventually the rank and file of parapsychologists will rush to join the UFO ranks.[6] He also believes that professionals in other fields — science, theology, history, philosophy, psychology, and medicine, will do the same. Trevor James, another respected UFO researcher, believes that the new tools needed for UFO study are the occult sciences.[7]

Even the Aerial Phenomena Research Organization, one of the oldest and more scientific of UFO groups, had an article in its 5th Annual Symposium Proceedings which spoke over and over again of psychic phenomena and the link between UFO's and parapsychology. It was suggested that, until one familiarized himself thoroughly with the legitimate parapsychological findings, he had better not speak in terms of an "extraterrestrial" hypothesis. It was also mentioned that the UFO scene will never be understood until *all* its aspects are admitted, researched, and correlated, and that this would detail the investigating of a great deal of odd data at variance with the typical "lights in the sky" viewpoint.[8]

THINGS TO LOOK FOR

If this surmise is correct, it is relevant to ask, "What should we look for? What will be the developments?" The following list is suggested as a starting point.

a. Increasing revelation on UFO's and UFO encounters from official files. Much of this will be surprising and even startling.
b. More acceptance generally of the UFO's, UFO study, and the contactee phenomena, both by laymen and those in the scientific community.
c. Increased sightings, with more "physical evidence" being provided by UFO's.
d. A worldwide increasing interest in the occult, parapsychology, psychic healing, and Eastern thought and mysticism.
e. A correlating tie-in of UFO study with parapsychology and the occult.
f. More expression of the idea that, if contacted, these beings could help

humanity solve all its problems and usher in a new age of advancement, both material and spiritual. More lay and scientific interest in the idea that man could be the result of a planned breeding experiment carried out aeons ago by extraterrestrials (a la von Däniken), and that they may return for us.

g. Increased attempts to contact the UFO's. Right now many scientists are either interested in or actually pursuing possible methods of contact.

h. Possibly eventual acceptable contact with "superior beings" on a significant scale. There is the serious chance of their contacting a few key world governments. It is not outside the realm of possibility for "proof" to be offered, either through "actual craft" or the sending of interstellar representatives. Christians should remember that "great signs and wonders" will be seen, and they should resist the strong delusion referred to at II Thessalonians 2:11.

THE UFO IMPACT

Dr. Carl Jung remarks:

These rumors [of UFO's] or the possible physical existence of such objects, seem to me so significant that I feel myself compelled . . . to sound a note of warning . . . . It is not presumption that drives me, but my conscience as a psychiatrist that bids me fulfill my duty and prepare those few who will hear me for coming events which are in accord with the end of an era. As we know from ancient Egyptian history, they are symptoms of psychic changes that always appear at the end of one Platonic month (a Platonic year is 26,000 years) and the beginning of another. They are, it seems, changes in the constellation of psychic dominants, of the archetypes, or "gods" as they used to be called, which bring about, or accompany, long-lasting transformations of the collective psyche. . . . I am, to be quite frank, concerned for all those who are caught unprepared by the events in question and disconcerted by their incomprehensible nature.

One can hardly suppose that anything of such worldwide incidence as the UFO legend is purely fortuitous and of no importance whatever.[9]

Vallee, Keel,[10] and others have already

theorized that the UFO landings are not in fact real craft from outer space, but are deliberately faked episodes to make us believe there are beings from another world. If the UFO scene is related to the Biblical last days, then this is also indicative of a demonic link with UFO's. In considering the historical aspect, Vallee concludes:

> For the time being, the only positive statement we can make, without fear of contradiction, is that it is possible to make large sections of any population believe in the existence of supernatural races, in the possibility of flying machines, in the plurality of inhabited worlds, by exposing them to a few carefully engineered scenes, the details of which are adapted to the culture and superstitions of a particular time and place.[11]

Elsewhere, he says that due to the large number of worldwide close encounter cases, a formidable impact is being made on our collective psyche."[12]

It seems that the UFO's are having an impact on mankind which could help pave the way for a world dictator. More on that later. If demons have plans to come upon the earth again (as possibly in the days of Noah), then their maneuvers are cunning indeed. The dramatic increasing of the

UFO sightings and encounters in our generation is significant, to say the least. This is especially so when there are reports of scientists becoming contactees (like Dr. A. Puharich who wrote *URI*, the book on Uri Geller) and the extraterrestrials forcing their contacts into politics.[13]

THE COMMUNICATION QUESTION

Many people are interested in communicating with the UFO's and some day the beings might contact earthlings in greater numbers. In 1958, Canada's Defense Research Board reportedly attempted with a top secret plan to make contact. Fortunately it failed.[14] More recently, Major Donald Keyhoe suggested *Operation Lure*, an attempt to arouse their curiosity by a specially designed UFO base. They would land and humans could then enter into communication with them.[15]

This is no small matter. Even Dr. Edward U. Condon stated, in *The Scientific Study of Unidentified Flying Objects*, that actual contact with extraterrestrials would be the single greatest scientific discovery in the history of man. [16] Along these lines, we can see that many scientists are interested in the extraterrrestrial communication aspect. The conclusions of the First International Conference on the subject (held in Russia) made the following recommendations:

a. The search for extraterrestrial intelligence should be an internationally cooperative endeavor undertaken by "representatives of the whole of mankind."

b. To continue expanded research on the subject.

c. The idea that contact with aliens from space "can positively influence the whole future of man," and that the results would justify "the expenditure of substantial efforts" at contact.[17]

If man does succeed in contact on a worldwide scale, it is sad to realize that despite his dreams for a "new world," he will be communicating only with his spiritual enemy. The new world will come, but it will be one ripe for judgment, as it was in the days of Noah (Genesis 6).

It is interesting to notice that in October, 1973, the Soviet Union's official news agency, TASS, reported that three eminent Russian astrophysicists had established contact with alien beings in outer space. They could not determine the exact location of the signals, but they knew it was within our solar system and possibly "from the upper layers of the atmosphere" of the earth. The signals could not have come from a natural source or an earthly satellite but had "to be transmitted by civilized beings with sophisticated transmission equipment."[18] Not much has resulted from this announcement, but we should note that demons do have control over electromagnetic phenomena, and they could easily send communications to scientists the world over if they wanted to. At present they seem to be waiting, *but* more extensive communication might not be far away. They are telling some of the contactees to involve themselves in politics,[19] and in at least one well-documented case aliens are saying they will soon offer proof of their existence by bouncing signals off a lunar satellite to a group of waiting scientists on the earth.

Incredible? Not when you consider that all over the world, right now, scores of scientists are attempting to communicate with extraterrestrial civilizations. Many people have a great hope that aliens will be contacted, that they will come to us, and that they will unite the world and solve its problems. Some scientists and political leaders even see this as man's best hope.

Dr. Jacques Vallee refers to ". . . the increasing number of people who are turning to a belief in UFO reality. We are, as a society, developing a great thirst for contact with superior minds that will provide guidance for our poor harrassed, hectic planet." He goes on to state:

Time and again in the history of

civilizations, there arises some wonderful untruth around which magnificent energy crystallizes, and great deeds are done. Such a time has come again. *It has become very important for large numbers of people to expect visitors from outer space.*

It may not be true that flying saucers represent visits from outer space. But if large enough numbers believe it, then in some sense it will become *truer than true,* long enough for certain things to change irreversibly.

Some of the best informed sources of gossip in Washington are convinced that UFO's will be increasingly prominent in coming years. There are persistent rumors highly placed officials in the U.S. government have long had evidence that another form of intelligence was contacting us.

He queries, "It is nonetheless interesting to ask what will happen to our civilization if the next step in the development of the [UFO] phenomenon is a massive change of human attitudes toward paranormal abilities and extraterrestrial life."[20]

THE LATEST ON GOVERNMENT DISCLOSURES

In *UFO's: What On Earth Is Happening?* coauthor John Weldon, speculated in relation to an official government disclosure regarding UFO's. Today he still believes this will come about. There have been numerous incidents which lend credibility to this possibility. For example, UFO authority and nuclear physicist Stanton Friedman had the following dialogue in a late 1975 interview:

UFO REPORT: There have been rumors and predictions about a confrontation in the near future. How do you envision this occuring?

FRIEDMAN: I'm not saying the aliens are going to land, but I do say there is going to be an official announcement from on high about it. Preceding any kind of confrontation, there will have to be a gradual loosening, a changing of the attitude, and getting the country and world ready. There are television specials in the works now about radio contact and Universal Studios filmed the Barney and Betty Hill story, *The Interrupted Journey* which appeared on NBC-TV. I think there will be all kinds of propaganda, like ministers who say what does this [alien visitation] mean to our concept of God.[21]

In mid 1976 the Spanish Air Force Chief, General Carlos Castro Cavero, stated he believed the world would eventually be told about the reality of UFO's. *Flying Saucer Review* summarizes his statements:

> The General went on to assert that the fact that Governments do not publicly recognize this reality is not due to fear on their part, but due to a certain sense of misgiving in the face of an intangible fact on which they are being asked to venture an opinion. . . . General Castro [Cavero] also went on to say that at the present time many countries are collaborating in research on the subject of the UFO's and that when definite conclusions have been arrived at, then will be the moment when it will be possible to inform the world about the existence of the UFO's.[22]

On April 18, 1977 *U.S. News and World Report* carried this statement in their "Washington Whispers" section:

> Before the year is out, the Government — perhaps the President — is expected to make what are described as "unsettling disclosures" about UFO's — unidentified flying objects. Such revelations, based on information from the CIA, would be a reversal of official policy that in the past has downgraded UFO incidents.

On April 31, 1977 The Center For UFO

Studies contacted the editor of this feature "who refused to reveal any additional information, but he did affirm that their unnamed source was sufficiently reliable to warrant the comment."[23]

James Mullaney, writing in *Science Digest*, July, 1977, stated:

Whatever the true origin and purpose of the great mystery of things seen in the sky, the UFO phenomenon has all the signs of being one of the most momentous topics ever to face mankind. One indication of this is the remarkable comment once made by the UN's late Secretary General, U Thant. In an address he is quoted as having said that the most important *problem* facing the world next to the Viet Nam war (at that time) is that of the UFO's.

Another sign of its import is that many nations appear to be preparing their citizens to accept the reality of UFO's. France — a country with one of the highest rates of sightings in the world — was the first to make an official statement to this effect.

Here at home, reliable sources such as *U.S. News & World Report* and ABC News have recently indicated that our government is expected to make an announcement on UFO's by the end of the year.

Can it be that an eventual understanding of the UFO mystery will bring us into closer touch with reality and even the universe itself?

Finally, in a nationwide radio interview on February 21, 1974, Robert Galley, the French Minister of Defense, stated:

There has been an extremely impressive increase in the number of visual sightings of luminous phenomena, sometimes spherical, sometimes ovoid, traveling at extraordinarily high speeds. . . . my own profound belief is that it is necessary to adopt an extremely open-minded attitude towards these phenomena. . . .

I must say that if your listeners could see for themselves the mass of reports coming in from the airborne gendarmerie, from the mobile gendarmerie, and from the gendarmerie charged with the job of conducting investigations, all of which reports are being forwarded by us to the C.N.E.S. (National Centre For Space Studies), then they would see that it is all pretty disturbing . . . in fact the number of these gendarmerie reports is very great, and they are very varied.[24]

What is clear from all this is that the entire issue of the world's possible involvement with UFO's is today an open one. It is obvious also that there are possible Biblical ramifications in this area. If the futurist school of prophecy is correct, there are some interesting possibilities relating to the idea of the Biblical "last days" Antichrist claiming to be in association with extraterrestrials, or even claiming to be an alien himself. Perhaps, in order to further his plans, he would use the concept of UFO's in a totally unexpected way. Could the world be united more readily by a benevolent alien entity of tremendous capacities than a mere earthly dictator? If the Anti-Christ were to claim contact with extraterrestrials, could he advance his cause in the guise of *their* benevolent purposes for mankind? It is noteworthy that in the prepublication release of Bruce L. Cathie's and Peter N. Temm's *UFO's and Anti-Gravity,* it states:

> The evidence amassed by Temm and Cathie strongly suggests that scientists in a number of countries not only know a great deal about UFO's but also know how to maintain contact with them. The authors believe there has already been a considerable exchange of information between UFO's and these scientists.

We could well ask, "Is this true for

some political leaders also? Just how many individuals who serve in important offices around the world have been contacted? Is a plan being laid for future open contact with world governments?"

Conversely, if UFO's should assume an evil design, few events could be more powerful than the idea of "a common enemy that threatens our survival" in uniting even hostile nations.

As early as 1955, we find statements like the following by W.J. Brown in the September-October issue of *Flying Saucer Review:*

> If "invaders " from another planet came with hostile intent they might well be expected to bring with them weapons and types of strategy which would make nonsense of all the weapons and military dispositions of Earth. We should have to combine for the first time as *"Earthmen"* resisting attack, say, by Martians. We should have to drop all the differences and competing ambitions which divide nations and groups of nations today. The Atlantic Charter, the European Defense Force, the Communist power-bloc, would become meaningless irrevelances to the new situation. The "curtains" would have to come down all over the world. Plainly the political impact

would be immense in every country. Most of our domestic differences within each country, the Party struggle for power, the exciting of class against class, would have their content taken from them. Just as during the last war we had to drop internal Party wranglings and concentrate on survival, so it would be again. But this time it would not only be domestic differences within countries which would have to be dropped, but differences between one country and another and one continent and another.

That same year, General Douglas McArthur stated:

The nations of the world will have to unite against attack by intelligent beings from other planets, for the next war will be an interplanetary one.*

More recently, an editorial in the *Los Angeles Times* of August 22, 1975 stated:

If those who believe in UFO's are right — if Viking does stumble onto flotillas of Martian spacecraft — earthlings might just put aside their differences and unite against

---

*The UFO Reporter, March-April 1975, p. 7; *FSR*, Nov.-Dec. 1955 p. 5; *New York Times*, Oct. 7, 1955.

what could be a common danger.

According to The Center For UFO Studies, *International UFO Reporter* (September, 1977), France has recently begun an official government study of UFO's that will involve "the active participation of some members of all the main Government Research Organizations, including the National Center For Scientific Research, the Astrophysical Institute, the National Meteorology Institute, the Universities, etc." The same issue noted that the Prime Minister of Grenada requested the inclusion of the following in the provisional agenda of the 32nd session of the General Assembly: "Establishment of an agency or department of the United Nations for undertaking, coordinating, and disseminating the results of research into unidentified flying objects and related phenomena." The government of Grenada is attempting to have 1978 declared the United Nations International Year of Unidentified Flying Objects during which time there would be established a United Nations UFO research branch and the holding of a Second International Congress on UFO's.

World governments will sooner or later have to deal with the problem, or risk serious consequences. Consider, for instance, the following statement from the

Mutual UFO Networks 1976 Symposium Proceedings. Dr. Ron Westrum, in an article on the social reaction to UFO's states:

But UFO's are not merely an object of research. They are also a potential threat to the existence of our society. If the rate of certain kinds of UFO manifestations dramatically increased, collective behavior in the form of panic, riots, and vigilantism could result. Whatever the nature of the UFO phenomena, we must recognize an increase in its magnitude could have grave consequences for all of us. The UFO phenomenon is a potential nightmare, and the fact that its serious manifestations have been local so far should not disguise its frightening possibilities. Thus studying UFO's is not like ordinary scientific research. The scientist who studies meteorites does not expect them to attack him or intentionally thwart his aims. But there is every reason to believe, on the other hand, that the UFO phenomenon is intentionally deceptive and occasionally attacks those who study it. But beyond the welfare of the individual researcher is that of a whole society whose members are coming to believe that UFO's are real. This society, which seems so stable today, could erupt into chaos tomorrow if people thought UFO's were landing *en masse*.

In this respect, the government has done very little to prepare either itself or the public for a crisis brought about by UFO's. By denying that UFO's are a reality, the government has based its credibility on the premise that UFO's foster the belief that something was taking place of which the government had no knowledge and was therefore powerless to control. This of course may never happen; UFO's may disappear tomorrow, never to return. But if it does, the government will suffer the result of a stupid and irresponsible policy. The public, especially the educated public, believes that UFO's are real. The least the government can do is make some efforts to help find out what UFO's are. By ignoring UFO's, the government simply assures that any massive manifestations will be met not with deliberate prudence, but with panic terror.

Hence, from all available data, it seems certain that UFO's are going to have a prominent function in the years to come.

Another relevant point to consider is that the existence of UFO's would offer a reasonable explanation for the disappearance of large numbers of Christians at the Rapture (or "The Translation" as it is known in the Bible). "The undesirable elements were in need of removal." An explanation will have to be given, and it will obviously not be the truth, or God would be glorified. Instead of "God took His own to be with Him," it will be "Those who are in the way cannot be tolerated — the rebellious have been removed."

Arthur Clarke's *Childhood's End* gives us a similar scenario. UFO's arrive on earth at a critical time to save us from nuclear Armageddon. The aliens proceed to rule mankind with an orderly dictatorship. One source of opposition to the plans of the overlords comes from a group of sincere but potentially dangerous religious fanatics, who must learn the truth. In this case, the "truth" is a combination of eastern-occult metaphysics. Karellen, the alien chief remarks, "Believe me, it gives us no pleasure to destroy men's faiths. . . ." (Dr. Carl Jung referred to his belief that in the face of contact with advanced extraterrestrial life," we would find our intellectual and spiritual aspirations so outmoded as to leave us completely paralyzed.")[25]

Nichols and Alexander comment on the

possibility that Clarke's scenario is not just science fiction — a feeling shared equally by Wilson and Weldon.

The apostle John, in the Revelation, says that the Dragon (Satan) will give his power and authority to the Beast (the Antichrist). It is not difficult to construct a plausible scenario of the future, in which the world's governments make contact with ETI's (Extraterrestrial Intelligences), as in *Childhood's End*, and receive instructions on how to conduct the affairs of our planet. We should not be surprised if Jesus Christ is not mentioned in his true Biblical identity by these ETI's. We should not be surprised if he is not mentioned at all.

But we should never forget that our Lord is Lord over all beings, whether in heaven or on earth, whether in outer space, or inner space, and that he is ruling the universe right now at the right hand of God. And let us not forget that we, as his people, have been given power over these ETI's and have overcome them by the blood of the Lamb![26]

SCIENCE IS BOUND TO WIN — HITLER

Relating somewhat to the correlation between Christian theology, potential dictators, and extraterrestrial notions is the

following perceptive comment by
philosopher and theologian, Dr. Rousas J.
Rushdoony:

Hitler for example, believed in
neither God nor in conscience,
which he called "a Jewish invention, a blemish like circumcision."
Man's hope was for him in scientific reason. During the war, he
stated, "The dogma of Christianity
gets worn away before the advances
of science. . . . Gradually the
myths crumble. All that is left is to
prove that in nature there is no
frontier between the organic and
the inorganic. When understanding
of the universe has become
widespread, when the majority of
men know that the stars are not
sources of light, but worlds,
perhaps inhabited worlds like ours,
then the Christian doctrine will be
convicted of absurdity. . . . The
man who lives in communion with
nature necessarily finds himself in
opposition to the Churches, and
that's why they're heading for ruin
— for science is bound to win."
SCIENCE IS BOUND TO WIN!
We cannot understand why the
German universities so extensively
supported Hitler if we fail to grasp
this central aspect of Hitler's faith.
Hitler's war time plans for

rebuilding Linz included a great observatory and planetarium as its centerpiece. It would become the center of a religion of science, and Hitler said, "Thousands of excursionists will make a pilgrimage there every Sunday. . . . It will be our way of giving man a religious spirit" (Alan Bullock: *Hitler, A Study in Tyranny*, p. 389 f.). There is no reason to believe that our universities will not be equally ready, throughout the Western world to receive another Hitler or Stalin.[27]

Footnotes: Chapter Three

1. *Redbook,* June, 1974, "Hands That Heal"; *Spiritual Frontiers Fellowship Bulletin,* Vol. 10, No. 9, Nov. 1974; *Psychic Magazine,* Feb. 1973, August, 1973.
2. Puharich, *Uri,* p. 92; *National Enquirer,* Sept. 24, 1972, May 12, 1974, Oct. 29, 1974.
3. Puharich, *Uri,* pp. 171-255-6; *Newsweek,* Oct. 28, 1974.
4. Blum, pp. 224-5.
5. *Screwtape Letters* (Macmillan, 1971), p. 33.
6. FSR, Vol. 16, No. 5, pp. 23-4.
7. FSR, Vol. 8, No. 1, p. 9.
8. Article by Dr. Berthold E. Schwartz, June 15, 1974, *Symposium Proceedings.*
9. Jung, C., *Flying Saucers,* pp. 15-16, 33.
10. *Flying Saucer Review,* Vol. 15, No. 4, Keel, *Our Haunted Planet.*
11. *Passport to Magonia,* pp. 150-5.
12. *Psychic,* Feb. 1974, p. 17.
13. Sagas U.F.O. Report, Summer, 1974, p. 29; Sagas U.F.O. Special, 1973, p. 46; Keel, p. 130; *Midnight,* Oct. 14, 1974, p. 24.
14. Keyhoe, *Aliens From Space,* p. 242.
15. Ibid. pp. 241-51.
16. E.U. Condon, *Scientific Study of Un-*

identified Flying Objects, p. 25, from the Summary Section.

17. Sagan, "Conference Resolutions," *Communication with Extraterrestrial Intelligence* (MIT Press, 1973), pp. 353-4.

18. Flindt, Max and Binder, Otto, *Mankind Child of the Stars* (Fawcett, 1974), pp. 50-51. See also Lawton, A.T., *Is Anyone Out There?* (Warner, 1974).

19. W.H. Smith of Canada; Ray Stanford of Austin, Texas, etc. Midnight, October 14, 1974, p. 24; Sagas UFO Special, 1973, p. 46, Keel, p. 130.

20. Vallee, *The Invisible College,* pp. 195, 207, 204.

21. *UFO Report,* Winter, 1975, p. 72.

22. FSR, Vol. 22, No. 3, p. 2.

23. International UFO Reporter, May 1977, Center for UFO Studies, Evanston, Ill.; *Chalcedon Report,* April 1977, No. 140, P.O. Box 158, Vallecito, Ca. 95251.

24. FSR, Vol. 20, No. 2, p. 4; Vallee, *The Invisible College,* p. 55-6.

25. Duncan Lunan, *The Mysterious Signals From Outer Space,* Bantam, 1977, p. 250.

26. SCP Journal, Vol. 1, No. 2, August, 1977, "The Modern Prometheus: *Science Fiction and The New Consciousness,"* p. 8. P.O. Box 4308, Berkeley, Ca. 94704.

27. *Chalcedon Report*, April, 1977, No.
    140, P.O. Box 158, Vallecito, Ca.
    95251.

---

*"The Soviet press reported yesterday that a strange,
starlike ball of light was sighted over Petrozevodsk
in Soviet Karelia early Tuesday, 'spreading over it
like a jellyfish' and showering down shafts of light
. . . . about the same time a similar phenomenon
was observed over neighboring Finland. No
explanation for the light could be given."*
San Francisco Chronicle
September 23, 1977

*"I foresee the day when American and Russian
scientists will combine forces to solve the mystery of
UFO's once and for all."*
Dr. Felix Ziegel, Professor
Moscow Aviation Institute
National Enquirer, *July 15, 1975, p. 4*

*"It's no wonder so many millions of ordinary
people want desperately to believe in the reality of
other worlds and other beings, free from the hype
and heartlessness that increasingly afflicts this
paranoid planet. The power of [the film] 'Close
Encounters' comes not so much from its careful
extrapolation of the most respectable UFO data, but
rather from the human reality that underlies the
whole saucer phenomenon."*
Newsweek *Nov. 21, 1977*

Chapter 4
A MAD PSYCHOLOGIST PLAYING TRICKS

In this chapter we analyze some of the psychological concepts associated with UFO's. It is relevant to state that Clifford Wilson is himself a Licensed Psychologist.

There are several "schools" of psychology, and the differences between schools are at times quite dramatic. Some psychologists regard man as an animal whose learning processes are simply optimum operations of the same functions in lower species. Others say man is purely a near-machine that will function according to predetermined rules: a certain stimulus leads to a known response, and if sufficient reinforcement is applied, predictable learning patterns will follow.

Some psychologists stress nurture (environment), and others stress nature (hereditary factors), while others take a more balanced view and recognize the great importance of each factor.

There are points of departure, but there also are areas of essential agreement. This even extends to the realm of ethics, for there are well defined codes laid down, and licensed psychologists must remain within the prescribed bounds. Anybody clearly stepping outside would be liable to investigation and possible de-registration.

All this is relevant to our chapter heading, "A Mad Psychologist Playing Tricks." Lecturers in psychology find it is relatively easy to discover those who have already undertaken some formal training in psychology. There are basic principles recognized and an avoidance of conclusions that the less informed tend to make without knowing they are in obvious error, or in opposition to other known psychological principles.

PSYCHOLOGICAL PRINCIPLES IN UFO EXPERIENCES

In a somewhat similar way, when a person with some training in psychology analyzes the UFO phenomena, it is clear that psychological principles are known and utilized. Even hypnotism, telepathy, and various other parapsychological concepts are all involved. At first the use made of psychological principles seems incredible and the stories are totally disbelieved. Then the consistency of those stories, the convincing credibility of the witnesses, and the recognizable symptoms in the victims make one stop and think. Disbelief gives place to confusion, for the facts staring us in the face do not make sense.

That confusion is constantly found in the reports of UFO researchers, as some of the incidents in this chapter will show.

At last a pattern becomes discernible, and, when it is acceptable, the same pattern is seen right through the whole spectrum of UFO relationships with human beings. The perpetrator is indeed a master psychologist, but he does not confine himself to any ethical standards set by a National Psychological Association. Nor does he set out to understand problems and then suggest remediation appropriate to the particular diagnosis. The psychological practices stem from a being who is not "normal" by human standards. He is thoroughly versed in parapsychology and is able to choose persons who will be suitable assistants (albeit unwittingly) in his nefarious schemes. The person with an open receptivity is a special target for this evil genius who would, if possible, bring all men to utter destruction.

UFO'S AND TERROR . . . "ABJECT HORROR"

The fact of terror associated with UFO's has been recognized for many years. Ivan

Brandt wrote an article entitled "The Problem of the Frankensteins,"[1] and in it he refers to the fact that the visitors appear to be various types, "some of whom are so formed as to strike terror into the hearts and minds of us who have encountered them. For *this* is the fact that is presenting a *seeming* chaos."

"A seeming chaos" — confusion associated with Frankenstein-like beings striking terror into the minds of the contactees.

John Keel is another who recognizes the problem, and he suggests that the usual investigations as to the physical nature and "proof" of UFO's ought to be put aside: "Throw away your worthless 'sighting forms,' " he urges, for physical particulars of vehicles are not of major importance. He suggests instead that people should be asked personal questions — such as the kind of phone calls he has been getting, or memories about his childhood. "You may be astonished with what he comes up with. And after you've talked to enough people and visited enough flap areas, your astonishment would turn to abject horror."[2]

Abject horror. Those are strong words from a highly respected researcher. Yet the language is justified, especially when we realize that even our children can be — and often are — involved as dupes in this Satanic strategy.

CHILDREN ARE IN DANGER

It is well known that children are pliable, often ready to believe in areas where adults are more skeptical. Many Christian people will testify to the fact that they came to know Jesus and entered into a real spiritual experience as early as five years of age. If these UFO entities are to deceive the world, then they have a great mission field open to them with the young people of the world. They will do their utmost to convince children of the greatness of the UFO power, and in this way lead them away from God.

John Keel elaborates further, reminding his readers that poltergeists generally "operate in the presence of children, usually a boy or a girl at the age of puberty."[3] He states that in most cases he has investigated of UFO's involved with automobiles, either there was a child in the car, or the driver or passenger was a schoolteacher; and that many "touchdowns" were in school yards. He warns strongly against youth involvement with UFO's.

Sometimes the child in the automobile is paralyzed while the UFO is present, and possibly the UFO entities are utilizing an energy source from the helpless child. Many adults also are temporarily paralyzed for the duration of their experience. Such reports are too consistent and too widely dispersed to be ignored as incredible.

In *The Edge of Reality* by Drs. J. Allen Hynek and Jacques Vallee, the first chapter is entitled "I thought they were coming to get us!" As we have noted, the opening paragraph states that the UFO phenomenon demands an extension of our imaginations as never before, thinking things we have never dared think before. The authors suggest that such thinking is frightening to many people and even a threat to their intellectual security.

THE INCREDIBLE OF TODAY MIGHT BE BELIEVED TOMORROW

This is entirely true. The authors of this book recognize what is being said, and although they have no fear in this area, they do recognize the "threat to intellectual security." To be identified with the UFO phenomena at all is still somewhat unacceptable in many circles, and certainly to go out on a limb in the matter of demons is asking for ridicule.[4] Nevertheless, history has many examples of concepts being true despite ridicule and mockery. The present day electronic miracles are in that category. Even the great scientists of the past would have considered may of the achievements of today as fantastic impossibilities, ideas to smile over but not to take seriously. Who could have imagined television becoming reality, let alone men walking on the moon, or using laser beams? The incredible of today is likely to be believed tomorrow.

Later in that same book, the authors discuss the paradox of the UFO phenomena, for the behavior of UFO entities is not consistent with what would be expected of space visitors, nor is it consistent with known laws of physics according to Earth Science. An antigravitation theory does not explain the phenomenon, and the psychic effects are simply not understood — "the UFO's seem to be 'a crime without a motive' " — by beings who "don't have any purpose in coming here."[5]

We suggest that the crime *does* have a motive, and there *is* a purpose in coming here. "They don't take anything. Apparently they don't pose a threat," the authors continue. But they do at least attempt to take something. They are attempting to usurp the powers of God and to steal the allegiance of all His subjects. They *do* pose a threat against the eternal goodwill of those whom they can deceive. We may not understand all the psychic effects, but we do recognize the theological implications as these evil entities continue their daring challenge against Almighty God. Running parallel with that challenge is their implacable hatred against man, the crown of God's creation. There are many incidents known to UFO researchers illustrating this. We elaborate this in Chapter Six.

THOSE REPAIR STORIES

John Keel suggests that even the matter of repairs to UFO's may be part of the same game that has been played with us, and that in fact UFO's want to be observed, and so their "broken down spaceships" will continue to land in front of isolated witnesses while their "repairs" are effected.[6] Elsewhere Keel discusses the "superior" technology of UFO's and points out that bits and pieces keep dropping off. However, when examined this debris is usually in the form of an oil-like composition made up of silicon and aluminum. He talks about repairs by many UFO beings and states, "One of the most intriguing 'repair' stories I have seen comes from Seattle, Washington, in the summer of 1965. The witness awoke around 3:00 A.M. to see a small, football-shaped object fly through her window. She suffered akinesia and was unable to move or scream as tripod legs extended from the object and it landed neatly on her bedroom floor. Half a dozen tiny people climbed out, and went to work making repairs on their craft. When they had finished the job, they hopped back in and flew off into the night."[7]

Keel draws some interesting conclusions from this story. He says that in such cases the witnesses nearly always suffer paralysis (akinesia) during the sightings, and he states, "This same phenomenon is found in the many psychic accounts of bedroom visitants." Then Keel makes an interesting suggestion: "Parapsychologists have long speculated that the entities somehow manage to materialize by utilizing some form of energy radiating from the percipient. The more intelligent contactees speak of this as an 'energy exchange.' It is so common that I have labelled it 'kinetic vampirism'. . . . feasting upon the motivating energy of the percipient, thus inducing temporary paralysis."

THE ATTEMPT TO ESTABLISH CREDIBILITY

Many contactees have voluntarily undergone hypnotism after their experience and tell stories that are convincing but not really important. They describe the interior of a UFO and the occupants. They give messages about other civilizations and warn about man's potential self-destruction. However, they do accomplish one thing: in the minds of many people they establish credibility. Very many of the incidents themselves, and of the methods employed, appear to have no other purpose. Hostility, paralysis, kidnapings, messages, implanted visions, and all the rest — one common purpose is to cause mankind to believe in UFO's. A further step will be to regard them as the means of ultimate deliverance when the world's chaos demands it.

Consider this hypothesis against yet another example which highlights the confusion of researchers. John Keel discusses the use of various forms of earth energy. He suggests that such transmogrifications of energy would not actually be mechanical, but would appear to be so. Once they had completed a mission (such as leading a police officer on a wild goose chase), they would again revert to an energy state, and so disappear from our field of vision forever. Thus, most of these "objects" would be unseen in daytime because of the ultraviolet and infrared radiations of the sun pouring down on us, but when those natural radiations were absent at night time the objects would become visible and ready, according to Keel, to "play outrageous games with our senses. The intelligence behind them remains to be defined, just as their real purpose may be incomprehensible to us."[8] Keel states that only one real truth is becoming evident, and that is that we are being hoaxed.

While we agree with the conclusion as to hoaxing, we believe there is a very real danger behind that hoax. The hoax is part of a pattern as spiritual powers try to deceive the world, and even totally committed Christians, into believing that these beings are themselves the greatest powers ever known. This is all part of a Satanic master plan, an evil genius utilizing psychological principles in his opposition to the eternal plan of God.

MESSAGES FROM "GREAT POWERS"

Messages come from all sorts of beings supposedly associated with great powers. Sometimes the message-bearers claim to belong to a long-since extinct race, or to be associated with those who built the Pyramids, or were responsible for Stonehenge. "Others pretend to be from lost Atlantis or mental projections from a secret temple high in the Himalayas."[9]

A typical case is reported by Horacio Ganteaume.[10] He wrote an article entitled "Landing at San Pedro de Losaltos." It contained a typical feature of UFO beings giving a message of telepathy. There was no movement of their lips, and the witnesses heard the messages inside their heads. One of the witnesses was a gynecologist, and his first questions were, "Who are you? Where do you come from? What do you want here?" The answer was, "We are from Orion. Our mission on this planet is one of peace. We are studying the psyches of the humans, to adapt them to our species."

They went on to say there were seven inhabited planets and claimed among other things that they had a wave compressor capable of disintegrating the moon with only one discharge. Their spaceships, half the size of the moon, lay behind the planet Mars. (This reminds us of contactee Truman Bethurum's planet "Clarion" which was hidden from us behind the moon. However, talk about such a planet Clarion is nonsense. The earth's path is not perfectly elliptical, and because of the principle of precession, such a supposedly hidden planet must ultimately come out from "behind the moon" and be seen by humans on earth.)

When the gynecologist asked the UFO beings, "Are the inhabitants of all seven planets equal or alike?", the answer given was, "No. There are the Morphaus and the Amorphaus. We the Morphaus, possess greater similarity among ourselves, with the exception of those who originate in the Outer Dipper, who are diminutive beings approximately 35 inches in height."[11] This is suggesting that there are intelligent beings, literally without form. The author of that article relates this to "cosmophilosophical" systems of India where form and nonform are at times fundamental. Beings could appear to be formless and, therefore, nonexistent so far as our physical senses were concerned, but they were not without existence in relation to other beings composed of that particular kind of matter.[12]

"DIMINUTIVE BEINGS" . . . STRANGE CLOTHING . . . LOCAL LANGUAGES

We referred above to "diminutive beings, approximately 35 inches in height." There are many reports of strange beings giving messages to humans.

One report is that on April 30, 1962, Eugenio Siragusa met two individuals on Mount Etna. They had on diver's suits made of some sort of metal in one piece and having on lights that gave out intermittent yellow-green-blue beams. "One of the individuals dictated to him in Italian a message for the powerful ones of the earth,"[13] and it urged them to peace. The report said that the voice did not have a human timbre, and seemed to be from a tape recording, having a metallic tone. At a second meeting on September 5, 1962, he received another message dictated in Italian, but once again the local language was the medium of communication.

Gordon Creighton tells of yet another examination by miniature men, involving a Brazilian civil servant whose story was published in *Gazeta de Noticias* of July 21, 1968. [14] Creighton reports that the witness heard the little creatures talking, and it was, so he tells us, "Incredible as it may seem — in Portuguese, and he decided they must be doing it telepathically inasmuch as he never managed to make out any mouths in their strangely shaped heads."[15]

Strange clothing . . . no mouths . . . telepathic communication . . . making use of Italian and Portuguese. At other times it is Spanish, as reported in the *Flying Saucer Review*, Vol. 15 No. 4 of July-August, 1969. A man in Argentina was suddenly overcome by his watching a group of UFO's maneuvering, and he went and sat down in a neighboring room. He began to write at a very high speed in some incomprehensible language, and this was followed by a brief message in Spanish saying when other contacts would take place. Those contacts have continued. The report states that during the sessions of communication with these visitors, the man's pulse stops and he seems as though he is dead.

Other examples could be quoted, the entities using such languages as German and English. These beings adapt themselves to the tongue of those with whom they are in contact. Yet even this is a ploy, for, in fact, if their contact is successful, they do not need to speak in any language. They utilize mental telepathy and are able to direct their message into the thinking processes of their victims.

COMMUNICATING HALF-TRUTHS . . . AND "MISLEADING NONSENSE"

The UFO beings follow the principle of giving part truth, for they know well if a half-truth is communicated often enough it will be believed as the total truth. After that, whatever else is given is likely to be accepted as truth. In the same way, if minor prophecies come to pass, the UFO entities are more likely to dupe those whom they are spiritually pursuing. The minor communications are followed by greater messages about atomic warfare, the end of the world, and all the rest of it.

We (the authors) have been surprised at the number of people we have met who believe they have a special message. We have been sent screeds from such people, with long details of supposed messages and revelations that have come either from beings associated with UFO's or from other occult-type sources. John Keel tells the same story, of lonely people all over the world laboriously writing their great revelations, believing that they alone have the true message for the world. He says, "These people — and I have been directly in touch with many of them — sincerely believe that they, they alone, have enjoyed a very special privilege: contact with God or Gabriel or Ashtar. . . ."[16]

We have seen that investigators are puzzled by the paradoxes associated with UFO's. We see this again as John Keel comments on the "misleading nonsense" in the reports of contactees. He tells us that, in his investigations, he has been troubled to find that thousands of people who had contact experiences have not later remembered them. Their minds have become a blank, and it is only when they are probed by a competent investigator — such as Keel — that they begin to remember the experience. "Those who do seem to remember the experience are programmed to remember only misleading nonsense about spaceships and eerie medical examinations. This ploy has been very effective, and has kept most self-styled UFO investigators off the track for years."[17]

"Misleading nonsense . . . has kept . . . investigators off the track. . . ." Such statements are highly suggestive as to the nature of the beings under investigation. It is all part of a complex plan as Satan continues his battle that can only end in his own utter defeat. The "misleading nonsense" has its source in a perverted power from another dimension.

THE MAD PSYCHOLOGIST

Keel makes the startling observation, "Few have dared to confront the obvious truth: the source of all these subhumans and parahumans is not sane. We have wasted the time of our greatest scientists, philosophers, and theologians for centuries. . . ."[18]

The fact is, Satan and his demonic powers are not "sane" by human standards. They have pursued the great madness of rebellion against God, and they are now pursuing it to its illogical end. As we have already said, they know their time is short and their activities have been intensified in this generation. Soon they will be consigned to "their own place," and their wild strategies will be forever ended.

The tricks of the mad psychologist have about run out. They have been exposed for what they are, but they will still be effective against many people. It is tragic that many people prefer Satan's lies to the truth of God, personified in Jesus Christ.

Footnotes: Chapter Four

1. FSR, Vol. 13, No. 3, p. 16-19.
2. FSR, Vol. 14, No. 3, p. 23-4.
3. Ibid.
4. Their reality is, however, attested to by hundreds of historical records and the personal accounts of thousands.
5. *The Edge of Reality*, p. 25, c.f., p. 142-3, 154-61, 240-62.
6. FSR, Vol. 15, No. 5, p. 26-27.

7. Ibid.
8. FSR, Vol. 15, No. 4, p.31, "The Principle of Transmogrification."
9. Keel, *The Eighth Tower*, p. 136.
10. FSR, Vol. 15, No. 2, p. 21-4.
11. Ibid.
12. FSR, Vol. 14, No. 6, p. 11.
13. FSR, Vol. 14, No. 6, p. 11.
14. FSR, Vol. 15, No. 5, p. 32.
15. Ibid.
16. Keel, *The Eighth Tower*, p. 184.
17. Ibid., p. 139.
18. Ibid., p. 128.

"Almost unanimously, all the participants agreed that there is overwhelming evidence to indicate that the solution to the flying saucer enigma lies at least partly in the area of parapsychology . . . .
"It's interesting to note that all 10 psychics — despite conflicting opinions on the nature of the phenomena — seem to agree on a few major points: (a) UFO activity is increasing and sightings will become more commonplace; (b) the next two decades will see major changes on Earth — as a result of contact with the intelligences behind these craft; and (c) alien entities will make themselves known in the near future, and — as the telepathic messages from these psychics seem to indicate — will help educate and enlighten mankind."
Results of interviews with top professional psychics
by Timothy Beckley
UFO Report, September, 1977, p. 42, 56

Chapter 5
MOTIVES AND METHODS

THE UFO PHENOMENA

The UFO phenomena are both historical and worldwide. In the last few years they have increased dramatically in interest, research, and sightings. A computer analysis of 50,000 UFO sightings over the last 30 years revealed definite patterns of behavior. There is a peak activity every 61 months. Every five years and one month they have been moving across the globe from west to east in 1,500-2,000 mile leaps. Thus they are very deliberately revealing themselves to the entire planet. Sightings during these peak periods range from 10 to 100 times the normal number of sightings, and they are leaving mankind little choice but to believe in them.[1] UFO's have taken every conceivable shape, size, and characteristic possible, as have their occupants. There have been millions of sightings and thousands of contactees.

It is reasonable to ask, "Would they be going to all this trouble, if they were not planning something on a vast scale?"

MAKE IT LOOK GOOD

Obviously they want us to believe in them. If we do not believe in them, their plan will not work. Overall they have been very successful, and the small minority who do not believe them to be extraterrestrials are comparatively insignificant. The vast majority of people who believe in UFO's are convinced they come from other planets, for many sightings conform more or less to what we would expect from visitors from other worlds. Knowing that in a perplexing situation humans will take a majority view, they have acted appropriately. They know what they can get away with and are confident that the demonic and evil aspects of ufology will not damage their present purpose, which is to make mankind believe in extraterrestrial contact. The world is clearly in a desperate situation, and the thought of deliverance by advanced intergalactic visitors is increasingly attractive. The entities use the present confusion as a means of insuring belief in them as benevolent space visitors.

A STANDARD UFO INVESTIGATION

In some cases the physical evidence they leave appears so real that all an investigator can conclude is that there has been an actual visit by a physical craft from outer space. Often many witnesses see the craft, and these are followed up by questioning and a comparative investigation. There have been over 700 recent incidents reported where a UFO has left physical traces, just what would be expected from a material craft. [2] These traces are of a wide variety, and they have been examined in different ways. Indentations are measured by an instrument which can tell the amount of pressure exerted on the soil, and thus the probable weight of the craft can be calculated. (Strangely enough, indentations are usually not left by the craft even when it has been seen on the ground. Analysis of 301 *landings* shows only 47 left any traces at all!)[3] Other instruments check for radiation in the area of a landing, and higher levels are sometimes found. A soil analysis may find that changes have been made in the soil, and that bushes and grassy areas have been singed or matted out. If possible a photograph is taken. At times the UFO leaves behind a visible residue of something, as a car would leave oil spots. This residue has been known to evaporate after a short time. Most of the "debris" left behind by UFO's includes very normal earth materials such as silicon, aluminum, magnesium, etc.

Occultism has parallels in all these areas. Demonic capacities clearly include exerting great pressure, causing fires, producing radiation, material teleportations, residues, and so much more. This is UFO evidence, however, especially impressive to those who do not believe in a demonic reality. It is a convincing array of data, and that is why the U.S. Government and some other world governments are changing their position on UFO's, for their existence cannot be denied anymore. The physical "evidence" is there, and yet the physical is not all the evidence.

MOTIVE

The Bible is God's revelation of Himself to mankind, and has been shown to be remarkably accurate and reliable.* On the other hand, UFO messages are invariably designed to lessen confidence in the Scriptures, and the accompanying UFO phenomena are purposeful deceptions. This fits the Biblical pattern of spiritual warfare — fallen spiritual beings who were once holy angels are engaged in a war of deception against humanity. They distort the truth concerning God's person and as to what Christ has done (Ephesians 6).

---

*J. McDowell's *Evidence That Demands A Verdict* is one book with highly relevant material. Another is Clifford Wilson's *That Incredible Book, The Bible*.

This hypothesis of UFO deception is consistent with what the Bible teaches concerning spiritual warfare. Thus, when we accept that the Bible is God's Book and that its teachings are to be accepted as truth, we then realize that UFO deception is what one would expect. For example, they masquerade as visitors from other planets. Who else would know more about truth, God, and reality than extremely advanced and intelligent beings from the other parts of our universe? As such, these beings would obviously be far superior to us in technology and power, and far beyond us in intellect, and they *must* know more about the vital questions of life. How can *advanced* beings give you "backward" information? That would not be expected. So this masquerade is a ploy on the part of demonic powers. They want to make people believe UFO's are real so that their own messages will be accepted.

INDISPUTABLE CONTACT REVELATIONS

In 1961 Betty and Barney Hill were allegedly taken aboard a spacecraft. Betty had considerable conversation with the crew captain, and during this time she was shown a star map of alleged trade routes together with exploration paths between a grouping of stars.

After they were released the Hills suffered nightmares for three years until they decided to submit to time-regression hypnosis. These nightmares were probably induced by the aliens to cause the Hills to undergo hypnotic regression, otherwise they would not have been able to produce the "evidence" of interstellar civilizations they were trying to provide. Under posthypnotic suggestion by a Boston psychiatrist and neurologist (Dr. Benjamin Simon), Betty Hill reproduced the star map she was shown on board the spaceship. That was in 1964, three years after the original star map was observed by Mrs. Hill.

The fact is, no one on earth could have drawn that exact sequence of stars between 1961 and 1964. Twenty-seven stars appeared in Betty Hill's map. In 1969, after five years of work, Marjorie Fish found nine of the main stars correlating to a known pattern of stars in the constellation Reticulum. In 1972 a triangle of background stars (Gliese Numbers 86.1, 95, 97) was located, and this completed Mrs. Hill's drawing. This resulted from the updated *Gliese Catalogue of Nearby Stars,* which came out in late 1969. Prior to 1969, these three stars could not have been identified. (In 1964, two of the stars appeared in incorrect parallax positions.) Experts admit that no earth astronomer could have drawn so accurate a map in 1964. Marjorie Fish says that "only contact with extraterrestrials" could have produced this map. The conservative Aerial Phenomena Research Organization (APRO) calls Miss Fish's task of identifying the star pattern "one of the most important accomplishments" in UFO research.[4]

While it is true no human could have made that map, it is obvious spiritual entities could have. They clearly have access to the stars of the heaven: they know their locations, and could easily produce a star map that is not yet fully catalogued.[5] Such a happening does add to the evidence, and it is relevant to notice that it also lends credence to the reports of UFO abductions, which we will discuss in the next chapter.

HYPNOSIS

Hypnosis is a common method used in UFO investigation. Its usual function is to cause a contactee to relive forgotten UFO experiences. There is usually a pattern. Sometime after the first contact with the supposed extraterrestrial, the contactee's life "falls apart." He becomes very anxious and confused, and things become somewhat chaotic. This usually causes him to see a psychiatrist, who often uses hypnosis as a counseling tool. Under hypnosis the UFO encounter is "uncovered," and the person's life then returns to normal.

Hypnosis is possibly the next level of standard UFO investigation. In most of the cases, it seems that amnesia is induced by the UFO entities for the express purpose of causing hypnotic methods to be utilized. Contactees, like mediums, are very often excellent hypnotic subjects. The first time they are hypnotized they generally go into a deep trance and stay there.[6] This is not the normal human experience. For some reason demons can function much better with an individual who is in an altered state of consciousness — be it trance states, drug states, meditation states, or hypnotic states. Os Guiness mentions that the two most common ways that members of the youth culture have ended up contacting the spirit world are by misapplied meditation techniques and LSD use.[7] Transcendental Meditation for instance, is not the innocuous "cure-all" it is made out to be. Contact with vicious spirits, insanity, involuntary astral projection, and other dangers, have been encountered by TM practitioners. John Weldon's *The Transcendental Explosion* gives details.[8] Any method which opens up the mind — drugs, a mantra, hypnosis, or induced trances — can result in demon intrusion.

Hypnotism has a much stronger occult tie-in than most people realize. Even medical practitioners who are not involved in "reincarnation" or the occult have found their hypnotized subjects reliving "past lives." Possibly there is a medical value for hypnosis, but we have need for caution here. Its historic tie-in to occultism in

America and the East, the cases of demon possession resulting from hypnosis, the similarity to mediumistic trance states, and the recounting of reincarnation and UFO experiences that come through hypnosis, all point to the need for caution. However, if it can be statistically demonstrated that most hypnotic subjects do not develop psychic powers or ESP later on and there are usually no adverse effects, this would indicate that hypnotism is simply a neutral tool of which Satan has made much use.

If it be insisted that hypnotism has therapeutic value in many cases, it is yet true that many other cases demonstrate strange side effects that persist over a long period of time. Hypnotism has been known to induce supernatural occult powers of a wide variety, including astral projection, telepathy, general types of clairvoyance, supernatural diagnosis of disease, psychometry, and several others. Many mediums got started as hypnotic subjects, and there are many parallels between hypnosis and mediumship. When the Society for Psychical Research was founded in 1882, six subjects were initially investigated, and three of them directly concerned hypnotic phenomena. Yogis have even used a type of hypnosis in their rope tricks. Photographs have shown that nothing unnatural occurs, but that is not what you see. You see a boy climbing a rope with no supports and then disappearing or being chopped in half, but it never happened. Certain black magic and voodoo rites also employ various types of hypnosis.

All the material mentioned here is well documented,[9] and such "side effects" occur not infrequently in hypnotic incidents. The possibility of some UFO close encounters being fabricated by the entities via hypnotic means has a very clear plausibility.

THE DREAM STATE

Some cases of UFO contact appear during the sleeping state. The person is awakened, or at least thinks he is. (This is not unlike the experience of having a dream so vivid that we cannot separate it from reality.) After awakening, the contactee has a variety of experiences with the UFO beings. Later, after the experience is over, he finds himself where he was originally wakened. Sometimes he may be teleported to another place.

In many cases like these there is nothing to indicate the experience was at all real, for it could have been implanted in the mind during the sleeping state. This idea of "dream feeding" is common in occultism, except that a person has experiences with "the spirits" instead of "extraterrestrials." Andrew Jackson Davis, the "John the Baptist" of the "Spiritualist Movement," and a bitter antagonist of

Christianity, had a similar experience. In a blasphemous dream he thought he was awakened in the night and was led outside by his mother calling him. After that he had many unusual experiences, including helping "Jesus Christ" several times, for He supposedly seemed unable to keep his flock in order.[10] Davis was also heavily involved in mesmerism, the early term for hypnotism.

ELECTROMAGNETISM

There are many things we cannot perceive with our senses, although they do in fact exist. Electric, magnetic, and radioactive fields are among them. The "foo fighters" or Kraut balls of World War II (early UFO's) produced electromagnetic effects which interfered with radar and airplane ignition systems. B-29 bomber engines would sputter in and out.[11] A common characteristic associated with modern UFO landings is having car ignitions and other electrical apparatus go dead. In 1961 a rather startling incident reportedly occurred. A salvo of missiles was fired at a squadron of UFO's hovering over a Moscow defense network, but all the missiles exploded short of the targets. The second battery of missiles met the same fate. The third salvo was never fired, for the entire electrical gadgetry of the entire missile base was strangely short-circuited.[12] Entities having control over the electromagnetic spectrum would obviously wield considerable power.

Magnetic fields are known to be associated with electric currents. Strong enough fields can alter the currents or even reverse them. In one hypnosis experiment, the visual images the subject was experiencing were altered by the use of a magnet in the back of his head. A good deal of research has been carried out on the effects of fluctuating magnetic fields on the brain, and they have produced such effects as visual sensations and mental changes.[13]

Maxwell Cade demonstrated that UFO's and ghosts could be "experienced" as real by focusing electromagnetic fields on the human brain. He said there was evidence for both "subjective impressions and objective psychological changes" that were produced or set off by electromagnetic radiation of a certain range. (These effects can also be produced by hypnosis.) When related to UFO cases he implied this radiation could be the planned product of an alien intelligence.[14]

THOUGHT OR MIND CONSTRUCTS . . . AND PHYSICAL PHENOMENA

Several ufologists have toyed with the idea that UFO's are the creatures themselves. Either they are thought projections by them or actual "shells" of the creatures. According to this hypothesis they are the vehicle of the entity's body, produced with some kind of "etheric" substance. Actually this is possible, if we allow that demons can take any shape they want to. Possibly they could even project a part of their own being, but as that "substance" is not a matter in the physical or earthly sense, they would probably need to utilize an energy source from earth as well.

These entities do utilize physical phenomena, for man is proud of his insistence that "seeing is believing." Man tends to think that the physical world is the only real world. Demons know that the spiritual world is the real world also and will go on after the material has passed away, but they know, too, that most humans demand "evidence" of a physical or material type. Hence they leave some evidences behind them, and once again these are similar to "occult" evidences.

If nonphysical entities can stop bulldozers,[15] hew down trees,[16] control the weather,[17] beach whales against their will,[18] plus do the other things that are mentioned in the Bible, their power is obviously great enough to allow for the reported variety of UFO evidence. All this has the effect of being apparently convincing physical phenomena as to their reality.

The production of UFO residues can

result from teleportations and materializations of matter across distances, and these also are well documented in the literature. It is not impossible to teleport "debris" and other "craft residues" so that they can be utilized at a landing site. The production of "ectoplasm" is common among mediums. This "cheesy" material comes out of the medium's body when the spirit is in them, and it can take a variety of forms. Whether the spirit produces it alone or in conjunction with the medium's body is a matter of debate, but the material has actually been analyzed.[19]

One marine pilot, retired Lt. James Mayhew, observed a UFO to the side of his jet. He noticed that it had a green-yellow "lubricating oil" coming off of its surface at the midpoint all around it. He claimed it was egg shaped and very similar to the one Astronaut McDivitt photographed onboard Gemini IV.[20] The UFO was clearly intended to seem physical, yet it had no jet blast, wings, or rotor. Most curious of all, it did not disturb the cloud surface, even though it came from inside one.

The fact is, the UFO incidents include a wide spectrum of physical phenomena. Among them are the starting of fires, scorching of treetops and landing sites, healing abilities, "oil" residues, mutilated animals, draining of water reservoirs, sexual assult, paralysis, death, red welts, and many others.[21] Demonic powers can account for them all, but the physical evidence is so impressive that anyone who refused to believe in demonic power would be forced to believe UFO's were in fact real and probably extraterrestrial. That is just what they want.

PRINCIPALITIES AND POWERS

Some of the other powers which the "extraterrestrials" have demonstrated are remarkable, and they would indeed be classified as "great signs and wonders" (Matthew 24:24; II Thessalonians 2:9). Besides producing large radiation and magnetic fields, such as those through Uri Geller, they have caused winds to come up around his house, not only swaying the trees but also actually rocking his house. A grandfather clock was thrown across a room and "smashed into a thousand pieces."[22] Geller (or really the "extraterrestrials" who admittedly work through him) has bent a steel bar three-fourths of an inch in diameter, and that requires over twenty tons of force. In one UFO case on October 18, 1973, Captain Larry Coyne and his crew actually had their helicopter lifted over 2,000 feet by a UFO that nearly collided with them.[23]

ANOTHER URI GELLER?

Ted Owens is a contactee who claims to have had 294 miracles performed through him, all of them documented by scientists. He is a member of Mensa, the high I.Q. society. He claims that his UFO friends have used him to produce three independent hurricanes for a group of scientists (somewhat reminiscent of Satan's whirlwind in the book of Job), to stop and freeze an exploding volcano, to control a government radar installation with his mind, to steer and control hurricanes, to destroy a huge military exercise, to control weather, and even to control a city for a week.[24] Much of this will be written off as nonsense, but let us be careful about total disbelief. Satan is described in the Bible as a roaring lion, walking about, seeking whom he may devour. Much of his power will necessarily be manifested through humans, and he seeks those who will use this power to his ends.

Ted Owens claims that the extraterrestrials have "modified" his brain so that he could communicate regularly with them, and in one article he discusses how any well-meaning individual can establish contact with these beings. Self-hypnosis is one key to the space intelligences giving him supernatural powers. One of the "formulas" for contact involves repeating a statement about sending your mind back through time to gain the wisdom of the ancient Egyptians, Incas, and Aztecs. All three cultures were involved in idolatry and demonic worship, and their "wisdom" can be expected to align itself with the "doctrines of demons" (I Timothy 4:1).

Owens also speaks of rejecting the Devil and serving God, which most occultists (i.e., psychic healers, mediums, etc., but not Satan worshippers) also speak of. He also mentions that the extraterrestrials have guided various aspects of his life, even choosing him to be their representative as a child. He went through the "standard" mediums' training period with these space intelligences, and the task they are training him for supposedly involves the fate of every person on earth. He fully admits, like Uri Geller, that his powers come from these so-called space intelligences.

Various articles about him seem to indicate that his powers are actual, and that he has done much of what he has claimed. He has successfuly predicted many events, saying that the aliens were responsible for them. These include plane crashes, natural disasters, exploding a Russian Mars probe, a power failure on the Gemini 5 flight, difficulties on the Mariner 4 spacecraft, extensive UFO flaps, a lightning bolt to hit the Apollo 12 spacecraft, and others. All these did in fact occur: whether or not the "aliens" were responsible for them, or they

are simply a case of foretelling the future,
is uncertain.

Owens is supposed to have an accuracy
rate in predicting future events of around
85 percent, this being above average for a
good psychic. He says that all these events
happened because the space intelligences
"want recognition" for themselves. (Now,
if they were *really* aliens from outer space
who wanted recognition [one wonders
why], they could easily attain it by landing
and openly disclosing themselves, yet they
remain "hidden." Obviously, this is
another indication of the validity of the
demonic theory.)[25]

In the Bible we have been warned about
such people: "For false Christs and false
prophets will arise, and will show great
signs and wonders (i.e., great miracles —
cf. Hebrews 2:4, the same Greek words), so
as to mislead, if possible, even the elect"
(Matthew 24:24).

In other words, the believer in Christ
should expect to see many great miracles
undertaken by the power of Satan. He is
trying to mislead even the elect of God, but
in the end result this will not be possible.

Footnotes: Chapter Five

1. *National Enquirer*, Sept. 27, 1974.
   Analysis by Dr. David Sanders, Pro-
   fessor of Psychology at University of
   Chicago. Confirmed as accurate by

phone. Cf. *International UFO Reporter*, Dec. 1976.

2. Phillips, T. *Physical Traces Associated with UFO Sightings* (Evanston, Ill. Center for UFO studies, 1975).

3. Olmos, V. B., A Catalogue of 200 type — IVFO Events in Spain and Portugal, (Evanston, Ill., Center for UFO Studies) 1976; FSR, Vol. 17, No. 5 and 6. Analysis by Weldon.

4. Blum pp. 209-19 *Proceedings of the 5th APRO Symposium*, corresponding article.

5. More extensive evidence showing that the map could not be a hoax (because of the information it contains) is to be found in the MUFON 1974 Symposium, pp. 69-80, esp. pp. 74-76. See also the discussions in *Astronomy Magazine*, December 1974, and its publication *The Zeta Reticuli Incident*, T. Dickinson.

6. *5th APRO Symposium*, p. 17.

7. Guinness, *The Dust of Death*, p. 300.

8. Harvest House Publishers, Irvine, California, 92707.

9. Edmunds, Simeon, *Hypnotism & ESP*, (Wilshire Books, 1969) pp. 61-155; S. Edmunds, *Hypnosis: Key to Psychic Powers* (Aquarian Publications Co., 1968), p. 9-63; Koch, K., *Christian Counseling and Occultism* (Kregel 1972) pp. 113-121; C. Matthews, *Hypnotism For the Millions*

(Sherbourne Press) pp. 3-129.

10. Brown, Slater, *The Heyday of Spiritualism*, pp. 1-100 and A. J. Davis, *A.J. Davis and the Arabula*, 1859.

11. Blum, pp. 66-7, Vescoe, p. 81.

12. Blum, p. 189.

13. FSR, Vol. 12, No. 1, p. 4.

14. FSR, Vol. 15, No. 6; Hynek, Vallee, *The Edge of Reality*, p. 107-118.

15. Twichell, Paul, *All About ECK*, 1973, p. 44.

16. Ibid.

17. Steiger, *In My Soul I Am Free*, p. 13.

18. Rose, R., *Primitive Psychic Power*, (Signet 1968) p. 128.

19. *Encyclopedia Britannica*, 1959, Spiritualism article.

20. *Modern People Magazine*, Oct. 13, 1974, p. 14; FSR Special No. 2, p. 30.

21. *The Flying Saucer Review* has hundreds of examples in their magazine which span a period of almost 25 years.

22. Puharich, pp. 199-200; Blum, p. 225.

23. *5th APRO Symposium*, pp. 21-22.

24. McWane pp. 113-116.

25. For several articles on Owens, see *Saga*, August, Sept. 1971; *Saga's* UFO Special, Vol. 3, p. 32; *Saga's* 1973 UFO Special, p. 24; McWane, *The New UFO Sightings*. Warren Smith, *UFO Trek*, p. 196-209; *Argosy UFO*, Jan. 1977, p. 21, etc.

Chapter 6
ABDUCTION CASES AND THE EVIL ACTIVITIES OF UFO ENTITIES

In this chapter we look at several other cases of UFO abductions and the evil activities of UFO entities. More and more people are claiming they have been forcibly taken aboard a UFO and have undergone various horrifying experiences: there are probably hundreds of such incidents. Some are even more bizarre than those we examine here.

CASE NO 1: THE MOODY INCIDENT

Case No. 1 involves Sergeant Charles L. Moody of the United States Air Force.[1] He holds a high security clearance at Holloman Air Force Base in New Mexico. He has been with the Air Force for thirteen years, having had over seven hundred hours as a flight mechanic. He had never seen a UFO before.

On August 12th, 1975, he heard there was a meteor shower due to occur early the next morning, and he went to see it. He saw about eight or nine bright meteors at 1:00 A.M., and at approximately 1:20 he saw a dull metallic object that just seemed to drop out of the sky. It hovered with a wobbling motion, roughly a hundred feet in front of him, about ten to fifteen feet off the ground. He was at first very frightened, and the object slowly moved toward his car. He attempted to get back in the car and tried unsuccessfully to start it. It was as if there was no battery at all. This was strange, for he kept his car in top condition. The object then stopped absolutely still and hung there in the air. It was completely motionless, about seventy to eighty feet away and about fifteen feet off the ground. Its approximate size was fifty feet across and eighteen to twenty feet thick at the center.

NUMBNESS ... THEN "FLOATING LIKE A CLOUD"

Next he heard a high-pitched sound resembling a dental drill, and he noticed at the right of the center of the object what seemed to be an oblong-shaped window. (We should note that certain auditory frequencies may alter perception.) At the window he saw the shadows of what looked like human forms. It was not too clear, but he could make out that they looked humanoid, and there were two or three of them at the window. He heard another high-pitched sound and a feeling of numbness came over his body. The fear that he had felt now left him and he felt "a very peaceful calmness over my body, it was like floating on a cloud."

Then the object lifted very fast and was gone, making no sound. The sighting lasted anywhere from one to two minutes, but later Sergeant Moody discovered that one hour and twenty-five minutes were unaccounted for. The day after the sighting he felt fine, except for feeling a minor back pain, and he was a little bit light-headed. L. J. Lorenzen of the Aerial Phenomena Research Organization phoned Moody on October 21, 1975, and found that he had begun to break out on his lower body with something similar to a heat rash. His lower back was giving him pain, as though "someone had hit him with a baseball bat." Earlier, in September, Moody reported to Lorenzen that he had heard from an old friend, a doctor named Abraham Goldman, a former flight surgeon in the Air Force and now a consultant in neurosurgery. Moody had told Dr. Goldman of his experience and Goldman advised him of a method of meditation or self-hypnosis which, he felt, might restore his lost memory. It partially worked, and after recalling some of the missing period, Moody remembered being told that he would not remember anything for a couple of months (this implies a programmed recall). He later remembered the rest of the data. He was still interested in pursuing hypnotic regression, and this is his account of his communication with the entities and some of the other things he remembered.

Moody states:

There was definitely a contact made. I can tell you that the people of this world have really misunderstood UFO's and what they are doing. It's not only just one advanced race that is studying this planet earth, but a group of them, and within three years from now they will make themselves known to all mankind. It may be as early as midsummer 1976. I can also say that it will not be a pleasant type of meeting, for there will be warnings made to the people of this world. Their plan is for only limited contact, and after twenty years of further study and only after deeper consideration will there be any type of closer contact. They also fear for their own lives and will protect themselves at all costs. Their intent is a peaceful one, and if the leaders of this world will only heed their warnings, we will find ourselves a lot better off than before. And at this time, it is not up to us to accept them but for them to accept us.

A FORM OF MENTAL TELEPATHY

Moody also stated that the beings were about five feet tall and similar to us except their heads were larger. They had no hair, their ears were very small, they had very thin lips on the mouth, and they weighed between 110 and 130 pounds. They wore skin-tight clothing. There was speech, but their lips did not move. They apparently could read his mind, for the leader or elder of the ship would speak sometimes before Moody would ask questions.

Moody goes on with what happened on the ship:

I was taken to a room, and the elder or leader touched my back and legs with a rod-looking device. When I asked him what he was doing, he said there had been a scuffle when they first made contact with me, and he only wanted to correct any misplacement that might have happened. I do not remember any type of scuffle or fight, but I do know my back hurt the next day.

The inside of the craft was as clean as an operating room. The light was indirect, and he did not see any source for the light, though there was light. He was also told they could find him any time they desired, and in a short time they would see him again. He states, "I then asked the leader or elder why I was so sluggish and clumsy, and he told me that I was quite hostile at the first contact, and they had to use a type of sound or light on me to calm me down. The effect would go away in a short time." The leader also asked him not to remember what he had said or what had been said, or what he had seen, for at least two weeks. The next thing Moody knew was that he was sitting in his car watching a strange object lift into the sky, and trying to start his car, which this time did start.

At the initial sighting when the craft came within 50 feet of his car, Moody reports: "Suddenly an odd glow enveloped my car and I felt numb all over. . . . I remember that while the car was engulfed in the glow, two beings came towards me from the craft. They didn't walk, they glided." Moody then apparently knocked one of them down and the lights went out (he himself went unconscious). When he came to, he was lying on a table while an alien studied him. He tried to get up, but could not. He reported that the creature's head was about one third larger than a human's, with no hair.

CASE NO. 2: THE TRAVIS WALTON INCIDENT[2]

There has been much controversy surrounding this case, but after reading numerous accounts of it, we conclude it is a legitimate case. It occurred in Arizona on November 5th, 1975, and Travis Walton was among a crew of the U.S. Forest Service who were consigned to do a job of thinning trees for the Forest Service. After leaving the area they had been working, they had traveled just a few hundred yards when Alan Dalis, one of the members, spotted a yellowish glow ahead of them, to the right. Eventually they came to a clearing where they had a better view of the UFO. It was very close, being about seventy-five to ninety feet to their right. It was a large, glowing object hovering silently about fifteen to twenty feet above the ground, being about fifteen feet in diameter and eight feet high.

Upon spotting the object, Walton yelled to the truck driver (Rogers) to stop. While the truck was still moving he opened the door, jumped out, and proceeded toward the object and stopped underneath it. While Walton was going toward the object, the others in the truck heard a beeping noise like the warning buzzer in a passenger compartment of a commercial airliner. As Walton was looking up at the object, the men heard a noise which one of them described as a sound like a generator starting. Rogers also described additional rumbling noises, and the object started oscillating or wobbling on its vertical axis.

A RAY OF GREENISH-BLUE LIGHT

Just as Walton was walking around underneath the object, a bright narrow ray of greenish-blue light struck him, either in the head or on the chest, and a bright flash surrounded his body. However no sound was heard. This jolted Walton about a foot into the air, and he was thrown backward with his arms flung out and his head knocked back. Rogers saw the flash reflected from the trees, and turned just in time to see Walton thrown into the air. Rogers and the other men were terrified and drove off rapidly. Only one of them actually saw Walton hit the ground. The whole incident took less than one minute.

About a quarter of a mile away they stopped to consider the situation. Through the trees Rogers saw a light lift up and streak to the northeast, and they decided that they should go back and look for Travis. Within fifteen minutes they were back at the sight, but they found no sign of either the UFO or Walton. The men were very upset when they reported to Sheriff Chuck Allison, and one was weeping. They eventually took a polygraph test, and five of them passed, with one being inconclusive. There is no doubt that the men were convinced they did see something.

On the morning of the 11th of November (five days later), Travis Walton's sister received a call from him: he was in a telephone booth at a service station in Heber, twelve miles from the place where he had disappeared. Walton's brother went to Heber, and Walton was found slumped on the floor of the phone booth.

He claims that when the light hit him, it was like being hit over the head. When he regained consciousness, he was lying on a table. The ceiling seemed to be close to him, and light came from it. There was an apparatus lying on his lower chest, and he had considerable pain throughout his body, especially in his head. Around him were three entities about five feet tall, having large eyes, small noses, mouths, and ears, but no hair. Walton said they reminded him of human fetuses. They were dressed in loose-fitting brown coveralls. The air in the room seemed heavy and moist, and he had difficulty breathing. He was panicked both by his position and by the strange creatures, and he knocked the apparatus off his chest, striking out at the creatures. The object rocked back and forth when it struck the floor. The entities did not seem bothered by his reaction, and they simply left the room.

A TRANSPARENT WALL

Walton himself went through the door and turned in the opposite direction down the corridor. He went into another room where he found a chair with pushbuttons on the arms. The wall seemed transparent, and he could see what he assumed were stars. He sat on the chair and pushed some of the buttons, whereupon the stars started to move, and so he left them alone. Shortly thereafter, a man wearing blue clothing and a transparent helmet came into the room and motioned for Walton to go with him. He was smiling, but did not respond to Walton's questions or attempts at conversation. He took him out of the craft through an airlock, and down a ramp. Here Walton could breathe more normally. He found himself in a large enclosure, and saw several disc-shaped objects parked there, some which were smooth and metallic in appearance. His guide took him into another craft where he encountered three more humans, one woman and two men, who closely resembled one another. At this point something resembling an oxygen mask was put on Walton's face, and he lost consciousness. The next thing he knew, upon regaining consciousness, was that he was lying on his back on a road. He could feel the cold of the road surface, and he also felt the heat of a disc-shaped object which was rising into the sky above him, with the doors on the bottom just closing.

Because of the controversies surrounding the case a few other points should be mentioned.[3] Blood and urine studies on Walton determined there was no evidence of drug use. The Minnesota Multiphasic Personality Inventory test and other studies indicated no psychopathology. Walton did eventually pass a polygraph test, and he did have somewhat of an interest in UFO's. However, he had never read a book on UFO's and he did not know a great deal about the subject. Out of his missing five days, Travis Walton remembers only about two hours, possibly suggesting that his mind has been tampered with.

CASE NO. 3: KIDNAPPED BY BEINGS WITHOUT FEATURES[4]

This involves Carlos Alberto Diaz of the province of Buenos Aires in Argentina. On the morning of January 4, 1975, he was walking home after getting off the bus and noticed a brilliant flash of light which momentarily blinded him. Becoming frightened, he attempted to run but was paralyzed and could not move. His vision had faded, but he heard a humming sound like rushing air, and, although he tried to resist, he was pulled off the ground to a height of about eight feet, then became unconscious. When he regained consciousness, he was inside a semi-transparent smooth bright sphere. There was no furniture or devices, and the illumination seemed to come from the walls. Now he was completely conscious, lying on his side against several openings through which air issued. If he turned his face away from these openings, he felt sick, so he kept his face next to them. The sphere was roughly seven feet by eight feet in diameter.

Suddenly three creatures resembling humans came *sliding* into the sphere. They were approximately five feet ten inches high, and their heads were half the size of a human head, being *completely devoid of features*, having no ears, no nose, no mouth, and no eyes. Their heads were mossy-green in color, and they had thin bodies covered with something similar to rubber: it was light cream in color and was very soft. They were completely hairless. Their arms were almost straight, but very flexible and they ended in *stumps* rather than in hands and fingers. When the creatures entered the sphere, they immediately began to pull tufts of hair from Diaz's head. He did not know how they did this: he only knew that every time they reached out their arms close to his hair, they would have some of his hair pulled out. This seemed to give them great pleasure, for they would then jump up and down and wave their arms. He tried unsuccessfully to resist the creatures. During his struggle he felt the softness of their bodies and ultimately noticed they had suckers on their arms, and he assumed this was their method of hair extraction. He felt no pain when they pulled his hair, either on his head or his chest. The creatures moved slowly and were very strong and seemingly tireless.

When this part of the ordeal was over, he began to lose his sight and then fainted. He remembers nothing else of the experience, and several hours later he awoke and found himself lying on the grass, near a busy highway. He felt ill and remained ill for the rest of the day. A passing motorist took him to the nearest hospital where he found it was 8:30 in the morning. He realized then that he had been gone for several hours. For the next four days he was confined to the Ferroviara Hospital in Buenos Aires, where he was questioned and examined time and again by 46 different doctors, as well as the Federal Police who also questioned him. The examinations yielded no evidence of psysiological or psychological aberration except for dizziness, upset stomach, lack of appetite, and his missing hair.

WAS IT REAL?

Many other cases could be cited: we

have collected a great deal of evidence and
have, by no means, exhausted this topic.
We have omitted some of the better known
cases because they have already been well
publicized and can be found reported in
the recognized journals. But we must constantly ask ourselves, did the event actually occur? Obviously the cultural impact will be the same regardless of whether
or not the experince was real, if the culture
views it as real. However, by examining
the cases quoted in our previous chapters,
it can be seen that there is no *evidence* that
the abduction was a real experience.
Either, the remembrance is brought out under hypnosis, with only fuzzy details about
something unusual; or the only real thing
they see is the UFO and then they have an
experience of being inside. The use of
hypnosis, the dream-like encounters, the
unconscious states, the occurrence during
the sleeping state, etc., all indicate the experience did not actually occur but was implanted while the person was in a receptive
or altered state of consciousness. There is
also the strange noise heard after the UFO
is sighted (or the flash of light), which
could precipitate a hypnotic state wherein
the experience is implanted. This strange
noise is very common and seems always to
precede the abduction experience or to occur just prior to the person being back outside the craft. The onset of physical
symptoms, etc., is also accounted for by

hypnosis, as has been demonstrated many times by professional hypnotists.

FRIENDLY OR HOSTILE?

If these were benign beings visiting us, they would grant their host society certain measures of respect. We would reasonably expect that they would have the intellectual, technological, and moral capacities or will to abide by the rules of their host planet and not injure anyone. UFO's do not *have* to shoot out rays of light that maim or blind or even kill people: they are *clearly* capable of keeping these outbursts and manifestations in control, for there are enough incidents where this *is* kept under control. This holds true for UFO occupants as well. However, this benign approach is not what we find in many circumstances.

All too often contactees have been tricked, lied to, deliberately misinformed, made to look like fools, ruined psychologically, driven insane, and had their lives disrupted. The source behind the contactee phenomena is the same source that is behind the close encounters and the abductions, and when we realize this, the evil aspect of the close encounters and the abductions make more sense. Clearly, the existence of intelligence also allows for the volitional expression of self-control. In many cases, UFO's and their entities have deliberately engaged in activities harmful

to men, and it is clear that the phenomena
are not entirely benign.

PARALYSIS FOLLOWS A LIGHT BEAM — A TYPICAL CASE[5]

Benedito Miranda had an encounter
with UFO occupants, and one of the entities took from its belt a roundish object
from which a beam of blue or reddish light
was thrown in his direction. When it struck
him, he was lifted up and suspended in the
air, all the way up to a height of approximately 50 meters (55 yards). He was
totally paralyzed, unable even to cry for
help. He suffered mild shock from his
fright. The next day he had pain
throughout his whole body, had a cut on
his left arm, and in his left hand he felt a
numbness and a tingling. He had reddish-
purple marks in the region of the elbow,
and also on his left side. The following day
his eyes were watering, and they remained
bloodshot and felt hot. He had a headache
for six days, and suffered insomnia for
about a week. Over two months later he
still felt pain in his left arm after a hard
day's work.

A CURE FOR CANCER PROMISED

Another indication of the diabolical

deception of these creatures is touched on by John Keel. We quote:

One very prominent American researcher underwent the contactee experience in August, 1967, and he was promised that he would be given a cure for cancer which would lead to his receiving the Nobel Prize in 1972. His ego thus led him into a labyrinth of disastrous manipulations which nearly caused an emotional breakdown. He did not get wise to this ploy until it was almost too late. He has since abandoned his interest in the subject.[6]

Keel also notes that in most of the cases he has investigated, the people confess they are sorry they ever got involved as contactees. Instead of offering a cure for cancer and so benefiting all mankind, contact with these beings may even cause types of cancer such as leukemia.

On August 13, 1967, Inacio de Souza, 41, was struck by a beam of green light from a UFO which hit him in the head and shoulder. The case is reported in *Flying Saucer Review*, Vol. 15, No. 2. De Souza fell unconscious. On the first and second days after the incident, he complained of numbness and tingling of the body and of headaches and severe nausea. On the third day, the same symptoms continued, plus continuous tremors of the hands and head. He was taken to the doctor, and the doctor discovered burns on the trunk and head. The eventual diagnosis was leukemia, and the patient was given about sixty days to live. The doctor reported that the case "is a fatal one because it is cancer." Inacio eventually wasted away to skin and bone and was covered with white or yellowish white blotches the size of a fingernail which lay just beneath the skin. He suffered much pain and died on October 11th, 1967.

A PROFESSOR WATCHES A MAN DISINTEGRATE[7]

The victim in this case was Joao Prestes Filho. A UFO was seen in the area, and it was reported that Filho had been struck by a silent beam of light coming from outside his house. He himself apparently did not see the UFO. He fell to the ground for a few moments without losing consciousness, then picked himself up and went to the center of town in search of help. The physical effects are very strange: in fact, we hesitated to include this report. However, this is not an isolated horror incident, and we therefore submit it. We have no reason to doubt its factuality.

It was noticed that Filho's internal organs began to glow, and his flesh started to look as though it had been cooked for many hours in boiling water. The report states:

> The flesh began to come away
> from the bones, falling in lumps

from his jaws, his chest, his arms, his hands, his fingers, from the lower parts of his legs, and from his feet and toes. Some scraps of flesh remained hanging to the tendons and none of those who were present dared to touch them. Soon, every part of Prestes (his middle name) had reached a state of deterioration beyond imagination. His teeth and his bones now stood revealed, utterly bare of flesh. Prestes meanwhile vigorously refused the food and water that was offered to him, but at no time did he appear to be feeling any pain. Now his nose and his ears fell off, sliding down his body onto the floor, a terrifying specter of progressive dislocation and mutilation. His eyes bulging with terror, his speech already distorted in a mouth that had collapsed. Nothing more was to be heard from him now but sounds . . . the meanings of which were utterly lost. Amid scenes of general confusion, what remained of the body of Prestes, now nearing dissolution, was placed aboard a cart to be taken to the nearest hospital, the Santa Casa at Santana de Parnaiba. But no more than six hours after Prestes had been struck by the beam of light, a corpse was brought

back to Aracariguama. He had died
enroute without ever reaching the
hospital.

Subsequently, there were further
sightings of UFO's over the area. The article including this report was written by
Professor Felipe Machado Carrion, who
personally saw the victim disintegrate in
the manner described. Carrion is Professor
of Cosmography at a University in the
State of Rio Grande de Sul.

A PSYCHIATRIST'S
COMMENTS

Professor Carrion is not alone in
recognizing the reality of terror aspects of
UFO contacts, but most researchers (and
others) tend to steer away from such mind-
boggling events. However, the facts should
be faced.

As Dr. Berthold Schwartz, (psychiatrist)
states:

All too little has been done in
clinical and laboratory study of
such alleged UFO-related psychic
and psychological effects as anxiety
and panic reactions, confusion,
mood and personality changes, loss
of consciousness, automatisms, amnesia, paralysis, parasthesia,
weakness, wasting, burns, heat sensations, eye injury, transitory
blindness, hoarseness, skin lesions,

reported radiation effects, and healings.[8]

Dr. Bernard E. Finch writing in *Flying Saucer Review* of January-February, 1966, in his article "Beware the Saucers" refers to evidence collected over the previous twenty years. He states that the effects of relatively close UFO encounters include headaches, dizziness, hallucinations (including visual, auditory, and olfactory), emotional changes, delusions, and amnesia, with psychotic features. He says, "In several recent encounters there were symptoms of epileptiform discharge, with loss of consciousness."

Well known UFO researcher Charles Bowen, referring to the many ludicrous and bizarre, mind-bending, sickness-inducing, lethal UFO incidents, states that it is better not to be personally involved in UFO sightings rather than to be involved and risk a "50-50 chance of something nasty happening."[9]

On page 8 of *Flying Saucers Are Hostile* by Brad Steiger, he states, "There is a wealth of well-documented evidence that UFO's have been responsible for murders, assault, burnings with direct-ray focus, radiation sickness, kidnappings, pursuits of automobiles, attacks on homes, disruptions of power sources, paralysis, mysterious cremations, and destruction of aircraft."

Jerome Clark in his article "Why UFO's Are Hostile" in *Flying Saucer Review* of November-December, 1967, refers to some of the hostility cases and states:

> There are many similar cases. They usually occur in secluded areas in the darkness, and the witnesses are often paralyzed, as was Marias De Wilde, injured like Flynn or Jesus Paz, killed as were Miguel Jose Viana and Manuel Pereira de Cruz, kidnapped like Rivalino Mafra Da Silva.

Many of those who write about UFO's are by no means convinced that these things are friendly powers ready to help in any way they can. Those who study the subject very often come to quite different conclusions and agree with Jerome Clark that UFO's are basically hostile. Clark himself makes the point that the UFO's actually go to fantastic lengths to prevent us from knowing what they are doing, and states that in earlier articles he himself had approached the issue from the opposite corner, putting forward the argument that UFO's had shown they were friendly. He justifies his changed point of view on the basis of contact stories and argues at page 18, "The implication, then, is that the ufonauts are lying."

THE IMPORTANCE OF HOSTILITY INCIDENTS

According to Clark, it should be "very evident that the 'hostility' incidents deserve the greatest weight of all." He argues that in those activities the ufonauts are desperately covering up their own activities because there are some aspects which they dare not reveal. He claims that hundreds of humans have seen what they should not have seen, and that possibly thousands have lost their lives as a result.

Some of the incidents he quotes might seem farfetched, and yet if the hypothesis we are advancing in this book is correct then they are not beyond the bounds of possibility. Clark quotes the example of some African boys watching odd lights on Mount Kenya with some sort of intense activity going on. A few nights later a fleet of glowing objects swooped down over a nearby village and it was afterwards found that "the entire population of the village had been seared to death." Clark gives other documentation to suggest that these things and abductions are not uncommon.

MENTAL TREATMENT AFTER UFO CONTACT

The people contacted by UFO's are a normal cross section of the community: they are not crackpots or inmates of mental institutions. However, many are

hospitalized for psychiatric treatment AF-
TER being contacted. John Keel puts it
like this: "Millions of people have been affected at least temporarily by UFO contact, thousands have gone insane and
ended up in mental institutions after their
experiences with these things began."[10]

SEXUAL CONTACT WITH A UFO BEING

This episode involves a single woman
named Shane Kurz, a member of Contact
International, a worldwide organization of
UFO students.[11] After her initial sighting,
she began to change both physically and
mentally. In the two days preceding the experience she had noticed red marks on her
lower abdomen and had experienced pain,
nausea, and severe migraine headaches.
Later, she had nightmares and depression,
suffered loss of weight, and the complete
cessation of her monthly period. She now
found that she had developed psychic
abilities. Her eyesight grew worse, and
eventually, under hypnosis by parapsychologist Hans Holzer, Shane recollected
that she had been taken aboard a UFO and
literally raped. As is reported with the
Villas-Boas incident often referred to in
UFO writings, the attacker moaned like an
animal, and there was also a distinct cold
feeling. This also is common to other
incubi-succubi reports (sex with male or
female demons).

Incredible? There are many such reports. We have no desire to dwell on perverse sexual activities, but they are a part of the pattern. We are reminded of Genesis 6:2: "The sons of God saw the daughters of men. . . ."

Many other examples of hostility could be given. For example, John Keel has half a dozen in his book *The 8th Tower*. Dr. Jacques Vallee in *Passport to Magonia* lists some 20 incidents. They include the command to murder, murder threats, second and third degree burns, abductions, various types of threats, physical attacks, and possible deaths. Harold Wilkins, in his books *Flying Saucers Uncensored* and *Flying Saucers On The Attack*, gives numerous examples of UFO hostility, as does Brad Steiger in his book *Flying Saucers are Hostile*. John Keel in *UFO's — Operation Trojan Horse*, has many examples.

In *Flying Saucers* for September, 1962, as well as the preceding issue, there are about 60 instances of UFO hostility against aircraft, and other incidents. In *Flying Saucers* for December, 1958, there is an article entitled "Hostile Spacecraft" that gives several examples, and we could go on. There are at least several hundred cases of kidnapping have been reported. This is something that any benign alien society would probably not attempt. There are also numerous records of people lapsing into trance-states after the contact and many cases of power blackouts. There are teleportations, deliberate attempts to frighten people out of their wits, losses of consciousness, difficulties in breathing, and much more.

Still these cases are clearly in the minority when we consider the great number of potential UFO sightings and close encounters. However, this is in line with what we would expect from a source that is inherently evil. We would expect to find a minority of evil events and a majority of either innocuous or benign events. That is just what we do find. There are numerous cases of UFO-related healings which parallel the healings to be found in the occult and psychic literature. Satan masquerades as an angel of light, and that is the best method of deception. However, his true nature is revealed in the reports that we have enumerated.

If there is one thing to be learned from the above reports, it is that *it is a wise thing to avoid encounters with UFO's or their occupants.*

Footnotes: Chapter Six

1. This incident comes from the *APRO Bulletin* for June and July, 1976. Further details come from *The Canadian UFO Report*, Volume 3, No. 8, summer of 1976.
2. This is reported from the November, 1975 issue of the *APRO Bulletin.*
3. A refutation of the seventeen page copyrighted Phil Klass report claiming this was a hoax can be found in the *APRO Bulletin* for July and August, 1976.
4. From the *APRO Bulletin*, March, 1975.
5. *Flying Saucer Review,* Special Issue, No. 5, November, 1973, pp. 12-13.
6. *Flying Saucer Review,* Special Issue, No. 2, June, 1969, p. 64-65.
7. Reported in *Flying Saucer Review,* Vol. 19, No. 2, pp. 14-15.
8. From the *Canadian U.F.O. Report,* Vol. 1, No. 8, Fall 1970.
9. *Flying Saucer Review,* Vol. 19, No. 5, p. 27.
10. *Strange Creatures From Time And Space,* p. 189.
11. Recorded in the *Ufonauts* by Hans Holzer, Chapter 9.

"The examples of apparent absurdity are very numerous and we even find almost always one or two absurd details in every well reported case, especially in the [close encounter] category. Some cases . . . are veritable festivals of absurdity."
Aime Michel
Noted UFO researcher
The Humanoids, p. 255

"A lot of contact cases and close encounters show creatures that conform with earlier mythological and anthropological descriptions."
Parapsychologist Dr. Arthur C. Hastings
The Edge of Reality, p. 250

Chapter 7
MONSTERS, SMELLS, AND MINI-MEN

By now we are ready for anything; otherwise we would not be still reading. Electromagnetism that is not electromagnetism; physical activities that defy known laws of physics; real experiences that are known only in the mind; we have seen all this and so much more as we have tracked these elusive UFO's.

Yet another strange effect is related to lower forms of life. In an article entitled "Mysterious Physiological Effects of Flying Saucers,"[1] Gordon Creighton quotes from Dr. W. Buhler of Rio de Janeiro concerning a saucer sighting that involved two crocodile hunters. They saw a saucer-shaped UFO, and not only did they have the distinct feeling that they themselves were under surveillance, but they suddenly noticed another extraordinary thing. Tropical forests are never silent, and insects such as cicadas keep up a din in the

Brazilian Jungle. "But now, for a brief
time, all these noises were cut out: not a
cicada or any other insect was to be
heard."[2] A third member of the party had
also been strangely upset because of the
awful silence in the forest.

There are many examples of animals
whining and in other ways showing terror
when UFO's are sighted. This episode in
the Brazilian jungle could fit into the same
category.

A HORSE AND A DOG
PARALYZED

Another incident involving animals was
with 15 year-old Oscar Iriart. Near Buenos
Aires, he came across two beings who
gazed fixedly at him with deep-set eyes,
and he noticed the odd fact that "their legs
were semi-transparent."[3] They communicated with the boy in his own
language, Spanish, and also gave him a
message in Spanish, written on an en-
velope, "You are going to know the world
(signed) F. Saucer," but the spelling was
not correct, for the final "D" was not on
the Spanish word for "you" — "usted."

The machine that brought the beings
then disappeared. Oscar ran over to his
horse, only to find that both the horse and
his dog were temporarily paralyzed. Investigators ran to where Oscar claimed the

machine had stood, and to their astonishment they found three holes that formed a perfect triangle, the base being two meters (6 feet, 6 inches) and the other sides 1.58 meters (5 feet) each. Five skeptics, including the police, set out to investigate, believing it was all a fake, but they themselves were soon alarmed as a luminous something approached them across the ground, only a few meters in the air. As a result of this incident they became firm believers in UFO's.

Although in this section we are dealing with animals and monsters, it is relevant to notice several points about this incident:

a. "Their legs were semitransparent." We shall see that incomplete forms are common with UFO entities.

b. The beings communicated in the boy's language. There are many examples of the local language being known, either orally, by writing, or by mental telepathy.

c. The boy felt "as if he had been asleep" during the contact, and his eyes had a strange bulging and disoriented look, as though he had been hypnotized.

d. Animals in the area were affected.

e. The physical evidences left by the vehicles were sufficient to convince the skeptical.

"BIZARRE ANIMALS, WITH THE HEADS OF BIRDS"

Sometimes the incidents involving animals are bizarre and virtually unbelievable. However, they are reported by hesitant people who know they are likely to be ridiculed. No doubt many of the experiences are "only in the mind," but that does not lessen its reality to the one experiencing such an incident, nor the cultural impact.

Lionel Trigano reports the experience of a businessman who was driving along near Var in France, in November, 1962. He came across a group of figures, and as they moved away from the center of the road he saw "some kind of bizarre animals, with the heads of birds, and covered in some sort of plumage, which were hurling themselves from two sides towards my car."[4] He wound up his window and accelerated like a madman. About 150 yards further on, he looked back and saw these beings with "a sort of flapping of wings," moving toward a luminous dark blue object. It hung in the air over a field on the other side of the road.

At first sight these stories are totally unacceptable, but let us turn aside for a moment. At Job 1:6 we read of Lucifer (Satan) going to and fro in the earth and walking up and down in it. He has a preoccupation with Planet Earth, and it is

therefore not surprising to find the constant interest of UFO occupants in this
planet. In the last Book of the Bible,
Revelation 12:7, we read of Michael and
his angels fighting against the dragon:
"That old serpent called the Devil and
Satan, which deceives the whole world." If
the Bible describes Satan in this sort of
language, is it so surprising to find so many
strange forms associated with the Devil
and his fallen angels? That same verse tells
us that the Devil knows he has but a short
time, and he is manifesting his great wrath
by his evil activities on the earth.

It is relevant to notice that in the Garden
of Eden Satan appeared in the form of a
serpent; he was disguised as one of the
animal species as part of his strategy to
deceive mankind. It is, therefore, not surprising to find that such disguises are apparently still being used in the weird
manifestations around the world. We read
elsewhere of Satan being transformed into
an angel of light (II Corinthians 11:13),
and lights are constantly associated with
UFO entities, another relevant "coin-
cidence" when we consider the whole matter of UFO's and their appearances to men.
The "angel of light" reference again implies that Satan and his demons cover
their evil intentions by appearing as
benevolent creatures, a common feature of
UFO stories.

THE LOCH NESS MONSTER

Not only are "normal" animals often involved in UFO encounters, but so also are great monsters. The question arises, "Fact or Fiction?"

In an article entitled, "Monsters and UFO's — Some Observations on Loch Ness,"[5] F. W. Holiday asks if it is justifiable, in view of his own research, to suspect that water monsters exist in the same dimension as UFO's, sharing a similar quality of reality, whatever that might be. He points to similar difficulties in photographing both the monsters and the UFO's. As typical evidence he tells us that "teams of volunteer cameramen, armed with 35mm cine cameras fitted with 20" or 36" telephoto lenses, have failed to film a monster even though the objects are visible during every watching season (May to October). By 1968, it was becoming obvious, at least to me, that there were factors involved of which we knew nothing."[6]

Holiday goes on to tell how he noticed unusual psychological effects on witnesses (including himself) when monsters were seen. At first he was unaware that similar effects had been noted in those who had been involved with UFO sightings. On the matter of repeated failures with cameras, he says, "The catalogue of unexplainable misses with high-power cameras at Loch Ness has now become absurd." He gives a number of examples of this and suggests that such effective secretivity can no longer be attributed to normal animal caution but must be seriously considered as paranormal. An organic creature cannot deliberately manipulate humans or machinery in order to preserve the mystery associated with its own identity, as the Loch Ness monsters appear to do.

Holiday testifies that he himself has been involved with blackouts for which there is no medical reason evident, and that in 1966 he had three experiences with UFO's. Three times during the last seven years he has found himself in houses containing a poltergeist, and eventually he recognized that monsters should be regarded as manifestations akin to UFO's and that psychic activity seemed to be a part of the total picture. He yet makes it clear that he is sure the Loch Ness monsters and other lake monsters are not shadowy apparitions, but they are solid objects that have great mass. He gives examples of the evidence such as when the Royal Navy "HSL" hit such a monster when the ship was traveling through Loch Ness in 1943. Its steel bow was damaged. He gives other seemingly convincing proof, but the strange fact is that there is little evidence that these things have been recorded on the usual recording equipment. He suggests that they never leave excreta on land, and yet some of the land patches associated with them are rather like the flying saucer "nests" that have been described and photographed.

MONSTERS HIDE THEIR IDENTITY

In an article entitled "Designed Anonymity — A Common Factor in UFO and Aquatic Monsters,"[7] Kenneth C. Bayman discusses *Holiday's* article referred to above. He discusses the parallels between monsters and UFO's, then states:

> Perhaps the most significant parallel between these two phenomena is that despite intensive and sustained investigation, both by scientists and lay persons, they have succeeded completely in hiding the secret of their identity. There have been many theories to account for them, but these remain unproven.[8]

He suggests that many contactees have been duped by the UFO occupants into believing that their vehicles are of interplanetary origin: "The imputation is that if UFO entities wish to keep their real identity secret, one effective way of doing so would be to lead people to think they were something else."

Bayman makes the point that the anonymity of these entities possibly "reflects a superimposed policy of the Deity, because throughout the Bible meddling with the 'occult' or hidden things is sternly forbidden." Mosaic law certainly insisted that contact with that world of familiar spirits was totally forbidden (Deuteronomy 18).

It is also relevant that the worship of a number of Israel's neighbors involved animals. Bulls were commonly worshipped and so were many other animals. Myths and legends included legendary dragons* and various other monsters. To the Babylonians even creation was associated with a monster cut in half, with the pieces supposedly used for the creation of heaven and earth. Monsters were very much a part of ancient religious motifs.

MONSTERS SMELLING LIKE SULPHUR

There are various other cases where huge creatures have been involved with UFO's. Psychiatrist Berthold Eric Schwarz wrote an article entitled, "Berserk: A UFO Creature Encounter."[9] The location of the incident was in the general area of Western

---

*Some scientists are now re-examining their position concerning the actual existence of creatures formerly assumed to be legendary or mythological, i.e. dragons. See *Dinosaurs: Those Terrible Lizards* (San Diego: Creation-Life Publishers, Inc., 1977), p. 50 ff.

Pennsylvania: in six counties there were a large number of documented creature cases. One of these was at 10:30 P.M. on Thursday, October 25, 1973, on a farm not far from Greensburgh. A number of witnesses saw two creatures, one about seven feet tall and the other a little over eight feet, completely covered with long dark grey hair and having greenish-yellow eyes, and arms hanging down almost to the ground. There was a strong odor present, described as something like burning rubber. When one of the creatures was hit by a bullet fired from close range, it moved its hand up toward the other creature. At that point their glowing vehicle disappeared, leaving behind a glowing white area. Then the creatures turned around and walked back toward the woods, apparently unaffected by the shot.

The police were brought in, and they too saw a huge creature. As the description goes on, we read that the witnesses "smelled a very strong sulphur, or chemical-like odor."[10] Once again they saw a strange being, this time a man in a black hat and cloak, carrying a sickle. According to the report, he told the contactee, a farmer named Stephen Pulaski, "If man doesn't straighten up, the end will come soon." The report also states that he said, "There is a Man here now who can save the world."

Some 13 people were involved in this

series of experiences, and five empty rifle shells were found at the site. The creatures themselves simply disappeared while walking back into the woods. Dr. Schwarz comments: "As in other alleged creature [and UFO] situations, it is amazing that after all the action there is such an overall paucity or even a total absence of tangible evidence for the events."

The farmer, Stephen Pulaski, reported many bizarre aspects, with UFO lights coming and going without any clearly discernible source, and with the creatures involving themselves in strange appearances and disappearances. Stephen entered into a state of fugue when his bullets were ineffective, and he was also virtually "possessed" by the creatures.

In view of these strange happenings, Dr. Schwarz raises the possibility that the myth of the ancient were-wolf could possibly have a germ of truth in it. Some of these more modern creatures have killed chickens, ripped off the hindquarters of a St. Bernard dog, and have even torn the throat of a pet deer.[11] Significantly, he refers to an entranced Polish medium named Kluski allegedly materializing a large bird of prey, a lion, and an anthropoid ape. He tells us that, as with UFO creatures, there were associated stenches.

Dr. Schwarz suggests that the greatest care should be exercised when collecting and reporting data about these creatures. He mentions that because the phenomenon is not explainable by any known technology of Planet Earth, there are those who say that, therefore, it must come from a different planet. He points out that such an approach appears to involve other vast and impenetrable possibilities.

SIMILARITIES BETWEEN UFO'S AND MONSTERS

Investigators have found some strange similarities between the UFO's and the monsters. There have been dozens of occasions when large numbers of men have gone looking for reported monsters. They have been armed with rifles, have been accompanied by bloodhounds and helicopters, and have thoroughly searched areas where the monsters have been reported being seen by credible witnesses. Despite thorough searching, no substantial trace of the animals has ever been found, and it would appear that these creatures are in the same category as the UFO phenomenon. Mysterious elusiveness has been the pattern right through the years, whenever strange monsters have been reported and hunted.

The monster in Loch Ness has consistently resisted scientific investigators. There have been many weird coincidences and strange happenings, such as the monster either appearing just after the photographer on duty had gone off for lunch, or for some other reason had temporarily left his observation post. Expensive cameras have failed to function just when the monster appeared, but were normal again as soon as it had gone out of sight. It is even a fact that films which should have been successful have been blank when developed.

THAT STRANGE SULPHUR SMELL

A number of times we have referred in passing to a strange smell associated with UFO appearances. They are part of these mysterious UFO phenomena, so we shall refer to several others.

In his article entitled "Trancas After Seven Years,"[12] Oscar A. Galindez describes "a penetrating odor resembling the smell of sulphur" associated with UFO's. Galindez comments that during the considerable period this experience was taking place, with a number of UFO occupants involved, "the farm dogs, renowned for their fierceness, never barked once. Nor did they bark after the objects had vanished. The dogs seemed dazed, as though asleep. The same effects were observed in the hens."[13] He also reports that a number of carob trees in the area were withered a few days later. Beams from the UFO had affected them, and those beams actually penetrated a solid building and reconstituted themselves on the other side of the wall of that building.

At the time the whole atmosphere was impregnated with a smell like sulphur, and Galindez compares this sulphur smell with various Argentine cases, for this had been a distinctive feature there. It is worth noticing that in this particular article the penetrating light from the UFO was reported as having some sort of passageway along which about 40 silhouettes of human type figures could be seen moving, as though inside a tube. Charles Bowen describes the smell in a rather different way. In an article entitled "More Unusual Humanoids,"[14] he tells of a young man whose first name was Peter. He was sitting with his young lady in a car when he noticed an intruder. On investigation he found it was between four and five feet high, but appeared to have no legs — "The thing was too low, squat, and square to be a man."[15] When it moved, it was with a gliding motion.

Peter drove off in a hurry, but he and his young lady returned to the same site about two weeks later. The report states, "When Peter opened the window to let in fresh air, he said an unpleasantly pungent smell, 'as of seaweed rotting in the hot sun,' assailed their nostrils. Although they saw or heard

nothing, he told the reporter they drove
away in some alarm."

John Keel is another who refers to this
awful smell, rather like rotten eggs, marsh
gas, or hydrogen sulphide. He mentions
that another characteristic activity of the
UFO beings is that they nearly always appear closer to water such as lakes, streams,
reservoirs, or swamps. He concludes that
this smell accompanies the entity, but is
not necessarily produced by it. Keel
suggests, "This smell is a by-product of the
chemical process which produces the
transmogrification" (i.e. the change to
visibility).[16]

That strange smell keeps turning up in
the sightings, and in fact it is referred to in
some reports included in this book for
other purposes. Traditionally, the Devil
and his demons have been associated with
sulphur. Perhaps there is a factual basis
for the tradition.

MONSTROSITIES WITHOUT
MOUTHS, HANDS, FEET

The strangeness associated with UFO
sightings does not end with the smell of
sulphur. Over and over again there are
reports of monstrosities, of beings without
mouths, not having hands or feet, only one
eye, and other abnormalities. Once again,
the reports come from widely separated
areas, with points so strikingly similar that

the whole matter needs to be taken seriously. Because of the strangeness of this concept we shall consider a number of cases.

In "Encounter With 'Devils,' "[17] Joel Mesnard and Claude Pavy tell of Francois Delpeuch, age 13, and his sister Anne Marie, 9, who suddenly saw four small creatures doing something near a large sphere. When the beings realized the children had seen them, they clambered back into their vehicle and took off. It made several circles, all the time climbing, with the intensity of its light increasing considerably. Then it flew off at full speed and "at the same time, a smell of sulphur began to spread, reaching the children. The cows started lowing. . . ."[18]

The article suggests that the smell of sulphur can be confused with that of ozone, and that such a smell has been noticed at a number of UFO landings. Some five and a half hours later, at 4 P.M. on the same day, the police were on the spot and confirmed the existence of that sulphurous smell. The children were separately investigated, but though the questions extended over a considerable period of time, at no point did they contradict their story.

"A WEIRD, UNBELIEVABLE PARANORMAL FORCE IS AT WORK"

Sometimes people who see monsters, UFO entities, and paraphysical phenomena, actually see only an eye, but their mind causes them to see the body surrounding the eye. John Keel says, "In occult lore, eyes — or a single huge eye — play a very important role. The eye is an ancient symbol for the deity. Persons suffering from paranoia (schizophrenia) see eyes everywhere."[19]

These are manifestations of false deities, and we are reminded of the eye of Horus in ancient Egyptian mythology. (Indeed, the eye is seen on every American dollar bill!) John Keel says, "A weird, unbelievable paranormal force is at work on this planet, and it is time we looked at it the way it is, not the way we think or wish it to be."[20]

Strange smells . . . paralyzed animals . . . light beams that pass through bricks . . . monsters that avoid being photographed . . . and still there is more. Often, the beings associated with UFO's are incomplete. Let us illustrate.

In *The Flying Saucer Review*, Vol. 17, No. 2, of March-April, 1971, there is an article, "The Question of Reality" by Luis Schonherr. He states a number of interesting things, including the fact that often UFO entities appear to have missing,

transparent, or indistinct extremities, or
that witnesses could see no arms, or they
appeared to be held close to the body.[21]
In other cases their legs are supposedly
transparent; sometimes the grass could be
seen through them, while at other times
the lower part of the body appeared to be
indistinct. Schonherr goes on to state:

> This kind of thing has frequently
> been reported about the
> phenomena of the seance room.
> Materializations of persons are
> seldom complete — often only the
> head appears, while legs and arms
> are either indistinct, or deformed,
> or partially missing.

SIMILARITIES BETWEEN UFO'S, THE SEANCE ROOM, AND DEMONOLATRY

Once again, we see a distinct
relationship between UFO entities and the
appearances brought into being at
spiritists' seances. It is relevant to notice
that these beings have great difficulty in
materializations at all times, and for this
reason they need to find human media if
they are to be reasonably successful. Over
and over again UFO's are blobs and indistinct in their features.

Once more we read of the missing
features, for Schonherr goes on to say,

"Some observers report non-moving lips and eyes, missing lips and noses, boneless structure, or a very hard (scaly) body surface." He suggests that the mechanical type movements and stiff gait and other actions of these beings "could point to a lack of coordination in the sensorimotor system, and it may be noted that the same behavior is often observed in hysterical or mentally deranged people." The entities are not real beings, and true human flesh is denied them, although in the occult literature at times they do *appear* as normal humans. It stands to reason that there are often coordination problems with their sensorimotor activities.

It is relevant to notice that Schonherr is suggesting that the UFO occupants are, in fact, creatures who are associated with the earth but belonging to a different time period. He agrees that their reported appearance or behavior points to mentally and physically degenerate mutants, "a rather gloomy outlook, if the entities should really be earthmen, i.e., time travelers coming back from what we call our future."[22] Schonherr suggests that this does not at present nullify the extraterrestrial hypothesis, but argues that some alleged incidents are more consistent with the facts of a time travel hypothesis than the extraterrestrial hypothesis.

We are certainly not arguing for a "time travelers" hypothesis, but indicating that the solid facts are demanding an answer. That answer is not provided by an extraterrestrial hypothesis: it is, however, provided from the spiritual realm.

This is touched on by Janet Gregory in an article entitled "Similarities in UFO and Demon Lore."[23] She states, "Other details from UFO cases spring to mind when reading *Demonolatry*. The demons which appeared to witches were by nature incorporeal, but could form for themselves a humanlike body whenever they wished. However, this body was always in some way imperfect, and witches have described the following characteristics of their 'Little Masters'. . . ."[24] She goes on to describe them as having features that were with deepset, flashing eyes, with thin and deformed hands. Their bodies were never in proper proportion, but were either unnaturally small or large. They always gave forth a sulphurous smell.

Demonolatry, the book referred to above, was a sixteenth century production by Nicolas Remy. Janet Gregory also quotes from Gordon Creighton in *The Humanoids*, which showed that these creatures were "giants, tall men, medium or normal size men, small men, tiny men, hairy bellicose dwarfs, greenish creatures, hairy giants." They were indeed coming in a variety of shapes and sizes. She goes on to show a number of cases where features such as a smell of sulphur and beings whose

limbs were out of proportion to their bodies
are commonly associated with UFO
reports. She quotes further from
Demonolatry as to voices being formed out
of the air and sounding in the ears of men.
She tells us that demons do not have
tongues, palates, or throat functionings,
but they can inform the air with any
speech they choose, and also that witches
insist that they are spoken to in their own
tongue quite naturally and idiomatically.

"HAS THEIR PHILOSOPHY CHANGED?"

Janet Gregory is not prepared to admit
that all UFO's are evil manifestations, but
she does agree that many UFO reports fit
in with visitations that were taking place
several hundred years ago, though "in
some details, such as dress and mode of
transport, the visitors have moved with the
times."[25] She concludes her article with
the question, "Has their philosophy
changed?" In this volume we are
suggesting that their philosophy has not
changed: demonic deceptions might
change in method, but not in philosophy.

Deformed creatures and incomplete beings appear very often in the UFO
literature. Professor R. L. Johannis of
Milan is reported as seeing a flying saucer
with two dwarflike occupants in it.[26] In his
statement he claims they came to within a

few paces from him and then halted. He states, "I had no strength left, I seemed to be completely paralyzed, or to be dreaming." Later he was actually felled to the ground.

He described the dwarfs as having no signs of hair, and the skins of their faces were an earthly green somewhat like sculptors' plasticine. Beneath their noses was a mere slit which "I saw opening and closing again at intervals, very much like the mouth of a fish. The 'eyes' were enormous, protruding and round."[27] They had hats on instead of hair, and he described their color as being like two well ripe, yellow-green plums.

GROTESQUE REPORTS ARE CONSISTENT

This description is typical of many others that are similar, with little creatures about four feet high and having strange openings for mouths, or no opening at all. Over and over again their extremities are deformed or grotesque — or simply not there. Twenty years ago these descriptions would have been regarded as funny by virtually everybody and not taken seriously. However, the great number of similar reports mean that these days they are taken seriously, even by many who would hate to be identified with such a viewpoint.

We shall give extracts from some other typical reports: the number could be enlarged considerably.

In *Flying Saucer Review*, Vol. 14, No. 5, of September-October, 1968, there is a description of a group of five figures. They had come from a light that approached a car in which there were a man, his wife, and his daughter on a road in Pennsylvania:

> They just stood there, about 10 feet from the car. They looked like human beings, but their faces were totally devoid of expression and unlike a human face. Their eyes, if you could call them such, were horizontal slits about this long (she extended her forefinger and thumb to indicate the length of their slits). I could not see any irises or pupils — just slits. Their noses were narrow and pointed, not unlike a human nose, and their mouths were slits like the eyes . . . the skin on their faces and hands was rough looking — it resembled scar tissue or skin which has been severely burned.

"IT'S ANOTHER WORLD"

These beings are often described as having no feet and with other parts of their body missing. As Drs. Hynek and Vallee put it, "It's another world, another realm, that seems to have some interlocking with ours. . . ."[28] They recognize that the beings are sometimes seen in various creature forms, and "certainly can't resemble the products of higher evolution as we conceive them. Who would think of a clawed creature coming down and being a representative of a very advanced technology? It just doesn't fit."[29]

In *Flying Saucer Review*, Vol. 19, No. 3, of May-June, 1973, Dr. P. M. H. Edwards, Professor of Linguistics at the University of Victoria, British Columbia, has a comment about coincidences in relation to a landing in Brazil, witnessed by Taago Machado. Every time Machado sketched the face of the ufonauts he placed their right eyes somewhat lower than the left eyes. He reported that their teeth were black, their gait was slow and stiff, their hands had four fingers, but "that they had thumbs which protruded from the arm but were much higher towards the elbow than is the case with human thumbs."[30]

Yet another description relates to a case in Belohorizonte, reported from Rio de Janeiro. There were four individuals, well over six feet in height, but they had only one round eye without any white to it, according to the three children who saw and described them.[31]

Charles Bowen tells of a report in which the description is of "a luminous man emitting a green glow from head to foot,"[32] and of another case in Brazil where there were "beings of approximately one meter (about 39 inches) in height, black, with heads shaped like potatoes and with inflated bellies."[33] Another Brazilian episode he quotes involved a medical doctor who had a conversation with a small visitor who "was dressed in something like evening (smoking) dress. He had a misshapen head, no mouth, and two enormous eyebrows."[34] According to the doctor, the visitor expressed himself in perfect Spanish. We again point out that over and over again we read that these visitors are thoroughly familiar with the language of the particular area they are visiting.

Bowen discusses the various types of beings that appear, ranging from "pilots" of small stature to giants and unearthly creatures such as mothmen, birds, and flatwoods monsters. He refers to a previous article of his own where he had suggested the possibility of a war in space. He then states, "I think we should consider there is still in a sense a 'war', but not necessarily in interplanetary or interstellar space. Could this struggle not be the ages-old one between what we know as good and bad?"[35]

With the last sentence we agree: a conflict continues between the forces of good and evil, between God Himself and the

great being who was once His special creation. That being rebelled, aspiring to be as
God, and ever since he has been trying to
take the throne of God. He knows his time
is short, and the conflict is intensified as he
engages in the preliminaries before the last
great conflict when he himself will be
forever defeated.

AND THAT WORLD IS SATAN'S WORLD

We have seen that partly formed beings
are often associated with UFO's and this
same strangeness is often mentioned in
relation to spiritists' seances. John Keel is
one researcher who discusses the reality of
seances and claims that some of these have
been genuinely photographed. He tells us
about the figure that materializes: "In the
majority of cases, the entity resembles an
Indian or an Oriental, with high
cheekbones, slanted eyes, and reddish or
olive skin."[36] Contactees often report that
aliens have oriental features. He says that
"fire elementals somehow utilize the
energy of flames and materialize in burning houses, fireplaces, furnaces. Then
there are water elementals, air elementals,
and elementals which feast upon the
energy of plants."

Our point is that here we have another
parallel to the UFO phenomenon. Both
UFO's and spiritism are manifestations of

the power of Satan. At seances, the materialization is more complete when the medium is in a deep trance than when he is only in a light trance. While sometimes the appearances of beings from UFO's are projections similar to hypnotic suggestion, at other times they are more literal appearances, at least paraphysical. Hence the need to paralyze a victim, or to utilize some other energy force, "borrowed" for the specific occasion.

Monsters, smells, and mini-men are frighteningly real. They come from Hell.

Footnotes: Chapter Seven

1. FSR, Vol. 13, No. 4, p. 5-7.
2. Ibid.
3. FSR, Vol. 14, No. 5, p. 26.
4. FSR, Vol. 14, No. 6, p. 18.
5. FSR, Vol. 17, No. 5, p. 12-14.
6. Ibid.
7. FSR, Vol. 19, No. 5, p. 29-32.
8. Ibid.
9. FSR, Vol. 20, No. 1, p. 3-12.
10. Ibid.
11. Ibid., p. 9.
12. FSR, Vol. 17, No. 3, p. 14-21.
13. Ibid.
14. FSR, Vol. 14, No. 3, p. 17-20.
15. Ibid.

16. *The Eighth Tower*, p. 124.
17. FSR, Vol. 14, No. 5, p. 7-10.
18. Ibid, p. 7.
19. Keel, *The Eighth Tower*, p. 124.
20. Ibid, p. 125.
21. FSR, Vol. 17, No. 2, p. 22-6.
22. Ibid.
23. FSR, Vol. 17, No. 2, p. 31-2.
24. Ibid.
25. Ibid.
26. FSR, Vol. 13, No. 1, p. 3-7.
27. Ibid.
28. *The Edge of Reality*, p. 155.
29. Ibid.
30. FSR, Vol. 19, No. 3, p. 23-6.
31. Ibid.
32. FSR, Vol. 14, No. 3, p. 17.
33. Ibid.
34. Ibid.
35. FSR, Vol. 14, No. 5, p. 12.
36. Keel, *UFO's: Operation Trojan Horse*, p. 232.

Chapter 8
UFO'S AND THE OCCULT

Part I

In this chapter we consider the high correlation between the occult and UFO phenomena. This is important because the province of demons is linked with the psychic or occult realm. This is not only a Biblical position, for it has justification historically and cross-culturally.[1] If the occult phenomena is demonic, and if the UFO phenomena is united to occult phenomena, it follows that the UFO phenomena is a demonic manifestation. In this chapter we will examine several research studies and their conclusions, show the correlations in the broad categories of the occult, and document over 150 specific examples. We have also documented the unity of the UFO phenomena to the occult in several categories, notably in five categories — Close Encounters I, II, and III, abductions, and contactee areas. We show that these UFO classifications cannot be arbitrarily divided (as many researchers have done),

but must be viewed as part and parcel with
the whole phenomena, each with similar
links to the occult. (Since this is a
"technical" matter, we have prepared an
appendix dealing with this subject.)

INVESTIGATION RESULTS

Although there are varying degrees of
frequency, we find the majority of occult
phenomena occurs in the UFO literature
on a common or semi-common basis. We
have already quoted numerous respected
researchers who have stated there is a close
resemblance in both fields. Now let us see
how well this research is supported.

CAPTAIN IVAR MACKAY

E. A. I. Mackay is a former chairman of
the British UFO Research Association, and
he has a profound knowledge of the occult
and parapsychological fields. He has
devoted almost half of his life to the study
of "occult and 'spiritualistic' physical
phenomena." As such, he is an authority.
However, Mackay gives a strong warning
about the "disastrous harm" that has
resulted to certain occult researchers, and
his warning should be taken seriously. It is
not an area in which to be involved. He
then gives dozens of parallels between
UFO and occult phenomena, noting there

are "very many more" subtle similarities
he does not mention. These parallels are
listed in his *UFO's and the Occult, Parts I
and II*, and are largely drawn from *non-
contactee* UFO phenomena. Many of his
correlations are found in the literature of
mediumism and in seance manifestations.[2]
Some of the parallels include the following:

a. Nauseous odors encountered in
   both seance rooms, haunted locations, and UFO landing sights.
   (They are also reported in contactee cases and are associated with
   the "monsters" that are found in
   both occultism and ufology.)
b. Falling materials or deposits of certain substances. These are found in
   both seances and poltergeist phenomena (e.g. ectoplasm and falling
   stones) and UFO phenomena (e.g.
   "angels hair" and oily fluids).
c. Aversion to strong light — both
   seance apparitions and UFO's
   share this characteristic.
d. Voices heard in the mind.
e. Levitation and teleportations.
f. Decrease (or increase) in temper-
   atures.
g. Instantaneous appearing, disappearing, enlargement, and reduc-
   tion of phenomena.

h. Similarity in entity characteristics — transparent, incomplete, semi-solid, solid, or vaporous.
i. Unusual noises and high pitched sounds.
j. Inapplicability of physical laws.
k. The dreamlike qualities of some encounters and the distortion and/or breaking up of normal time sequence.
l. Similar effects on humans physically and psychologically, e.g. control by another entity, prickly, tingling sensations, temporary paralysis, etc.

UFO ENTITIES

In another paper, Mackay further explores the relationships between UFO and occult entities. He divides each area into three categories and finds we are dealing with essentially one phenomenon. He concludes:

Further, if one sets the three occult groups against the three classifications of UFO entities and their characteristics it is rather surprising how complementary to each other they appear to be, not only through their appearance, activities, and level of behavior, but also in the quality of mental and, especially, emotional reaction and response that has been noted to have occurred on contact.[3]

THE RESEARCH OF LYNN CATOE

We have referred to Lynn E. Catoe, who was the senior bibliographer for the study commissioned by the Air Force Office of Scientific Research, *UFO's and Related Subjects: An Annotated Bibliography*. It was prepared in conjunction with the Condon Committee research of 1966-1968 and is the most comprehensive bibliography to date. Over 1600 books and articles are listed. This literature survey took two full years, and Miss Catoe had to read through thousands of books, articles, and publications to prepare the 412-page volume. As such, her conclusions are very significant. In her preface she notes that "a large part of the available UFO literature" is closely linked with the occult and the metaphysical and gives examples such as mental telepathy, automatic writing, poltergeist manifestations, demon possession, and general psychic phenomena.[4]

THE WORK OF JOHN KEEL

John A. Keel is considered by many people to be among the most authoritative researchers in the world. He has spent years doing firsthand research among UFO percipients of all classes and knows the field as well as any man. He has written several books and numerous articles on UFO's, reflecting over ten years of near-continuous UFO research. His books include *UFO's: Operation Trojan Horse, Our Haunted Planet, Strange Creatures From Time and Space, The Mothman Prophecies,* and *The Eighth Tower.* They are a goldmine of documentation, showing UFO's to be demonic manifestations, and they clearly indicate the superiority of the demonic theory. In fact, given the Biblical world view, his research (particularly in *Operation Trojan Horse*) leaves few, if any, other options available. We can summarize his research with his statement: "The UFO manifestations seem to be, by and large, merely minor variations of the age-old demonological phenomenon."[5] It is no exaggeration to state that his research encompasses hundreds of examples and parallels between UFO's and the occult.

THE RESEARCH OF JACQUES VALLEE

Dr. Vallee is another authority, one well acquainted with the two fields, being both a serious UFO researcher and a parapsychologist. In his third UFO book, *Passport to Magonia,* he describes 923 UFO landings from 1868-1968. Time and again there are references to numerous occult phenomena and the demonic is evident throughout the book. In his subsequent book, *The Invisible College*, he brings out dozens of other cases involving the occult and he states: "No theory of UFO's can be deemed acceptable if it does not account for the reported psychic effects produced by these objects."[6] He also notes the connection between close encounters and the occult: "In recent years, too, the report of paranormal events in connection with close encounters with UFO's seems to have become the rule rather than the exception."[7] This idea finds further support in *The Humanoids*, a compilation and analysis of over 300 landings and contacts.[8]

OTHER STUDIES

Several other studies have brought out the correlations. Jerome Clark and Loren Colemans wrote *The Unidentified*, and it is another goldmine of occult parallels. Although interpreted in light of Carl Jung's "collective unconscious" theory, the parallels are still evident. In fact, the demonic theory would provide them with solutions to many of the perplexities they have encountered which apparently made them opt for the Jungian interpretation, about which they themselves are not so

sure. The independent existence of powerful paraphysical entities — having the
desire and means to confuse and deceive,
that are capable of manifestations on the
physical and psychic levels, and yet
nevertheless are ultimately restricted in
their influence and power — explains the
facts quite well without recourse to totally
subjective phenomena.

Another study is that by Bryant and
Helen Reeve. They spent two years and
traveled over 23,000 miles, interviewing
and living with UFO contactees. Their
book, *Flying Saucer Pilgrimage*, is another
virtual bonanza of occult parallels involving numerous cases of mediumism, occult
philosophy, and occult methods of contact.
We could mention other studies,[9] but
the point is clear. Solid research by respected UFO investigators points to the
occult explanation. It is significant that in
several of the above studies certain common ideas were expressed. These include:

a. The UFO's are not extraterrestrial
but originate on this planet.
b. They have been with us throughout all of human history, although
assuming different guises.
c. They are clearly capable of evil and
deception, although they may not
act that way.
d. They operate on both the physical

and psychic planes, primarily the latter.

e. They are nearly one and the same with occult phenomena.

The significant point is that the above five tenets are exactly and precisely what is expected in the demonic theory.

GENERAL OCCULT CORRELATIONS

If we examine the world of the occult in a very broad sense, we find half a dozen or so characteristics which are predominant. These include:

a. The contacting of a higher or supernatural entity, generally, but not always, while in a partial or full trance state, as in mediumism. This contact may or may not involve possession and may be precipitated by the person or by the entity.

b. The contact is often made through supernatural occult means — ouija board, automatic writing, altered states of consciousness, astral projections, yoga, hypnosis, etc.

c. The occurrence of both physical manifestations and violations of physical law.

d. Harmful physical-psychological effects.

e. Messages with a non-Biblical content.
f. Either the person has an occult background and/or psychic abilities before contact, or develops them soon after.
g. A "psychic transformation or illumination" is experienced, usually involving a new metaphysical and non-Biblical outlook.

We shall examine these in turn.

CONTACTING A SUPER-NATURAL ENTITY

Mediumism is the classic example, and numerous parallels are found in the UFO contactee phenomena. Parallels are noted by most of the researchers referred to earlier. Clark and Coleman state:

> In the considerable majority of cases the contact experience, which comprises the core of the enigma, occurs in a state of altered consciousness. . . . We see no alternative but to view the flying saucer contactee as a modern-day spiritualist medium, religious mystic, shaman . . . etc.[10]

Brad Steiger notes that many contactees, while in communication with the "extraterrestrials" are nearly indistinguishable from mediums in a seance.[11] Trevor James has noticed that some contactees establish communication "after preparatory measures closely resembling those of a seance. . . ."[12] Finally, we would like to comment upon Dr. Nandor Fodor's *Encyclopedia of Psychic Science*. Recognizing this as a wealth of accurate information on the occult world and its manifestations, much of it coming from mediumism and the seance room, we decided to see just how much UFO overlap there was. To say the least, the parallels are very numerous. As an example, we have listed fifty pages wherein scores of parallels are evident.[13] One could even call the volume a storehouse of knowledge on ufology. We are not the only ones to notice the connection. After making our examination, we encountered this statement by psychiatrist, parapsychologist, and top UFO researcher, Dr. Berthold E. Schwarz. He has spent a lifetime of study in these areas. He says:

> Well studied spontaneous cases where the parallels between psi [psychic] and UFO phenomena are striking. You can read Nandor Fordor's masterful book, *The Encyclopedia of Psychic Sciences*, and many of the examples he draws on pertaining to the great mediums are right out of modern ufology, including luminous lights, entities, poltergeists, and the whole works.[14]

Hence, we can see that mediumism and

ufology seem to be part and parcel of the same phenomena. In fact, D. Scott Rogo, referring to Uri Geller says, "The history of mediumship is littered with accounts of such [UFO] contact."[15]

PLAYFUL POLTERGEISTS?

Poltergeists are often associated with both the occult and UFO's. There appears to be a parallel between UFO flaps and poltergeist outbreaks, both numerically and geographically.[16] Sometimes UFO percipients or contactees end up having poltergeist visitations.[17] Poltergeists are demons who pretend to be playful or bothersome spirits. One result is they get people interested in occult and psychic phenomena, seances, etc., and they tend to foster a false view of the next life.[18] Poltergeists are usually responsible for the so-called haunted houses. It was poltergeist phenomena that resulted in the tragic events occurring in the life of the late Bishop Pike.[19]

Finally, possession in general is a hallmark of the occult. There are thousands of documented cases, many involving very ugly endings for those possessed.[20] The phenomena is very similar, if not identical, to the possession of UFO contactees and some close encounter UFO cases. In both, the person is taken over by the invading entity, sometimes voluntarily, sometimes involuntarily, and controlled by the entity for whatever purposes it has in mind. There are hundreds, if not thousands of cases of possession among contactees or UFO percipients. They are mentioned by Keel, Steiger, Norman, Schwarz, Reeve, Catoe, and many others.[21]

CONTACT VIA OCCULT METHODS

Continued communications or contact with UFO's is almost always done by occult means. We could list numerous examples, but only a few need be noted. Ouija boards and automatic writing are two methods utilized. Dr. Vallee discusses several cases of contact via automatic writing — including Uri Geller.[22] This procedure involves mediumistic trance states in which the entity controls the individual and writes or types (or paints, composes music, etc.) through them. Bryant and Helen Reeve in their interviews with contactees around the world mention that communication with UFO's and the extraterrestrials is always done by occult means. They state:

> In fact we found that the most significant, interesting, and valuable information regarding outer space has not been coming through physical contacts but through other means.[23]

They then list the various types of communication. It is interesting that they discovered that "most physical contacts only last a few moments, and the information gained is usually negligible." The communication methods they found were:

a. Psychic emergence or materialization.
b. Projections of consciousness.
c. Automatic writing.
d. Dictation (recording voices heard in the mind).
e. E.S.P. (extrasensory perception).
f. Telepathy.
g. Clairaudience.
h. Clairvoyance.
i. Mediumship.
j. Samadhic (yogic) meditation.
(True yoga, contrary to popular belief, is documented as a dangerous form of occultism.[24] Even Dr. Carl Jung, sympathetic to occult-eastern teachings states: "Often one hears and reads about the dangers of yoga, particularly of the ill-reputed Kundalini yoga. The deliberately induced psychotic state, which in certain unstable individuals might easily lead to a real psychosis, is a danger that needs to be taken very seriously indeed.

These things really are dangerous
and ought not to be meddled with
in our typically Western way. It . . .
can let loose a flood of sufferings of
which no sane person ever
dreamed."[25])

k. Akashic records (an occult source
and guise for demonic manipulation).

l. Sound and sight rays.

m. Inspired writings (i.e. published
books done via automatic writing).

n. Electronic (reminiscent of Uri
Geller and the demonic Raudive
[electronic communication with
the dead] phenomena).

Without exception the above methods
are occultic, and it is most significant that
occult methods were the only ones they
found in all their contacts stretching across
23,000 miles and two years of travels. They
even go so far as to state: "Anyone who is
afraid to venture beyond the physical
world had best leave the subject of outer
space communication alone."[26] Another
important fact is that mediumship in its
various forms was the communication
method preferred most by the UFO beings.[27] Dr. Robert S. Ellwood of the University of Southern California states in
reference to UFO contactees and
mediumism:

Both types of groups employ the same manner of communication: vision and marvelous journeys, trance speaking and writing, seance circles, and telepathy. The close interaction between Spiritualism and UFO cults is not surprising, for one finds there is much exchange of persons between them. . . . in some cases, individual contactees have delivered trance messages from UFO's in a manner virtually identical to the trance-preaching of Spiritualism.[27a]

THE OUIJA BOARD

In passing we wish to sound a warning about using this so-called "game." While there are numerous cases of UFO contact,[28] this is not its only purpose. It is used for a variety of occult contacts. The ouija board is an exceptionally dangerous tool. People have become demon possessed through using it, and many have ended up in mental institutions because of it. Even William Blatty, author of *The Exorcist*, is well aware of this and refers to it as very dangerous. He says that mental institutions "are loaded with people" who got involved with the occult through the ouija board.[29] The ouija board is no game. Unfortunately it is a $20 million a year industry in the United States.

The best book on the subject, Edmond Gruss', *The Ouija Board* (Moody Press, 1975), shows that it is one of the easiest ways there is to become demon possessed.[30] There are thousands of cases. He also documents two cases of murder inspired by directions from the ouija board (i.e. the spirit behind it).[31] Murder has also been commanded by some of the extraterrestrials.[32] Hence, the ouija board, along with all forms of the occult, should be avoided.

We could go on to list numerous examples of other cases of UFO contact via the occult, but this has already been done in other sources.[33]

OCCULT MESSAGES

Literally tens of thousands of supernaturally received occult messages have been published in the U.S. since the spiritist movement began in 1848. We have personally studied hundreds of them and find they contain certain generally universal characteristics:

a. Denial of the key Biblical truths.
b. An appeal to human pride, either through a system of salvation by good works or reliance upon the "divine" within.
c. Urging the development of psychic powers and/or contact with

higher entities, beings, or "ascended masters," usually through altered states of consciousness; the encouragement to trust in these entities for their help and protection.

d. The giving of an important mission that only the contacted person or a select few can accomplish; control over them by the appeal to human emotions and experience.

e. The teachings of eastern and occult doctrines (e.g. reincarnation, Vedantic monism, impersonal ontology, universalism, the divinity of man, the dawning of a new psychic age, etc.).

When we study the UFO contactee phenomena we find *the very same messages revealed*. This has been noted by several other researchers as well. Brad Steiger, who has investigated hundreds of cases, states:

Whether men and women claim to be in contact with Space Brothers, Ascended Masters, or spirits from the astral plane, they are all independently coming up with largely the same communications. These emphasize that man may draw strength from a higher intelligence, that man has all the spiritual abilities necessary for this within his own being; that man is one with all things; that man is approaching a New Age, a period of transition; that other-dimensional entities are present to assist man in leaving the old and adjusting to the new.[34]

E. A. I. Mackay, quoted earlier, states essentially the same:

Now, it is an interesting fact that the information gained due to human involvement with extraspacial entities in the field of ufology is almost exactly mirrored by what has been understood within the Esoteric [i.e., occult] fraternities from time immemorial.[35]

Finally, John Keel observes:

The endless messages from the space people would now fill a library, and while the communicators claim to represent some other world, the contents of those messages are identical to the messages long received by mediums and mystics.[36]

A good sampling of this eastern-occult philosophy is found in the Reeves book, *Flying Saucer Pilgrimage*.[37] They found no exceptions and noted the ''extraterrestrials'' are anxious to move mankind into the realms of the occult metaphysics and powers.[38]

PSYCHIC INVOLVEMENT

In many UFO contact cases there is a history of prior involvement in the occult. When there is no prior involvement but the person seeks out contact, the entities attempt to involve them in the occult more fully. This opens them up as channels of communications. Many of the famous contactees had an occult or mediumistic background prior to UFO contact — Adamski, Van Tassle, Menger, etc.[39] And as mentioned earlier, often times mediums who are not even seeking UFO communication end up being contacted and becoming channels for both the "dead" and "extraterrestrials."[40] It is this fact of occult background, or the ensuing development of occult involvement, among UFO contactees which is one more connection to the realm of the demonic.

PSYCHIC TRANSFORMATION

UFO experiences can be life-changing. Generally speaking, the more profound the experience, the greater impact it has on the person. In both the world of the UFO's and occultism, percipients can experience a radical change in their lives that nearly always involves a new perception of reality in harmony with occult metaphysical or a non-Biblical epistemology or world view. Dr. Vallee notes:

> By "psychic effects" . . . I am especially referring to the fact that certain witnesses have been changed in a manner that is not explained by the events they claim to have observed.[41]

John Keel notes that this psychic transformation "often accompanies UFO sightings, particularly when witnesses are caught in a beam of light from the objects."[42] We believe that the thousands of cases of transformation represent one aspect of the ultimate purpose of the UFO's. They are part of a plan to deliberately move significant portions of an entire culture, or world, into acceptance of, or involvement in, the occult, and a collective alteration in world view. This is preparatory for and necessary to the events surrounding the rise of the anti-Christ. Man's concepts are being rearranged in such a manner that will allow for the welcomed rise to power of a world dictator with supernatural capacities who will plunge the world into Armageddon.

Dr. Vallee notes that UFO's seem to be irreversibly conditioning human society:

> The controversial work of psychologist B.F. Skinner has shown under what conditions an organism reacting to an external phenomenon *learns* a new behavior. We also know under what conditions this learning is irreversible.

These are similar to the pattern that the UFO phenomenon seems to be following. Is it trying to teach us something? With every new wave of UFO's, the social impact becomes greater. More young people become fascinated with space, with psychic phenomena, with new frontiers in consciousness. More books and articles appear, changing our culture in the direction of a higher image of man.[43]

This "higher image" of man is the image founded upon one basic ingredient: occult metaphysics and epistemology.

The two final areas of occult — UFO correlation (the violations of physical laws, i.e. the laws of gravity, motion, etc.) and the harmful effect of involvement (physical and psychological) — have already been discussed herein and are fully documented elsewhere.[44]

The exact relationship between the psychic and physical worlds is problematic at best. It does seem, however, that UFO's represent both worlds. They are primarily psychic, but sometimes physical. On the one hand, it is important to recognize that UFO's can leave physical evidence of their visits. However, many quotations can be cited from reputable writers demonstrating the belief that UFO's are not strictly physical in the sense we humans think of it. Thus John Keel writes:

The statistical data . . . indicate that flying saucers are *not* stable machines requiring fuel, maintenance, and logistical support. They are, in all probability, transmogrifications of energy and do not exist in the same way that this book exists. They are not permanent constructions of matter.[45]

Another who writes in the same vein is Dr. Curt Wagner, a physicist whose Ph.D. degree was taken in the field of general relativity theory:

Drawing from what we can know can happen in seances and poltergeist activity, it seems that these supernatural forces can manipulate matter and energy, extracting energy from the atmosphere, for example (which manifests as a local temperature change), to manipulate matter and produce an apparent violation of the second law [of thermodynamics], and I guess my feeling is that on a larger scale this is what a UFO could be. I'm not saying I know that it is, but only that it could be. It seems to me likely that UFO's are large-scale violations of the second law in which energy is arranged to take on enough of a forcefield appearance so that it appears to look like matter, yet

it's really just an energy concen-
tration — it's not really solid matter
in the usual sense.[46]

At the same time we need to recognize
the possibility that some UFO's may actually be *temporarily* solid, physical craft.

UFO'S AND THE OCCULT

Part II

OTHER CORRELATIONS

We now present a *generalized* "summary
correlation" of phenomena which continue
to show the extent of overlap between occultism and the UFO areas. Much more
could be added, but enough correlations
are made to make the parallel evident. If
one source is demonic, the evidence is
overwhelming that the other must also be
demonic. We will first list the correlations,
and then move on to document over 158
separate instances. Not all of the
phenomena occur with the same frequency
in the UFO literature: some are more common than others, but all do occur.

Topic	Occult, Psychic, and Para-psychological Literature	UFO Contactee Phenomena
1. Reincarnation and metaphysics	Common	Yes
2. Hypnotic regression	Common	Yes
3. General evolution-ary philosophy	Common	Yes
4. Automatic writing — the use of a human amanuen-sis by a spirit being	Common	Yes
5. Yoga practice	Common	Yes[1]
6. Evidence of decep-tion	Yes	Yes
7. Psychic healing or surgery	Common	At times[2]
8. Heightening of mediumistic powers, or the direct giving of super-natural powers	Common	Yes
9. Prediction of the future	Common	Yes
10. Denial of Christ's Deity	Common	Yes[3]
11. Denial of personal God	Usually	Most[4] of the time
12. Denial of the Trinity and/or the Biblical nature of God	Common	Yes[5]
13. Denial of the au-thority and/or in-errancy of Bible	Common	Yes[6]
14. Denial of Christ's	Common	Yes[7]

sacrificial death for salvation, or rein- carnation substi- tute.

15. Denial of Christ be- ing the only way to God, of God's judg- ment, heaven and hell, Satan, etc.	Common	Yes[8]
16. Trance states and/or loss of con- sciousness	Common	Yes
17. Tingling sensation or "light" before contact with the entity	Common	Yes[9]
18. Those involved with certain spirit con- tact usually do not have knowledge in the areas about which the entity proceeds to give in- formation.	Common	Yes[10]
19. Increasing "super- natural" philo- sophical knowledge on part of the con- tacted individual	Common	Yes
20. Unusual death, in- sanity, tragic occur- rences (See the writings of Dr. Koch in the bibliog- raphy)	Occur Regularly	Yes
21. Training period for the individual by the entity	Common	Yes
22. Implicit trust in the entity	Common	Yes

23. Told to publish the revelations	Common	Yes
24. Abilities in a wide range of occultism	Common	Yes
a. Automatic writing	Common	Yes
b. Visionary dreams	Common	Yes
c. Clairvoyance	Common	Yes
d. Clairsentience (supernatural diagnosis of illness)	Common	At times
e. Clairaudience	Common	Yes
f. General ESP	Common	Yes
g. Supposed communicating with the dead	Common	At times
h. White magic	Common	At times
i. Mental suggestion and/or manipulation of the thought processes	Common	Yes
j. Telekenesis	Common	Yes
k. Astral projection	Common	Yes
l. Levitation	Common	At times
25. A rotten smell like burning sulphur when the entity is near or present	Common	Yes
26. Family history of occultism back to 3 or 4 generations	Common	Yes, but not many cases have been reported

27. Usage of the subject's dream state	Semicommon (in terms of admissions by the entity)	Yes
28. A variety of physical ailments as a result of the initial contact	At times	Yes
29. A supernatural ability to compose music by means of a spirit control	Rosemary Brown's "Unfinished Symphonies"	Howard Menger's "Music from Another Planet"[11]
30. A ray emanating from the spirit	Occurs	Common (from the UFO)[12]
31. A strange noise occurring before teleportations	Common	At times[13]
32. A variety of weird creatures, "monsters," elves, dwarfs, ghosts, etc.	Common	Very similar
33. Mysterious fires	Common	Yes

ONE HUNDRED AND FIFTY INCIDENTS

The following represent 150 occult correlations divided into seven basic categories. Although there are over 50 different categories, they have been grouped for the convenience of the reader. The number of instances is listed in parenthesis after the category. John Weldon has previously listed over 150 specific correlations in *UFO's: What On Earth Is Happening?*[14] These are new listings for this book.[15]

1. General anti-biblical teachings or the encouragement by UFO entities to study eastern-occult philosophy and groups (7 cases).

2. Psychic powers before contact, or transmitted afterwards, or occult history (14 cases).

3. Contact via occult means; onset of occult symptoms (not powers) prior to contact or after contact (i.e. tingling, temperature alteration, paralysis, loss of consciousness, trance states, mediumistic exhaustion, etc.) (19 cases).

4. Various forms of mediumism, automatic writing, possession, seance entities (18 cases).

5. Numerous general psychic and occult incidents (30 cases).

6. Teleportation, astral projection, levitation, telepathy, precognition, poltergeist phenomena, author notation of occult correlations (47 cases).
7. General immorality by UFO entities (sexual, lying, evil actions, etc.) (18 cases).

This ends our discussion of the correlation between UFO and occult phenomena. It is clear that we are dealing with an essential unity between the two categories.

We began our chapter by stating that if UFO'S could be shown to be occult phenomena, then because the latter is demonic, so must be the former. This is our conviction, and we believe it is supported well by the evidence.

(Having come this far, there are some people who will object that no logical connection has been demonstrated or documented among *all categories* of UFO phenomena. They will say, "You can't lump them all together — the long-term contactee phenomena may be demonic but that does not make the close encounter temporary contacts or the abductions demonic." The interested reader may refer to the appendix where we document the essential unity between *all* UFO categories and the occult.)

Footnotes: Chapter Eight, Part I

1. Unger, Merrill, *Biblical Demonology*, (Scripture Press, 1971), *Demons In the World Today* (Tyndale, 1972), *Demon Experiences in Many Lands — A Compilation* (Moody Press, 1960); T.K. Oesterreich, *Possession Demonological and Other;* J.W. Montgomery (ed.), *Demon Possession; Principalities and Powers;* Nevius, *Demon Possession;* Shaw, *Oriental Magic;* Kurt Koch, *Demonology Past and Present; Christian Counseling and Occultism,* etc.

2. FSR, Vol. 16, No. 4, and Vol. 16, No. 5, we have added some material to Capt. Mackay's.

3. FSR, Vol. 19, No. 2, p. 28.

4. Catoe, L., *UFO's and Related Subjects: An Annotated Bibliography*, p. iv.

5. *Operation Trojan Horse*, p. 299.

6. *Invisible College*, p. 6.

7. Ibid., p. 17.

8. Bowen, Charles, (ed.) Henry Regnery Co., 1969.

9. Trench, Brinsley LePoer, *Mysterious Visitors*, Chs. 6-15.

10. Clark and Coleman, p. 236.

11. Steiger, *The Aquarian Revelations*, eg, p. 58.

12. *They Live in the Sky*, p. 25.

13. Fodor, pp. 3-9, 44, 113-117, 123-128,

135, 161, 200-202, 206-9, 214, 218-229, 250-55, 287-292, 406.

14. *UFO Report,* Oct. 1976, p. 28 (interview).

15. Ebon, Martin, (ed.), *The Amazing Uri Geller,* p. 131.

16. Keel, *Operation Trojan Horse,* p. 239-42; FSR Special Issue No. 2, p. 17.

17. *5th APRO UFO Symposium*, p. 18.

18. Cf. M.F. Unger, *The Haunting of Bishop Pike* with J. Bayly, *What About Horoscopes?* (1970) p. 60-66.

19. See previous note particularly Bayly, pp. 60-66.

20. Cf. J. Montgomery (ed.), *Demon Possession,* Kurt Koch, *Christian Counseling and Occultism.*

21. Keel, *Our Haunted Planet,* p. 128, 162; *Operation Trojan Horse,* p. 45, 199, 215, 220, 244-46, 252, 270-71, 290, etc.; Steiger, *The Aquarian Revelation,* p. 86; Eric Norman, *God's and Devils From Outer Space,* p. 120; B.E. Schwarz, *FSR,* Vol. 20, No.1, p. 3-11; Reeve, *Flying Saucer Pilgrimage,* p. 128; Lynn Catoe, *UFO's and Related Subjects: An Annotated Bibliography,* p. iv.

22. *The Invisible College,* pp. 67-89.

23. Reeve, *Flying Saucer Piligrimage,* pp. 185-6, 277.

24. Weldon, *The Transcendental Explosion,* appendices 2-3.

25. Wentz, W.Y. Evans, *The Tibetan Book*

of the Dead, (New York: Oxford University Press) 1976, p. XLVI.

26. Reeve, p. 186.

27. Ibid., p. 277.

27a. Ellwood, *Religious and Spiritual Groups in Modern America*, p. 131, 134.

28. Wilkins, *Flying Saucers Uncensored*, p. 40; FSR, Vol. 20, No. 4, p. 8.

29. *San Francisco Chronicle*, Jan. 5, 1973.

30. Gruss, p. 52-67.

31. Ibid., p. 86-7.

32. Keel, *Our Haunted Planet*, p. 128.

33. Cf. Weldon, pp. 95-100, 116-20, 158-66.

34. *UFO Missionaries Extraordinary*, p. 63.

35. FSR, Vol. 19, No. 2, p. 27.

36. *UFO's: Operation Trojan Horse*, p. 183.

37. pp. 13, 20, 22, 24-5, 62-3, 97, 144-9, 223, 231-49, etc.

38. Ibid., p. 224-49.

39. Reeve, pp. 9, 92, 95, 164; Coleman and Clark, *The Unidentified*, p. 203-12, cf. Keel, *Our Haunted Planet*, p. 128.

40. Examples are found in Steiger, *The Aquarian Revelations*, and The Academy of Atlantis in Los Angeles.

41. *The Invisible College*, p. 6.

42. *Our Haunted Planet*, p. 218.

43. *The Invisible College*, p. 197.

44. Weldon, ch. 4, appendices 1, 5; Emerson (ed.) *Thesis-Antithesis*, **AIAA**

publication, 1975, Los Angeles
Symposium Proceedings 9/27/75 p.
45 esp; Montgomery, *Principalities
and Powers,* p. 149; K. Koch
Christian Counseling and Occultism,
p. 187-8.

45. Keel, *Operation Trojan Horse,* p. 182.
46. Interview with David Fetcho reported
in *SCP Journal,* Vol. 1, No. 2, Aug.
1977, p. 20 (P.O. Box 4308, Berkeley,
Ca. 94704).

Footnotes: Chapter Eight, Part II

Note: Numbers 3-8 are direct and indirect
statements.

1. "A Brief Introduction," tract from
George Kings' Aetherius Society of
Los Angeles.
2. FSR, Vol. 13, No. 5, and Vol. 15, No.
5.
3. Menger, p. 160; Hewes and Steiger, p.
110-11, 91, 94-6, 52-4; Mustapa, p.
187; Dean p. 69; King *The Three
Saviors,* p. 60; Williamson, p. 426-7;
Adamski, p. 81; Mathes and Huett, p.
145; Yolanda, p. 4, 5, 163-4; Angelucci, p. 32 etc.
4. King, p. 24, 31, 56; FSR, Vol. 21, No.
2, p. 9; Adamski, p. 158; Dutta, p. 39,
etc.
5. Menger, p. 170; Dutta, p. 34;
Mustapa, p. 165; Fry, p. 74-6;

Puharich, p. 211, 218; Michael, p. 28; Angelucci, p. 112; Mathes and Huet, p. 30, 41, 134; Girvin, p. 114; Williamson, p. 48, 105, 150; King, p. 62; Dean, p. 68.

6. Mustapa, p. 109, 124, 167; Fry, p. 89; Puharich, p. 211, 218; Michael, p. 31; Adamski, p. 72-3; Dean, p. 69.

7. King, p. 60, 21-22; Dean, p. 70; Hewes and Steiger, p. 89, 36-7, 85, 96, 109-10, 143; Mustapa, p. 185-92; Puharich, p. 211; Angelucci, p. 34, 44; Menger, p. 7, 161, 115, 170; Dutta, p. 69, 70, 87, 95, 100; Yolanda, p. 53; Mathes and Huett, p. 139; Adamski, p. 94; Ibrahim, p. 177-8, 188-91, chapter 10.

8. Menger, p. 7, 56, 118, 137, 167, 169; King, p. 52, 62; Hewes and Steiger, p. 100-101, 139, 149; Adamski, p. 147, 150; Williamson, p. 154; Dutta, p. 29, 91, 112; Mustapa, p. 122, 163-4; Puharich, p. 218; Angelucci, p. 44; Mathes and Huett, p. 151; Geller, p. 270-271; Mustapa, p. 42, 47, 70, 71, 101, 109, 171; Yolanda, p. 6; Sanctilean, p. 38; Michael X, p. 58.

9. Keel, *Our Haunted Planet,* p. 217-219.

10. Ibid.

11. Menger, ch. 9, p. 113.

12. Ibid., p. 112-13.

13. Wilkins, *Flying Saucers Uncensored,* p. 98.

14. *UFO's: What on Earth Is Happening?*

Harvest House edition, 1975, appendix 5.

15. a) Contactee books: Menger, *From Outer Space* p. 87, 91, 114-24, 129; King, *The Three Saviors are Here*, p. 7; Ibrahim, *I Visited Ganymede*, p. 172; Mustapa, *Spaceship to the Unknown*, p. 15, 182-3; Hewes and Steiger, *UFO: Missionaries Extraordinary*, p. 3, 36-7, 58-9; Williamson, *Other Tongues — Other Flesh*, p. 444; Girvin, *The Night Has a Thousand Saucers*, p. 107; Yolanda, *Visitors From Other Planets*, p. 16, 22, 47, 113.

b) *Flying Saucer Review* articles: FSR, Vol. 19, No. 1, p. 3-6, 7-9, 15-23, 28-29; Vol. 19, No. 2, p. 2, 3-5, 9-11, 18, 21, 25; Vol. 19, No. 4, p. 13, 14; Vol. 19, No. 5, p. 12, 13-14, 16, 28-31; Vol. 19, No. 6, p. 7-14, 16-17; Vol. 20, No. 1, p. 3-11; Vol. 20, No. 2, p. 20; Vol. 20, No. 3, p. 18, 22-3, 27; Vol. 20, No. 4, p. 3-8, 14-16, 20-24, 28; Vol. 20, No. 5, p. 20-27, 30; Vol. 20, No. 6, p. 21; Vol. 21, No. 1, p. 9, 17, 30; Vol. 21, No. 2, p. 1, 3-10, 24-27; Vol. 21, No. 3 and 4, p. 3-7, 22-28, 39-42, 59; Vol. 21, No. 5, p. 8; Vol. 21, No. 6, p. 20, 22, 31; Vol. 22, No. 1, p. 3-9, 21-23; Vol. 22, No. 2, p. 10, 12-22 iii; Vol. 22, No. 3, p. 19-21.

c) Keel, *Operation Trojan Horse*, p. 205-6, 208-10, 213, 219-20, 245-7, 270, 275, 278, 281, 283-4, 295, 303, 305.

Chapter 9
URI GELLER AND "EXTRA-TERRESTRIALS"

Millions of people have heard about Uri Geller. He is the psychic who has mysteriously bent forks and spoons and even stopped department store escalators.[1] In the past several years he has demonstrated amazing abilities. The Stanford Research Institute as well as UCLA have both studied him and his psychic powers. He has not passed every test, but for at least some of his exploits there appears to be no explanation from a purely naturalistic premise. Uri himself claims to get his powers from extraterrestrials, or UFO beings.

In a television interview on *The Tomorrow Show* (June 18, 1974) with Kelly Lang, he stated that the source of his power comes from outside himself and that he is a channel for that power. In a *Psychology Today* article he was quoted as saying that the energy coming through him was intelligently directed from another universe.[2] Geller also has healing abilities, but he does not want to use them. As is common with most psychics, mediums, and occultists, Uri first noticed his supernatural abilities as a child (in his case, before age 7). As related in his book *My Story*, his first unusual experience was as a child in an Arabic garden. It involved a close encounter with a UFO ("a silvery mass of light") that knocked him unconscious.[3] Today, he relates his current powers and experiences with UFO's to this incident.[4] The Department of Defense and a number of high American officials apparently all have an interest in his powers.

Uri has demonstrated the ability to do the following:[5]

a. Powers of telepathy and clairvoyance.
b. Moving the hands of a watch and /or repairing a watch (without touching it).
c. Repairing electronic circuitry supernaturally.
d. Forming an image on film that is sealed in light-tight cameras.
e. Bending metal bars without touching them, or by "stroking" them lightly.
f. Erasing patterns from videotape "with his mind."
g. Making objects disappear and then reappear at another place.

h. Control over laboratory instruments and the ability to affect the performance of computers, radios, television sets, and audio tape recorders.

FILM DECEPTION

The fact that he can form images on sealed film, and his admission that these powers come from UFO beings, makes the following incident highly instructive. While aboard a Boeing 747, Geller reported that his Nikon-F camera, which was on the floor, levitated to his waist. He took this as a sign to use the camera, and he took several pictures of the airspace outside his window. Neither he, nor his friend, nor the pilots nor apparently anyone else on the plane, saw anything unusual, yet when the film was developed five frames contained UFO pictures.[6]

If these space creatures have worked through Geller before and have already produced images on film, why could they not have done the same thing here with the UFO's? If they can produce images on film, can they also produce "images" on radar? It seems that spirit beings, such as angels or demons, can purposely make themselves identifiable on radar at times, much like they can materialize in human form (see Genesis 19:1, 5; Acts 12:1-15). No one on the flight, including Geller, *saw* the UFO's. It was as if something appeared on film which really was not there. Geller and his friend took pictures of what they saw as empty sky, but later they found the images on the film. He states: "As I was shooting the picture, I saw nothing outside."[7] It is again logical to deduce that these "space beings" want people to believe that UFO's exist even if in fact they do not.

This whole incident of producing images on film is very similar to demons producing the supposed voices of the dead on tape recorders. This is fully documented in Raudive's *Breakthrough: An Amazing Experiment in Electronic Communication with the Dead.* The demons produce voices (up to six different languages in one sentence) on magnetic tape, and there are over 72,000 audible voices, of which 25,000 have been analyzed. The religious element plays an important part in the voice recordings,[8] and there are outright contradictions of the Bible. We read that Jesus wandered around in the afterworld in loneliness, and the Roman Catholic doctrines of purgatory and interceding for the dead by prayer are evident.[9] There is no Biblical heaven or hell.[10] The whole basis of this book (i.e. communication with the "dead"), is forbidden by God in Scripture (Deuteronomy 18:10-12; Leviticus 19:26, 31; Zechariah 10:2). The similarity to Uri Geller's film episode is clear: if demons can imprint voices on tape, it is reasonable to believe they can make imprints on film.

THE URI GELLER STORY

The fact is, Uri Geller is a very significant man. He and others like him may prove to be a bridge between science and parapsychology — the connecting link which could sink much of Western society into occultism. Many scientists are seriously considering his powers as indicators of a new type of reality. Leading scientists have recently conducted secret experiments on him and have come away convinced. Theoretical physicist Dr. Jack Starfatt called the results "staggering" and said a new step had been taken in psychoenergetics (mind energy). Dr. David Bohn, the eminent theoretical physicist, Professor John Hasted of London University, and authors Arthur C. Clarke and Arthur Koestler, were also involved in the research.[11]

Andrija Puharich (M.D.) has recently (1974) written a book on Uri. He is a distinguished neurologist, expert in medical electronics (56 patents), and one of the world's top parapsychologists. Despite these credentials, he has been accused of dishonesty in his reporting on Geller. However in Uri's own book *My Story*, written in 1976, he confirms that Puharich's book is fully accurate and without any exaggerations as some have claimed.[12] He first became interested in him in 1971, and today they are good friends. Puharich originally studied Geller to determine something about his extraordinary powers. After eliminating all physicalistic hypotheses by experimental tests, he was faced with a dilemma as to the origin of Uri's abilities. Then, on December first of the same year, the problem was solved.

During a routine hypnosis experiment with Geller, a voice sounded near him, announcing itself as a representative of an extraterrestrial power.[13] Puharich went on to devise a way of communicating with the voice by placing a tape recorder on the table. Next, an invisible hand would press down the buttons to start the machine recording. After this, a voice would imprint itself on the tape. Puharich discovered that if he questioned the voice, it would answer his question. When the conversation was over, he would transcribe the tape and the cassette would then mysteriously vanish. Other means of communication were also used — the telephone, mysterious letters, cables, T.V., radio interruption, and others. Even though he has never seen one of them, Puharich says that several classes of beings have communicated to them:

a. Robot-computers inside the spacecraft, with various identifying names like Rhombus 4-D, Spectra, etc. The voice on the tape is similar to synthesized speech.

b. Living creatures claiming to be humanoid in appearance from a planet called Hoova, which exists outside the Milky Way of our Galaxy. The recorded speech is like a human voice, and their life-span is a million years.

c. Living beings who exist trillions of years in the future. (Yet their prophesied dates for the end of the world have consistently proved wrong.)

d. Other creatures who will not identify themselves. (Adding a note of intrigue!)

Puharich was told that the extraterrestrials from Hoova had been observing the earth for 20,000 years, but they made contact with men only sporadically during this time. Some of their contactees were well-known figures in history, but now, for unknown reasons, a pledge to secrecy has been lifted in our time. Puharich was asked to reveal the communications from these extraterrestrials to mankind.

"REVELATIONS" ABOUT UNKNOWN SCIENCES

The supernatural feats by Geller result from the advanced science of Hoova. Its inhabitants claim to have solved nearly every problem that Earth has, and their achievements result from three unknown sciences. Those three "unknown sciences" are:

a. The ability to make objects disappear, translocate, and reappear
   at different locations.
b. Complete control over biological systems, including their appearance, reproduction, healing,
   and implanting of feelings and
   ideas to the mind.
c. The ability to travel across time as
   we travel across space.

It is interesting to note that science fiction (e.g. Star Trek) has had a significant
impact on the public consciousness in
viewing such things as possible future
science. This may well turn out to be the
case. Much of what used to be considered
science fiction is now coming to be seen as
science or possible science. The problem
here is that once science, or its concepts,
are extended into the non-physical (or
"spiritual") realm, it becomes impossible
to distinguish occultism from science and
what is truly occult becomes viewed as
science. We can see the beginnings of this
in something like parapsychology and the
use of technology and scientific
methodology in psychic experiments. Unfortunately, this allows Satan a more or
less free reign to pursue and accomplish his
particular ends. The need for spiritual dis-
cernment becomes obvious. Christians are
exhorted to "test the spirits" (I John 4:1)
and to discern matters by Biblical standards. A good tree cannot produce bad

fruit (Matthew 7).

These advanced "scientific" achievements of Geller's extraterrestrials are obviously meant to help spread the idea that science and the occult form a unity, i.e. to help spread occult philosophy as "legitimate" and "scientific." (They also want to spread belief in extraterrestrial life. They told Puharich "whenever Uri talks about his powers, he should mention that he believes in life in outer space."[14]) All three of these achievements fall clearly in the realm of demonic powers. The first is well documented.[15] The second achievement is more interesting: that the demons have the power to heal[16] is evident, but that these UFO beings actually claim to imprint feelings and ideas in the minds of their contactees is more revealing. This fits with the previous explanation of intended deception and is backed up by considerable literature.[17] Dr. Puharich tells us of the personal impact this power made on him. He refers to a series of events of two days' duration that was totally controlled by the Intelligence from Space or "IS," as he calls them:

> These two days' events numbed me. Sarah and Uri experienced one sequence and Ila and I experienced another, in the same time frame. I had discovered the truth about Uri's deepest secret, had had a gun in my hand that felt real, and had

had a phone call experience that is real in my mind to this day. But most of all I realized that the four of us had had an experience imprinted on our minds by what could only be the agency of IS. I finally learned that, given the existence of IS, I could never again know which of my experiences were directly imposed upon me by IS and which were not. I have never been so deeply shaken in my life as when I realized the full implication of this power of IS."[18]

Obviously, it is not hard to see that UFO abductions could easily fall into the same category of implanted experiences, and hence are unreal.

Achievement number three would explain how psychics and occultists can predict the future with anywhere from 30-85% accuracy. Often they claim help from a spirit being and basically any theological or spiritual information coming through them is anti-Biblical. The "revelation" is always inspired by the demon spirit, and it is written down and often published. The statement made by Gellers' contacts about "God" being only an "idea" is obviously not true in relation to the Biblical God. In fact, these entities claim to be God, "There is no God other than what we are together, the Nine Principles of God . . . These are God's words."[19]

As a result of his space contacts, Geller believes reincarnation is a fact of human existence, however no philosophy could be more anti-Biblical.[20]

In considering all this, it is wise to be as objective as possible. We recognize that to the anti-supernaturalist and the rationalist, in this book we have long since left the "objective" sphere, because their presuppositions on reality do not allow for the supernatural even to exist. However, such presuppositions are seen as foolish today. The overwhelming evidence demands attention.

We agree with Dr. Puharich that UFO's do exist, but we differ in our interpretation. He believes they are real beings from other planets, but we believe they are intelligent spirits existing in another dimension who are trying to deceive us about the true God as revealed in the Bible.

HEALED BY A PSYCHIC SURGEON

Let us consider some of the material in Dr. Puharich's book. He has been interested in psychic phenomena for a considerable time, as some of his earlier works show. He has investigated the famous medium Eileen Garrett, as well as Peter Hurkos, the Dutch occultist. He was even healed once by the Brazilian psychic surgeon Arigo,[21] and it was Arigo's death in

1971 that caused him to seek out Uri Geller.[22] Investigating and promoting Uri has consumed much of his time.

The first time he hypnotized Uri, a voice came from somewhere in the room. This was the "extraterrestrials" making their first contact, and they said they had plans for both Uri and Puharich.[23] Uri recalls his fear at the strange "almost computer-like voice coming through me in the trance. It said that this was the power that had found me in the Arabic garden and that I had been sent to help man. It said I had been programmed by these forces . . . to forget exactly what happened in that garden."[24] Subsequent hypnotizing produced the voice again, with another message. Uri was told that he was the "only one to save mankind" and that he had been given enormous powers.[25] Uri also astral projected while under hypnosis,[26] and at one time was actually teleported over 30 miles to another location.[27] Eventually the aliens were telling Puharich *when* to hypnotize Uri so they could speak through him.[28] Uri Geller had become a medium.[29] Dr. Vallee confirms this as he relates an interview with Uri:

> Listening to Uri as he explains his power is very similar to reading those old records by a nineteenth century medium describing the source of his knowledge. In both cases we are told that the power

does not lie within the man himself, but emanates from one of two sources, either a higher spiritual center or a race of extraterrestrial beings.[30]

Geller is often controlled by unusual impulses or urges to do something. He recalls one incident where he was urged to drive to a field and approach what seemed to be a pulsating light. He felt his mind getting fuzzy, went into a trance and found himself apparently inside a UFO, although everything was as if he were in a dazed condition. An object was placed into his hand which turned out to be the very object Geller had caused to disappear several days earlier.[31]

Both Uri and Puharich feel that these aliens have the ability to take any shape they desire for their purposes — from people, to ants, to UFO's. They believe that it is possible for them to transport themselves anywhere in the universe and to assume a form of "matter-energy" which could be transported anywhere, invisibly stored, or recalled to or from various places in the world. This would explain many of the UFO characteristics (vanishing suddenly, radar sightings, etc.).[32] Puharich also says that the results of his tests show conclusively that psychic energy can be localized.[33] Obviously, the powers of fallen angels are supernatural (which very often means "psychic" to humans), and their power is localized in the demons themselves. The concept of men storing psychic energy for future work is probably making use of a cooperating demon and his power. In numerous cases, however, the demon may draw off energy from a human host, as seems to be the case in seances. Several UFO researchers feel this is a likely possibility in many contactee cases. Uri feels they are using energy from him somehow — he gets very bad headaches even when he is doing nothing.[34]

The aliens are most anxious to get their message out. They had Puharich write his book, and they told him he was to tell the world everything about them, including how information comes from them (i.e. by tape recorders, etc). This is so others will try experimenting in the occult and get "hooked" — just as with the ouija board. Seth, the spirit control for Jane Roberts, recommended several experiments in one of her books for developing ESP powers. Demons obviously know the best way to trap unsuspecting humans. If people would leave the realm of the psychic-occult world alone, demons would have much less of an influence.

Another common feature of spirit contact is the phenomenon where they dictate material through a human medium for publication, and it seems that this will occur with Uri and Puharich also. *The Knowledge Book* may take years (the usual time is one to two years), but when it is done they say it will be "the most historical event" of human history.[35] They also claim there will be a mass landing in the next few years, but that it may be an invisible landing.[36] This is similar to the teachings of "the Great White Brotherhood," an occult society which has several books written by a being from the "other side." The *Second Book of Azrael* states that visitors from other planets *will* come, but not everyone will know them because they will come through our consciousness.[37]

IS URI THEIR SLAVE?

Obviously "something" is going on. Exactly what that is, Uri and Puharich themselves do not know. Throughout the book they see scores of UFO's that apparently only they can see. Several times they have an uneasy feeling that there is something "funny" or "wrong" about the whole situation, and they wonder whether or not they are being played with — if it is not all a big joke.[38] Several times the aliens have changed their "set and fixed" plans and have done very foolish things. Uri wonders if they are not stable or even if he is their "slave." At times he thinks they really do not care about the world.[39]

We can tell him that it is not a joke. It is deadly serious business, and possibly they *are* being played with. Fallen angels do have a sense of humor, but it is like that of a sadist. They are cruel in their hatred of God and man. Many times we read in their writings and see in their comments how dearly they love the human race and would sacrifice all for man's welfare. There are many statements like, ''We are trustworthy Friends of Light who will never mislead or forsake you.'' "You will have your reward for helping in this book which is done for a sacred purpose." "We love you. We love you, never doubt our love for you.'' But all the time they fully realize they are sending people to spiritual destruction. They always make certain the person is given a false idea of God and that there is no salvation through faith in the sacrificial death of Christ. This is not a game. It is spiritual warfare.

It is interesting to note that Uri seems to have gotten over most of his doubts about the entities since Puharich's book was published. In *My Story* he says:

> If I know one thing, it is that these intelligences are working and communicating no matter how hard it is for anyone to believe. . . . what I'm trying to achieve is this: I think it's important for the world to know about these intelligences because they are real and they are going to prove out even if it takes

time. . . . I know that these forces will only work for the good of mankind and that nothing sinister is going to arise from the situation.[40]

We wish Uri was aware of the fact that "even Satan masquerades as an angel of light, and his servants as ministers of righteousness" (II Corinthians 11:13-14). Geller came to believe in and trust these beings and their messages, because of all the miracles they have done and continue to do through him.[41] Again, it is crucial to realize that Satan is a supernatural being; he does miracles all the time. Miraculous events are not always an indication of truth, but only of power (Matthew 24:24; II Thessalonians 2:9). Unfortunately, Geller urges that everybody develop the same powers that he has. These beings can and have triggered his power in audiences all over the world while Geller is demonstrating his abilities on television or radio.[42] Regretfully, people will only be linking up to demonic power, thinking it is some great new ability or "gift from God."

An interesting note relates to the psychic surgeon, Arigo, who healed Puharich. It seems that the extraterrestrials using Geller have confirmed that the "dead" Arigo is now "with them."[43] This sort of teaching is again in line with the false premises of spiritism and is a further evidence of the oneness of the UFO phenomenon and the false teaching of demonism.

Footnotes: Chapter Nine

Note: Puharich references are from both editions of the book.

1. Puharich, *Uri* p. 181; Geller, *My Story*, p. 227.
2. June, 1974, p. 46, 48.
3. *My Story,* p. 93.
4. Ibid., p. 277.
5. Puharich, "Uri Geller and Extraterrestrials" *Psychic,* May-June 1974, p. 13-16.
6. Ibid., p. 16-17, *My Story,* photo section.
7. Geller, p. 152.
8. Raudive (Lancer, 1971) p. 131.
9. Ibid., p. 131-6, 147-57.
10. Ibid.
11. Charles Panati, *The Geller Papers,* 1976; *National Enquirer,* October 7, 1974.
12. Geller, p. 216, 222.
13. Note 5, p. 16.
14. Puharich, p. 147 (Bantam).
15. Ernest, *I Talked With Spirits;* Gasson, *The Challenging Counterfeit;*

Koch, *The Devil's Alphabet, Between Christ and Satan, Christian Counseling and Occultism;* Unger, *Biblical Demonology, Demons in the World Today;* Nevius, *Demon Possession.*

16. Unger, *Demons in the World Today,* chapter on healing; Pedro McGreggor, *Jesus and the Spirits.*

17. e.g. The Jane Roberts' Seth books; *The Urantia Book,* etc.

18. Puharich, p. 112.

19. Puharich, p. 218.

20. FSR, Vol. 19, No. 5, p. 11: for reincarnation and the Bible, see Weldon, *The Transcendental Explosion* (Harvest House, 1975) Appendix 4.

21. Puharich, p. 25-35.

22. Ibid., p. 7.

23. Ibid., p. 94-6.

24. Geller, p. 218.

25. Puharich, p. 100.

26. Ibid., p. 99-100.

27. Geller, p. 264.

28. Puharich, p. 125.

29. Ibid., p. 78, 87-88.

30. FSR, Vol. 21, No. 5, p. 13.

31. Geller, p. 223.

32. Puharich, p. 71, 126-7, 152.

33. Ibid., p. 92.

34. Ibid., p. 208.

35. Ibid., p. 161.

36. Ibid., p. 174, 182-3, 224, 248.

37. De Vorss publishers, 1961, p. 121.

38. Puharich, p. 173.

39. Ibid., p. 188-9.
40. Geller, p. 276.
41. Ibid., p. 252.
42. Ibid., p. 260.
43. Blum, *Beyond Earth,* p. 151; Puharich P. XXXIV.

"The one inescapable fact that emerges is that, despite the millions of UFO landings that have supposedly taken place on earth, not a single piece of tangible evidence — neither a nut, bolt, artifact, instrument, or defector from a flying saucer, nor even a convincing picture of one has ever been produced."

Ronald Schiller
Reader's Digest, *Nov. 1977, p. 112*

"What does [Dr. J. Allen] Hynek himself believe UFO's might really be?' We have the questions, not the answers,' he says. . . . UFO's, he says, may be psychic phenomena and the 'aliens' may not come from outer space but from a 'parallel reality.'"

Newsweek *Nov. 21, 1977*

Chapter 10
FALLEN ANGELS AND THE TEACHINGS OF "EXTRA-TERRESTRIALS"

We have said that Uri Geller and others receive their "messages" from fallen angels. In this chapter we compare the teachings of such beings with those of the Bible.

The word "angel" means messenger and includes an innumerable host of spirit beings directly created by God. A great multitude of these spirits rebelled against God under the leadership of a very high archangel, Lucifer (Satan). There are apparently various angelic ranks, implying some have more power or authority than others.[1]

In the course of this study we have listed a number of powers exhibited by the occupants of UFO's, and these are the same

capacities that are exhibited by the
Biblical demons. Even though demons are
rebellious angels, they would probably
retain the innate powers of unfallen angels.
It is important to recognize that out of
some 70 examples listed below, all but
three or four are the same as, or similar to,
the powers claimed or demonstrated by
UFO's or UFO occupants. Even these three
or four are potentially similar, but are not
known to the reviewers from the literature.

A few of the listings are logical exten-
sions from angelic power to UFO power. If
a UFO can wipe out an entire African
village,[2] then it can potentially do much
more damage. One angel, a minister of
vengeance, destroyed many thousand people in David's kingdom in three days, and
another destroyed tens of thousands of
Assyrian soldiers in one night. Out of the
70 listings, the ones apparently *not* the
same as in UFO reports include *imitation*
of the dead (although communication with
the dead is mentioned) and two relating to
animals. One would not expect extraterrestrials to imitate the dead, for
Satan uses spiritism as his major method
of deception this way. The two animal
cases, where there was possession and
speaking through animals, do not appear
to have parallels in the UFO literature.
However, UFO's and their occupants do
have a very weird effect on animals, often

causing sheer terror.³ Perhaps they are fearful of being possessed. Strange, erratic behavior and extreme fear have also been reported among animals in the presence of a possessed medium.⁴

POWERS AND SEDUCTIONS

We give below a listing of the powers of angelic beings, according to the Bible.

The Abilities of Angels (Mostly Fallen)	Found in UFO Literature
1. Rev. 9:1-11; Matt. 12:22 — Power to torment (See Luke 8:31 re: demons from the abyss). Blindness and dumbness.	Yes
2. Rev. 9:14 — Four angels released to kill ⅓ of mankind.	Yes (ability to murder).
3. II Cor. 4:4 — The world is said to be partially under Satan's authority. In Matt. 5 Jesus did not question Satan's right to give Him the world's kingdoms.	UFO's represent the great power who will save the world and rule it.
4. Gen. 3:1-13 — Purposeful deception.	Yes

5. II Cor. 11:14-15 — Evil spirits imitating good spirits.   Yes

6. Gen. 6:1-4 — Sexual involvement and cohabitation (according to some scholars, although others interpret this as not relating to fallen angels).   Yes

7. Luke 8:26-35 — Producing insanity and having great physical strength.   Yes

8. Luke 13:11-17 — Sickness for 18 years; producing suffering and deformities.   Yes

9. Rev. 13:13 — Satan produces fire from heaven in the presence of men and great miracles.   Yes

10. Job 1:16-18 — Satan produces fire from heaven, great whirlwinds.   Yes

11. Job 2:7 — Satan produces painful boils or welts all over the body.   Yes

12. Matt. 9:32-3; 12:22; 17:15, 18 — Dumbness, blindness, and epilepsy, attempted murder by fire and water.   Yes

13. Luke 8:30; 11:24-26 — Multiple possession (Matt.   Yes

12:43-5). They seek rest by possessing humans.

14. Luke 9:39 — Convulsions, child possession, mauling.	Yes
15. Matt. 8:30-32 — Animal possession.	Possible
16. Acts 16:16 — Predicting the future, fortune-telling.	Yes
17. Psalm 103:20; Acts 19:16 — Anger, great strength.	Yes
18. Judges 9:23 — Treacherous natures.	Yes
19. They give supernatural revelation — Heb. 1:1; 2:2; Acts 7:53; Gal. 3:19; etc.	Yes
20. Numbers 22:23-7 — Animals can recognize them.	Yes
21. Gen. 3:1-5 — Ability to speak through an animal (a serpent).[5]	The serpent symbol (ancient worship) is on the "uniform" of some UFO entities.
22. Job 1:7 — Supernatural power to travel.	Yes

23. Matt. 4:8 — Projection of a false reality instantaneously. .   Yes

24. John 13:2; Matt. 13:19, 39 — Apparent ability to remove thoughts, to plant thoughts, and manipulate the mind.   Yes

25. John 8:44 — A great liar and murderer.   Yes

26. Matt. 8:28; John 13:27 — Possession of humans.   Yes

27. Rev. 12:12 — Great wrath.   Yes

28. Luke 22:21 — To "strip" a man mentally.   Yes — usually temporarily.

29. II Cor. 12:7 — Physical ailments.   Yes — a wide variety.

30. Eph. 6:10-16 — Supernatural power. Schemes wickedly, attacks humans.   Yes

31. II Cor. 4:4 — Deception, blinding minds.   Yes

32. Rev. 20:8 — Deceives the nations — demanding great power.   Yes — (there were reports of a Vietnam battle started by UFO's.)

33. Job 4:15 — Invisibility, but   Yes
    awareness of their presence.

34. I Sam. 16:14-15 — Ability to   Yes
    terrorize.

35. Gen. 19:1-10; Luke 1:26;   Yes
    John 20:12; Acts 12:9; Heb.
    13:2 — Angels assume
    human form.

36. Ex. 7:10, 11, 21, 22; 8:7 —   Yes
    Duplication of God's mira-
    cles: men having demonic
    powers changed sticks to
    snakes, water to blood, and
    had control over frogs (the
    animal kingdom). Control
    over matter/energy.

37. Deut. 18:10, 11 — They can   They im-
    imitate the dead. (cf. R.   personate
    Gasson's *The Challenging*   the living,
    Counterfeit).   as with
                                   strange
                                   telephone
                                   calls.

38. Acts 8:39-40 — Teleporta-   Yes
    tion (by God). Matt. 24:31;
    Luke 16:22 — Human beings
    can be transported.

39. II Kings 6:17 — "Chariots of Fire."	Yes
40. II Thess. 1:7; Ps. 103:20; II Peter 2:11 — Great power, might.	Yes
41. II Sam. 24:17; Acts 12:23 — Can induce the death process.	Yes
42. Rev. 9:15; I Chr. 21:1; Dan. 10:13; I Thess. 2:18 — Ability to "prevent" and to a limited extent control events and human actions.	Yes
43. I Cor. 5:5 — Can destroy the flesh.	Yes
44. I Cor. 7:5 — Can influence a person toward evil.	Yes
45. Rev. 12:9 — Deceives the whole world.	Yes
46. Deut. 32:17; Col. 2:18 — Involved in being worshipped.	Yes
47. Ps. 106:37 — Child sacrifice and murder (indirect).	Possibly
48. Acts 10:38 — Oppression.	Yes
49. Heb. 2:14 — The power of death.	Yes
50. Rev. 2:10 — Can control humans to secure their own ends.	Yes

51. Acts 13:10 — Seek to pervert the ways of God.　　Yes

52. Gen. 19:13, 24 — Fire and brimstone rained down upon a city, destruction of Sodom and Gomorrah.　　Yes

53. Gen. 31:11 — Influence upon the dream state.　　Yes

54. Judges 6:27 — Causes fire to spring up.　　Yes

55. II Sam. 24:15-16 — Sends a pestilence, has power to destroy a city.　　Yes

56. I Kings 13:18, Acts 23:9 — Can communicate by speech to humans.　　Yes

57. Gen. 1:10, 16; I Kings 19:5 — Physical contact with humans.　　Yes

58. Ps. 78:49 (literal) — A band of evil angels.　　Sometimes several UFO beings act together.

59. Heb. 1:7 — Possible explanation for UFO fireballs. (Ps. 104:4 — Angels of fire?)　　Possibly

60. Gen. 19:11 — The ability to strike a human with blindness.　　Yes

61. Luke 2:9, 14, 15 — Can materialize and dematerialize at will.   Yes

62. Luke 24:23 — A vision of angels.   Yes — (visions).

63. Heb. 12:22; Matt. 26:53 — They are innumerable.   Yes — apparently.

64. Luke 1:19-20 — Speak to men; control of vocal chords (paralysis and possession).   Yes

65. Rom. 8:38 — Subject to God.   Yes

66. I Cor. 13:1 — Different languages, speech.   Yes

67. I Kings 22:19-23; Gal. 1:8; I Tim. 4:1; I John 4:1 — Can preach a false gospel and deception about God.   Yes

68. Rev. 8:6-8 — Loud sounds.   Yes

69. Jer. 17:9; 23:16; Ezek. 13:1-9; Col. 2:18; Gal. 1:8; Matt. 24:24 — False visions and experiences.   Yes

BIBLICAL WARNINGS AGAINST INVOLVEMENT

1. Deuteronomy 18:10-12 — Do not participate in spiritism, magic, etc.

2. Zechariah 10:2 — Beware of lying visions and false dreams.
3. Ezekiel 13:9 — Do not be deceived by lying divinations and false visions.
4. Acts 13:10 — Judgment — God will finally judge demonic powers (Rev. 21:8).
5. I John 4:1 — Test the spirits.
6. I Timothy 4:1 — Be aware that there are deceitful spirits.
7. Leviticus 19:26, 31 — Mediums defile and must not be listened to.
8. I Samuel 15:23 — Rebellion is in the same category as divination.
9. Galatians 5:20-21 — Sorcery is evil.
10. II Corinthians 11:3, 14 — The imitation of good by evil is associated with evil powers.

THE URANTIA BOOK: A CLASSIC EXAMPLE OF DECEPTION

The Urantia Book is a large volume, comprising 2,097 pages.[6] It was supposedly "authored" by some 23 extraterrestrial beings around 1955 (probably by the mediumistic technique of automatic writing). They claimed to be a commission sent from Uversa, the capital of the super universe Orvonton. They came to the earth for the purpose of formulating the Urantia Book, for Urantia is the planet earth. Nearly one-third is devoted to a *new* interpretation of the life and purpose of Christ, and this new interpretation opposes the Bible at nearly every major point: the Trinity, the unique Deity of Christ, the fall, blood redemption, fiat creation, Noah's flood, the nature of the Holy Spirit and the Father, hereditary transmission of the sin nature, the nature of Christ's substitutionary work on the cross, and more. "Extraterrestrials," it seems, always seek to distort Christ or to attack Christianity, but not other religions.

The extraterrestrials seem quite anxious to get across the idea that the Christian religion is full of errors. Again, if these beings are demons, what we find in the Urantia Book is just what we should expect. If not, why does the book have so many historical blunders? Why is it geared so much towards Christianity and takes so much trouble to reinterpret it? Why do genuine spirit (demon) communications always deny what the Bible says about God, Christ, and salvation? The Urantia Book has redefined nearly every Christian distinctive, making it much harder for a person to come to a saving faith in Christ, or to believe in what the Bible teaches. The following is only a selection of the many statements opposing Biblical Christianity. Biblical corrections are added. (Page numbers are references in *The Urantia Book*.)

1. Creation is a legend: Moses never

taught such a distorted story (pp. 836-7). Man is the result of directed panspermia (alien originated life) (p. 709). [Genesis 1-3].

2. Man has not fallen (pp. 845-6) [Genesis 3; Romans 5].

3. There is no hell — only annihilation (p. 37) [Revelation 20; Matthew 25:46].

4. Noah's flood was not universal[7] (p. 875) [Genesis 7, 8].

5. The Jews' Messianic kingdom is a false hope (p. 1071) [Romans 11].

6. The resurrection of Christ was figurative (p. 2091) [I Corinthians 15; Luke 24:39; Acts 1].

7. "God" is in every man (p. 17) [Romans 3:10-17].

8. The Christian concept of the trinity is wrong (pp. 1144-5) [cf E. Bickersteth, *The Trinity*, Matthew 28:19].

9. Christ did not die for the sin of the world (pp. 60, 41, 67, 984, 2002-3, 2016, etc.) [Luke 24:25-7; 46-7; Romans 3:23-6].

10. The Holy Spirit appears in all human personalities (p. 1003 [Romans 8:9].

11. Jesus "achieved" divinity (p. 2092). He is not the incarnation of God (p. 1083) [Colossians 2:9; John 1:1].

12. The God of the Old Testament, Yahweh, is a "savage demon" (p. 1076) [Nehemiah 9]. This is the God Christ Himself claimed was His

Father, and the one true God [John
5:18].

13. Evolution is a fact ("man's primor-
dial ancestors were literally the slime
and ooze of the ocean bed. . . .") (p.
731) [Mark 10:6], See J. F. Coppedge
Evolution: Possible or Impossible?

14. The two great blunders of the early
church were (a) The Christian doctrine of atonement, and (b) the
overemphasis upon Jesus to the exclu-
sion of Eastern religion (p. 1670) [John
3:16; Acts 4:12; II Corinthians 5:21;
John 14:6].

Again, if these extraterrestrials are telling us the truth —

1. Why do they never follow proper and
accepted methods of Biblical and
literary interpretation?

2. Why are their writings full of errors?
For example:

   a. Genesis is a spurious document
   (p. 838).

   b. The Psalms was authored by a
   score or more of authors. Many
   were Egyptian and Mesopota-
   mian teachers (p. 1060).

   c. The New Testament writers perverted the Old Testament and distorted Hebrew history (p. 1071).

   d. Unfallen angels do not possess
   people (p. 610).

   e. The greatest distortion of Jewish

        history had to do with King David
        (p. 1072).

f. The early church compromised with Mithraism (one of the Mystery Religions).

g. The New Testament is not the Word of God, and Paul never intended it to be so (p. 1084). (See I Thessalonians 2:13 where Paul says just the opposite.)

h. The book of Isaiah has two authors (pp. 1066-8).

i. The Gospels have been changed considerably. Numerous passages have been added and deleted, and they are not very reliable documents (pp. 1341-3). (This goes against all that we know about the gospels and the study of historical documents. See F. F. Bruce, *The New Testament Documents: Are They Reliable?*) Jesus said His word would never pass away (Matthew 24:35).

j. The 10 commandments are completely different from the ones God gave to Moses, as recorded in Exodus 20 (p. 1599).

k. There never were twelve tribes of the Israelites. The Hebrew nation resulted from the union of the so-called Israelites and the Canaanites (p. 1071).

Many others could be listed. However,

this is enough to demonstrate deception on the part of these "extraterrestrials." All except d. are open to historical investigation. References a., b., c., e., f., h., i., j., and k. would be admitted as erroneous by any non-Christian scholar who is fair in his assessment of the historical and textual evidence. All would be admitted false by any scholar who is a true Christian. One could consult Dr. Gleason Archer's *A Survey of Old Testament Introduction*, Wenham's *Christ and the Bible* and the bibliography on Christian evidences in support of this.

The book also takes many Biblical passages out of context (e.g. p. 977). In one sentence it "does away" with the Christian religion: it says that the primary religious ideas of incarnation, inspiration, revelation, propitiation, repentance, atonement, intercession, sacrifice, prayer, confession, worship, survival after death, sacrament, ritual, ransom, salvation, redemption, covenant, uncleanness, purification, prophecy, original sin — all go back to the early era of primitive ghost fear. (Hence they are, supposedly, false beliefs.) (p. 1005). All but a few of the terms mentioned here are central to Christianity.

If *The Urantia Book* is not written by demons, one could not find a better example of what would be *expected* from demons anywhere else. What is obvious is that they have lied to us. We surely, then, cannot trust them when they say they are extraterrestrials from other galaxies.

BLATANT ERRORS

At times the "extraterrestrials" have made absurd errors of judgment, knowledge, and common sense: this obviously does not help their credibility. The theology of the UFO beings is also very important. Not only is it consistently unbiblical, but it is absurd. The following list summarizes some of the major errors.

TRANSMITTED BELIEFS OF UFO OCCUPANTS

1. Reincarnation, Karma, Maya, Pantheism (Eastern beliefs).[8]
2. The Brotherhood of Man, Fatherhood of God.[9]
3. God does not punish anyone.[10]
4. Jesus was a highly-developed Venusian.[11]
5. The will of the Father ("God") is to express love in all dimensions (John 6:40).[12] (Love without salvation will not help a person eternally — it will damn him. Demons always speak of "love" but never the right way.)
6. Biblical angels are the UFO occupants.[13]
7. Christ is not God.[14]
8. Death does not end in judgment — it is just a transition[15] (e.g. Hebrews 9:27).

9. Evolution is fact, involving the continual perfection of man.[16]
10. UFO's delivered the Jews out of Egypt.[17]
11. Man's real inner nature is his God-self or God-consciousness (Eastern).[18]
12. Christ is a space being.[19]
13. Satan is mythical.[20]
14. Extraterrestrials appeared to Abraham at the time of Sodom and Gomorrah.[21]
15. God is the same as gods.[22]
16. Denial of the sinfulness of man.[23]
17. God is really "Nine Principles" or nine extraterrestrials.[24]
18. God did not speak through the Old and New Testament prophets (indirectly implied).[25]
19. A Oneness with the Infinite Father (non-Biblical Sense).[26]

The following are theological statements given by several UFO beings or the people who contacted them.

1. Jesus was an exalted person from another planet.[27]
2. The brothers in space answer our prayers.[28]
3. Christ will return near the Great Lakes.[29]
4. We are branches of the Creator.[30]
5. The God spark is in all of us.[31]
6. Twice they mention the coming of a great world leader.[32]
7. Pre-marital sex is permissible.[33]

8. Jesus is from Venus.[34]
9. We are all on the road to perfection.[35]
10. Belief in the Cosmic Christ, the Great White Brotherhood (a group of demons), the messages of avatar Jesus, Buddha, Krishna and the spiritual masters, the Second Coming of "Christ."[36]

WHAT ABOUT GEORGE ADAMSKI?

Perhaps one final aspect should be mentioned. George Adamski was a famous UFO contactee. Although he himself has been seriously challenged and his "space journeys" ridiculed, his claims to "revelations" from UFO entities are similar to others. He makes, however, a startling claim—that his contacts were not connected to "mystic phenomena," "psychism," or "spiritualism." However, in his book, contact is made by telepathy, and some of the *same* phenomena, beliefs, and procedure that occur with other contact cases, occur with him.[37] Some of his teachings are listed below.

1. The Bible contains "several hundred" reports of space visitations.
2. He was urged to make the aliens' messages public.
3. Venus and Mars are inhabited.
4. The plan is for a "united planet."

5. All planets within our solar system are inhabited.

6. Inside numerous craters on the Moon, there are very large hangars for large spaceships.

7. He claims that since the publication of *Inside the Space Ships* (his first book), people all over the world have turned to "virtual worship" of extraterrestrials (i.e., idolatry).

8. Reincarnation.

9. Venusians keep their clothes clean by a method similar to our ultrasonic methods.

10. The Garden of Eden in Genesis is a "word picture."

11. The account of Adam and Eve is allegorical.

12. Universalism — all will be saved.

13. Christ is from another planet.

14. Ezekiel described a spaceship. (see appendix)

15. Flying Saucers support the records of the Bible.

16. The Akashic Records are valid sources of information. (They are really occult sources.)

17. All religious faiths are the same.

18. God is impersonal.

19. There is no real devil — "Lucifer is symbolic of the mortal sense mind."

20. Works bring salvation — only man can change himself.

Thus by Biblical standards Adamski is

automatically put in the same area as those he feels are false prophets. It is clear that he himself was misled. In his book, *Inside Flying Saucers*, Adamski says he was taken to the other side of the moon in a UFO. There he saw forests, small towns, lakes, and much more. It is significant that a respected scientist, in referring to this case, suggests deliberate deception by the extraterrestrials, through hypnosis, projections, or by putting pictures into his mind.[38] He also suggests that by making such obvious errors, one result would be less investigation by serious scientists. In other words they have been controlling the minds of some contactees for their own sinister ends. Why? Possibly they are waiting for just the right time to begin their final plans.

THERE ARE "OTHER ADAMSKIS"

George Adamski achieved worldwide fame, but there have been many others like him. They have not become as widely known, but their messages are similar. George King of the Aetherius Society (a UFO contactee group) has stated in a trance that a New Master is to come "shortly" in a flying saucer. A new world is coming, and men are being prepared to enter it. His "new master's" power (the term

used is "magic") will be greater than any
on the earth, and in fact he will have more
power than the *combined* might of all the
world's armies. He will come openly in a
"flying saucer," and the whole world will
know of his coming. Those who do not heed
his words "shall be removed from the
earth."[39]

"AGENTS 666"

Allen-Michael Noonan, also a contactee,
refers to a "world plan" which will be im-
plemented around the globe by UFO's.
There will be "Agents 666" who will help
regulate all buying and selling. A "planned
artificial tribulation" will turn the anti-
God forces back upon themselves, and they
will be "destroyed." It is relevant to compare this with Revelation 13:18 where we
read that "the number of the beast" is 666.

According to Allen-Michael Noonan, at
a time when "everything comes under the
number 666," "One" will appear and bring
in true world government. He will have a
Master Plan to unite the earth's soldiers,
workers, students, churches, and temples,
and will deliver the world into its "long-
awaited reward." This will be done
without armaments and without destroying some progressive aspects that are
already built. A special "weapon" will be
used against Christians, or any others who
oppose them, for they are hindrances to the
plan of bringing in the "New Age."[40] We

will examine this UFO group in more detail in the next chapter.

A WORLD LEADER WHO WILL BRING "HIS DISCIPLES" WITH HIM

Another occult volume, *The Second Book of Azrael*, speaks of preparing the way for "communication with visitors from other worlds." The visitors will appear in human form, and they will work for the good of all. It implies the world leader who comes is an extraterrestrial (though human), and that he will bring "his disciples" with him.[41] Azrael (i.e. the demon) says that Christ was a visitor from space, that the crucifixion was only symbolic, reincarnation is true, and Jesus is not "the way, the truth, and the life."[42] (See John 14:6.)

These statements come directly from demonic inspiration such as trance states and automatic writing.

Many psychics speak of a coming world leader. Jeanne Dixon says he was born in 1962, somewhere in the Middle East.[43] Paul Twitchell, founder of Eckankar, says that the "new age Messiah" is likely in our presence right now.[44]

Fallen angels, as we have seen, have the capacity to materialize as men. If they can also transform matter into a UFO, they can assume human shape inside it. It follows, therefore, that there could be a "visit from outer space." If the meaning of Genesis 6:2 is that demons cohabited with women and produced offspring, it is at least theoretically possible again for mankind to be in direct "physical" contact with demons. The phenomena of sexual "union" with demons is well documented. N. Fodor *Between Two Worlds*, (Chapter on the Incubus); K. Koch, *Christian Counseling and Occultism*, p. 162; M. Unger, *Demons in the World Today*, p. 32.

Just exactly what the relationship of the UFO phenomena is to the "last days" is uncertain, but it would seem clearly to fit in somewhere with the anti-Christ, the Beast, the False Prophet, and the miraculous powers which they will display.

SOME RELEVANT BIBLE VERSES
(New American Standard Bible)

Here are some relevant Bible verses:
"Then we who are alive and remain shall be caught up together, with them in the clouds, to meet the Lord in the air. . . ." "in a moment, in the twinkling of an eye. . . ." (I Thessalonians 4:17; I Corinthians 15:52)

"and they worshipped the dragon [Satan], because he gave his authority to the beast, and they worshipped the beast, saying, 'Who is like the beast, and who is able to wage war with him?' " "And he causes all, the small and the great, and the rich and the poor, and the free men and the slaves, to be given a mark on their right hand, or on their forehead, and *he provides* that no one should be able to buy or to sell, except the one who has the mark, *either* the name of the beast or the number of his name. Here is wisdom. Let him who has understanding calculate the number of the beast, for the number is that of a man; and his number is six hundred and sixty-six." (Revelation 13:4, 16-18)

". . . 'Who is like the Beast, and who is able to wage war with him?' " ". . . and authority over every tribe and people and tongue and nation was given to him." "And I saw another beast. . . . And he exercises all the authority of the first beast in his presence. . . . And he performs great signs, so that he even makes fire come down out of heaven to the earth in the presence of men. And he deceives those who dwell on the earth because of the signs which it was given to him to perform. . . ." (Revelation 13:4, 7, 11-14)

"*that is*, the one whose coming is in accord with the activity of Satan,

with all power and signs and false
wonders, and with all the deception
of wickedness for those who perish,
because they did not receive the
love of the truth so as to be saved."
(II Thessalonians 2:9, 10)

Satan is referred to as "the prince of the
power of the *air* [emphasis added] (Ephesians 2:2), and Scripture says we wage war
against "the spiritual *forces* of wickedness
in the heavenly *places*." (Ephesians 6:12)

In our next chapter we analyze the UFO
phenomena in the light of a particular warning given by Jesus, recorded in Matthew
Chapter 24.

Footnotes: Chapter Ten

1. For an excellent discussion on the
   angels, see Vol. 2, *Systematic
   Theology,* L.S. Chafer, p. 1-121 or his
   volume on Satan. Also Matthew
   25:41, Jude 6, Revelation 12:9.
2. Steiger and Whritenaur, *Flying
   Saucers Are Hostile.*
3. See the special FSR catalogue
   starting with Vol. 16, No. 1.
4. Fodor, *Encyclopedia of Psychic
   Science,* "Animals" category.
5. Fodor, *Between Two Worlds,* chapter
   on Gef, the talking mongoose.
6. The Urantia Foundation, Chicago, Il-
   linois, 1955.
7. See Morris and Whitcomb, *The*

Genesis Flood, Presbyterian and Reformed.

8. Keel, *Our Haunted Planet*, p. 141; Menger, p. 88, 161, 170.
9. Menger, p. 7.
10. Ibid., p. 56.
11. Ibid., p. 60.
12. Ibid., p. 164.
13. Ibid., p. 169.
14. Ibid., p. 170.
15. Ibid.
16. Ibid.
17. McWane, p. 114.
18. Ibid., p. 123.
19. Ibid., p. 131.
20. Menger, p. 137.
21. Puharich, p. 134.
22. Ibid., p. 194.
23. Ibid., p. 241.
24. Ibid., p. 254.
25. Ibid.
26. Menger, p. 170.
27. Norman, *Gods and Devils From Outer Space*, p. 25.
28. Ibid., p. 29.
29. Ibid., p. 60.
30. Steiger, *The Aquarian Revelations*, p. 69.
31. Ibid., p. 71.
32. Ibid., p. 81, 132.
33. Ibid., p. 87.
34. Ibid., p. 141.
35. David, J., *The Flying Saucer Reader*, 1970, p. 76-80.

36. Steiger, *The Aquarian Revelations,* p. 93-95.
37. *Behind the Flying Saucer Mystery,* (Warner 1974) p. 48, numbered notes, respectively, p. 1, 14, 19, 22, 47, 56, 63, 64-5, 71, 72, 73, 80, 82, 88, 97, 100, 158, 147, 153, 96-7.
38. *The 5th APRO UFO Symposium,* p. 22.
39. "Some Basic Principles," tract from the Society.
40. *To the Youth of the World,* p. 1, 9, 11, 122, 130, 228, 349, 338, etc.
41. De Vorss and Co., 1961, p. 120-123.
42. Ibid., p. 19, 68-9, 120, 178.
43. Montgomery, Ruth, *A Gift of Prophecy,* p. 193 (Bantam); Jean Dixon, *My Life and Prophecies,* chapter 9.
44. *All About ECK* (Illuminated Way Press, 1973) p. 84.

"He was a murderer from the beginning, and does not stand in the truth, because there is no truth in him. Whenever he speaks a lie, he speaks from his own nature, for he is a liar and the father of lies."
Jesus describing Satan
John 8:44

Chapter 11
"FALSE CHRISTS SHALL ARISE"

At Matthew Chapter 24, verses 23 and 24, Jesus warned His disciples that in the last times false Christs would arise. "Then if anyone says to you, 'Behold, here is the Christ,' or, 'There he is,' do not believe him," Jesus warned, "For false Christs and false prophets will arise. . . ."

The role of Christ is from time to time associated with UFO's, but usually indirectly rather than directly. The disciples of Jesus look to Him as the Great Deliverer, the One Who will eventually rule the world when the forces of evil are overthrown. This is a theme "borrowed" by the UFO entities, masters as they are at deception. They have seized on the potential dangers from atomic bombs, atmospheric pollution, and international tensions as pointing to the urgent need for deliverance, a deliverance which man himself is unable to provide. Thus the UFO's offer the "only hope" for a world bent on destroying itself. Not Christ, but UFO's

have thus assumed one of the roles of
Christ Himself, and that is a fulfillment of
the prophecy, "False Christs shall arise."

Malcolm Dickson wrote an article entitled *"UFO's and Signs of the Times."*[1]
He says, "All quasi-eschatological warnings from flying friends and from their
earthbound public relations officers are
couched in Biblical doctrine and terminology, and therefore a challenge from
any but a Scriptural standpoint is not in-
trinsically relevant." Dickson states that
the "end of the age" prophecies that Christ
issued in Matthew 24 and Luke 21 have
been frequently abused "in the cause of
UFO salvationism."[2] The UFO entities
consistently misuse these prophecies.

Dickson goes on to say that these
"alleged extraterrestrials," who claim to
have our interest at heart, warn that our
planet is verging on its last days and that it
will be totally destroyed. Usually they
blame nuclear effects or mysterious
natural causes. The argument is that we
should believe in them, and so be chosen
and be saved by an eleventh hour pickup
by the UFO's: the ones so delivered will be
taken to a new heaven and a new earth by
the UFO's. Dickson points out that these
messages from the UFO's seem at first to
be compatible with Scripture, but as a
more exhaustive study is made it is seen
that deception is at work, "and one sees
that Christ has in fact warned us against it

in no uncertain terms."

THE COSMIC MESSIAH

There are also more direct claims to Messiahship, and one group that has set themselves up with clear statements as to their Messianic pretensions is the One World Family. Their book, *To the Youth of the World*, is the first volume of *The Everlasting Gospel*. Eleven more volumes are to be channeled through Allen-Michael Noonan who claims to be "the cosmic Messiah."[3] The group hail him as their leader. They propose further volumes dealing with such topics as, *The Ten Kings*, (who are ten great industrial complexes) (Vol. 4), *The New World Government* (Vol. 5), and *Revelations Revealed* — giving earth people their future in advance — (Vol. 9), and *Earth's People Meet the Galactic Command* (Vol. 11). Allen-Michael claims to have had his "cosmic initiation" in 1947 when he was "taken up to the throne of God." He claims that "Venusians from the 12th dimension" summoned him to "help save the world."[4] It is relevant to notice that 1947 was the year when the modern flying saucer era came into its own.

AUTOMATIC WRITING

The editor of the first volume, William

Hannaford, was also in contact with UFO's before he was "led" to contact Allen-Michael.[5] Hannaford edited the automatic writings of Allen-Michael for publication.

Automatic writing, again, is a common "tool" among mediums, spiritists, and many occultists. The spirit (a demon) takes full or partial control of its host and "uses" the human instrument to transmit messages. This is how Ruth Montgomery, Jeane Dixon's biographer, channeled information, supposedly from the dead medium "Arthur Ford" to produce the book, *A World Beyond*, and others. It is how Seth (the spirit) wrote through Jane Roberts to produce *Seth Speaks*. It is how the *Oahspe* volume was produced. It is also similar to, though not identical with, the writings of Edgar Cayce, Taylor Caldwell, Richard Bach (i.e., Jonathan Livingston Seagull), Patience Worth (through Mrs. Curran), Rosemary Brown's music (and the philosophy that came with it), Kahlil Gibran's *Jesus the Son of Man*, and hundreds of others. *All* deny the historic Old and New Testament writings, i.e. the Bible. Receiving spirit information can be by a full or partial trance state, by handwriting, or with a typewriter or ouija board. One or more spirits may be involved (23 in the case of the *Urantia Book*), and communications may continue for a few months or for a lifetime.

A NEW WORLD COMING

Allen-Michael claims to be "the Messiah," "the very spirit of the Archangel Michael," and to be in telepathic communication with UFO's.[6] He claims that "The Everlasting Gospel" fulfills the Scriptures, reveals the true purpose of UFO's, and fulfills the "Godhead's" promise of heaven on earth. UFO's will go into direct action to spread the Everlasting Gospel throughout the world.[7] The plan is to use voting precincts, churches, and temples to teach the Everlasting Gospel, and to get the Worldwide Passive Resistance Movement (WWPRM) underway. Each city is to be oriented into their New World Structure. The "Agents 666 will do collective buying for each district." Eventually, "the Kingdom" will be brought about.[8] Once again we are reminded of Revelation 13:18 where the number of "the beast" is given as 666. Interestingly enough, Michael states: "Galactic Beings, who are the main force of the UFO's that are here now, have a great plan to intervene directly into affairs here to bring on an artificial tribulation in order to insure the success [of world unification]."[9] The tribulation is coming, but it will be headed by forces of evil, not good, as Michael thinks.

THE FALSE PROPHET

Allen-Michael himself says that his

writings have caused him to be called the
False Prophet of the Book of Revelation.
He admits that "The Master Plan" does
end all buying and selling for secular
profit. A new world economy is to be
brought about and he sees "the real need"
for I.D. cards. He has his "Agents 666,"
and he will demonstrate how, in one day,
every person in the world will either be
healed, or put on the road to healing. As
his WWPRM grows, they will occupy the
White House, the Pentagon, the United
Nations, and other top organizations.
However, he says his group will not be a
dictatorship,[10] although you get the distinct feeling that if anyone gets in their
way, they will be "taken care of." Obviously, they have a long way to go. At present, they appear to be struggling and to
have various practical problems.[11]

WOULD YOU BELIEVE?

Their basic beliefs are a synthesis between communism, occultism, UFO
philosophy, and drug use. When world
Communism arrives with the help of
UFO's (usually referred to as "Christ's
communism") "the promise of 'heaven on
earth' will be fulfilled."[12] They believe
UFO's come from Jupiter and Venus.[13]
Our recent space probes should be enough
to convince anyone that whoever inspired

these writings is a liar. This is further
borne out by the fact that the being who
channeled the writings through Allen-
Michael calls himself, *"I AM THAT I
AM,"*[14] a Biblical Name for God. God does
not contradict Himself; and these writings
are undoubtedly opposed to God's Word in
the Bible. No one who loves God would
claim for himself God's name. Their other
beliefs include the following:

a. Love is equivalent to socialism.
"Universal Joy" is everyone doing
what is natural.[15]

b. The United States is the tribe of
Joseph.[16]

c. Each person has his own God-self.
Human nature is divine.[17]

d. Pantheistic beliefs: God = the Universe.[18]

e. The Spirit of Truth (One of Jesus'
terms for the Holy Spirit) is God
personified in men, women, and
children. "He" is a connected channel into the Universal mind.[19]

f. Sodom was removed by a laser
beam.[20]

g. Syncretistic beliefs, i.e., all
religions are truth.[21]

h. The channeled writings of Allen-
Michael provide the keys for understanding the "Scriptures" (not just
the Bible, but *all* religious, occult,
and communistic writings).[22]

i. Stalin and Hitler are not to be con-
demned for "eliminating many of
the people around them"! Hitler
was one of "the Lord's faithful"![23]
Also, 90% of the people in prison
don't belong there. They would let
all people out of jail. The real
criminals are those people who
obey the laws of their society.[24]

j. Reincarnation.[25]

The theology of the sect involves the
beliefs that there is no sin and no sin-
nature. People have never needed a
Savior.[26] There is no judgment ("The
Godhead condemns no one.");[27] and Jesus
is a being of the "United Planets Organization of Jupiter" (this is similar to the
Urantia book's teaching about Christ).[28]
The Jesus of the church Christians,
Orthodox Christians, and "cross" Christians, is not the Jesus they claim to know:

"The Father God in heaven and the Savior
Jesus stories become so ridiculous that
intelligence doesn't even want . . . to try to
liberate those hallucinating people from
their . . . daydreams." Christians who
believe in Jesus as Savior are false
prophets teaching witchcraft.[29] "Repentance" is to deny that you are part of a
mixed-up civilization.[30] They also claim
usage of the Akaschic records.[31] (A
"psychic source" of knowledge often used

by occultists. It is most likely demonic inspiration.) They also believe extraterrestrials "staged" the crucifixion.
The following statement clearly shows how
anti-Christ they are: "The erroneous head
games of right and wrong (same as the
Biblical duality of good and evil, or the
rather silly games of the good guys and bad
guys) shall be put out of our heads. We
shall be given a new heart and mind
through our good works (cf Ephesians
2:8, 9). In our Universe, there is *right on
procedure*, and right on procedures
automatically usurp all that is out of harmony with natural law. The wicked will
not understand, but the wise shall understand."[32]

Enough has been given to demonstrate
the false teachings within this group. It
should be remembered that they claim
contact with UFO's and extraterrestrial
space beings and this is where they get
their philosophy.

THREE AREAS OF SPECIAL CONCERN

Three areas in particular cause concern
about this group. First, despite volumes of
contrary evidence, they teach that drug
use is beneficial, and they advocate its
widespread use. Second, they have a
positive attitude toward occult teachings,
and they practice and see them as truth.
Third, they have an antagonistic attitude

toward real Christians. These will be briefly taken up in order.

DRUG USE

To the One World Family, drugs are "nature's potions," religious sacraments, and "the elixirs of the fountain of youth,"[33] and the family plans to help set up "proper" use of drugs throughout the entire world.[34] Remember, this is not only Allen-Michael speaking. These are "UFO beings" giving their teachings through him, by automatic writing. One of their statements advocating drug use says that no person under the influence of drugs can harm others or commit serious crimes. The user is under controlled "yin and yang" (two cosmological principles supposedly regulating the body's positive and negative life forces). Even if the users become psychotic, they hurt only themselves, and the pain they bring upon themselves teaches them "right procedure." However, it is admitted that "nature potions" either kill a person or cure him, and it is claimed that 95 percent of the people presently using psychedelic drugs (hallucinogens) are healed. Very few of them have "cashed in" (died) because of using them. The harm being done is that about 1 percent are "spaced out," and it is only the "blind who lead the blind" who refer to drugs as "dangerous."[35] Actually, as this teaching implies, they aren't too concerned about the physical body: "Bodies, we could say, are a dime a dozen. . . . the destroying of bodies doesn't destroy . . . the eternal souls evolving in them, but sets them free of situations imposed upon them by their national society."[36]

The above statements are outright lies, but then lying is not all that negative a thing to this group.[37] Police records are full of cases where people on drugs *have* harmed others and committed serious crimes. As for the idea that those who "flip out" on drugs only hurt themselves, this does not take into account those who love and care for them, such as parents, relatives, and friends. Apparently, they do not matter. Psychedelic drugs do *not* heal. Their effects can mimic psychotic states and, for this reason, they are designated "psychotomimetric drugs."

There is also a chemical relationship between serotonin (a chemical related to schizophrenia), LSD, psilocybin, and other psychedelics. Historically, hallucinogenics have been used in ceremonies for divination, communication with supernatural powers, and for meditation purposes.[38] Besides precipitating psychoses, drug-induced experiences can be so disturbing that a residue of fear and depression takes years to wear off.

The common experience that so many users speak of — a feeling of unity with all that is, or "God" — is also common among Eastern metaphysical experiences. This feeling that "all-is-one" could not be further from the truth, for man is separated from God by a great gulf that only faith in Christ can span.

Salvation to the Eastern mind is *first* of all realizing there is no separation between you and God. To them, illusion is believing there is. On this essential point both certain drug experiences and the Eastern way of thinking are hazardously deceptive as to the nature of reality and man's relationship to God.

Many who take LSD regularly have ended up demon-possessed. Even Hugh Lynn Cayce, Edgar Cayce's eldest son, describes drugs as a "dangerous" pathway to the unconscious or expanded states of consciousness.[39]

It is reported that in the One World Family contact with "intergalactic beings" is *aided* by taking LSD or marijuana. The OWF have admitted that these beings are not human, but are extraterrestrials. Contacting the spirit world is also a regular practice. They see Christians as "the main threat to uniting the world into one government."[40] Allen-Michael himself says that taking LSD, psilocybin, and mescalin (hallucinogenic drugs), open up your "body centers of light." He says that nothing you encounter while on your "trip"

can touch you, unless, that is, you begin to
participate with astral beings.[41] The
danger involved in all this is self-evident.

THE POSITIVE ATTITUDE TOWARD OCCULTISM

The positive attitude toward occultism
is the second aspect that is particularly
dangerous. The One World Family claim
that "higher beings," as channels of their
Galactic Command Space Complex
(GCSC), would have entered into the
bodies of such persons as Hitler, Stalin,
and Roosevelt in order to set up the stage
for their movement.[42] Their "scriptures"
include occult writings, as previously mentioned. They believe that "the occult circles had the greater truths all along,"[43] and
refer to "the high cosmic science of parapsychology."[44] Their use of the "Akashic
Records," involvement in fortune telling,
and automatic writing, are all occult practices that are extremely dangerous. Psychic abilities are considered to be good,
and it is acknowledged that the twelve
volumes of the "Everlasting Gospel" are
contained in the Akashic Records — an obviously demonic source. The group does
not believe in real demons, as do most (if
not all) others who have written demon-
ically inspired books. Despite the unbe-
lief, they yet practice spirit communication.[45]

THEIR ANTAGONISM TO CHRISTIANS AND THE BIBLE

The third serious problem is their antagonism to Christians and the Bible, and the following beliefs speak for themselves. The One World Family believes that "nothing good" comes out of orthodox evangelical preaching ("Jesus propaganda").[46] There will be no judgment of sinners, and the "pseudo-Christians" who say there will be, are wrong. These pseudo-Christians (i.e., true Christians) should also "drop all their thinking about what they think Jesus stood for."[47] The whole Bible, except for some prophecy, could just as well drop out of the picture.[48] As far as Allen-Michael and the extraterrestrials are concerned, the Bible does not give any genuine working knowledge of practical value as to what is wrong with people.[49] It is implied that Christians give false prophecy, and that if they persist in trying to prove their claims, they will seal their doom.[50]

How will this doom come? This is how the "extraterrestrials" put it:

So in order to control the people who persist in doing things that can actually result in disaster for many, though they think they are right, [this is the Christians] the high beings have developed a righteous secret weapon [which] are radio-controlled, to attack negative vortexes of energies. They are harmless to the righteous people, but those who are out of the discipline and screwing up the works — could end up in disaster. . . . all sane people will understand that there must be a way of policing things in the beginning days of our WWPRM, until we, the World People, have all things under control. No one should have ill feelings about the tactics used by Higher Beings, if necessary, to bring about the right kind of discipline that will bring in our complete New Age.[51]

Let Allen-Michael and the One World Family be judged by their own words:

a. "We pledge to one another that we are the church of God."[52]
b. "We have no false Gods." — "We shall inherit the earth."[53]
c. "Our New Age Slogan is to know the truth and live by it."[54]
d. "The fewer things we say to men of which God is not the author, the better off for us."[55]

Compare this with their anti-biblical teaching above, and we see how these four declarations are empty nothings that are

void of truth. They are part of the fulfillment of Jesus' prophecy that false Christs
would arise. Allen-Michael Noonan, "the
Cosmic Messiah," is one of them.

Footnotes: Chapter Eleven

1. FSR, Vol. 15, No. 5, p. 30-32.
2. Ibid.
3. Starmast Publications, 1973,
   Berkeley, Calif. prior to "p. 1."
4. Ibid., p. 345 and *Spiritual Community Guide of North America,
   1975-6*, p. 95 (San Raphael, Ca.
   94902).
5. See the introduction.
6. Ibid., p. 1.
7. Ibid., back inside cover.
8. Ibid., p. 326.
9. Ibid., p. 30, 36.
10. Ibid., p. 327-8, 335-40.
11. Ibid., p. 347.
12. Ibid., p. 21-22.
13. Ibid., p. 332.
14. Ibid., p. 117.
15. Ibid., p. 16, 21.
16. Ibid., p. 6, 17.
17. Ibid., p. 20, 12.
18. Ibid., p. 265.
19. Ibid., p. 112, 97.
20. Ibid., p. 133.
21. Ibid., p. 24, 26.

22. Ibid., p. 24-5, 11, 266.
23. Ibid., p. 8.
24. Ibid., p. 41, 168, 59.
25. Ibid., p. 126, 318.
26. Ibid., p. 3, 23, 5, 27.
27. Ibid., p. 335.
28. Ibid., p. 143.
29. Ibid., p. 121-2, 291, 348-9, 162, 32.
30. Ibid., p. 303.
31. Ibid., p. 13.
32. Ibid., p. 346-7.
33. Ibid., p. 148.
34. Ibid.
35. Ibid., p. 149, 339.
36. Ibid., p. 30.
37. Ibid., p. 10.
38. *Scientific American*, April 1964.
39. *Venture Inward*, Paperback Library, 1966, chapter 3.
40. Statement by Investigator Jill Shook, P.O. Box 4308, Berkeley, Calif.
41. *To the Youth of the World*, p. 220.
42. Ibid., p. 131.
43. Ibid., p. 73.
44. Ibid., p. 162.
45. Ibid., p. 107-8, 194, 228.
46. Ibid., p. 122.
47. Ibid.
48. Ibid.
49. Ibid., p. 130.
50. Ibid., p. 349.
51. Ibid., p. 338.
52. Ibid., p. 211.
53. Ibid., p. 212, 12.

54. Ibid., p. 228.
55. Ibid., p. 321.

"As a former Spiritualist minister and active medium, it is possible for me to say at the time of my participation in the Movement, I actually believed that these spirits were the spirits of the departed dead.

". . . at the time of my conversion, I half thought that now that I had a personal knowledge of the Lord Jesus Christ as my Savior, these 'good spirits' would now work closer with me than ever before.

However, to my surprise they stayed away completely! [They even attempted to murder him].

"Spiritualism is an attempt to communicate with what are presumed to be the spirits of the dead. Those who indulge in this cult give themselves up to demons who pose as 'spirit guides' and 'loved ones,' and spiritualists become ready to give obedience to what are actually demons whether they realize it or not . . . . They have no knowledge of spiritualism being forbidden by God (Lev. 20:27) and that He considered such practices as criminal and worthy of death.

"Many have suffered greatly because they started investigating into this thing . . . . Homes have been broken up; suicide and lunacy have afflicted those who were once in it and have dared to seek deliverance from its power.

"The way into spiritualism is extraordinarily easy. The way out is extremely dangerous."

Raphael Gasson

The Challenging Counterfeit, *pp. 36, 28, 32, 35*

Chapter 12

FOREWARNED IS FOREARMED: GUARDING AGAINST DEMONIC INTRUDERS

Millions of people around the world are involved in the realm of the occult. There is a surprisingly large number of people with great interest in this area, and these are more likely to be contacted by UFO entities than others. What follows is meant as a special warning to such people, for involvement can take place almost before one realizes what is happening, and no involvement of any kind should be permitted.

The facts that follow are given with some hesitation, but they are presented because knowledge of the methods commonly employed is necessary so that appropriate action can be taken immediately.

Raymond Buckland and H. Carrington in *Amazing Secrets of the Psychic World*[1] outline some of the practices and phenomena found in mediumism. They say that the first symptoms of involvement with these manifestations is when the psychic person sees tiny spots of light which form before him in space, and they come together, making a larger light. Progressively this light, cloudy mass becomes more definite in shape and outline and probably will begin to assume the form of someone standing in front of the medium, the person being contacted by these spirits.

As time passes it is probable that the medium will "be able to establish more or less intelligent mental communication and exchange messages."[2] Such a person with psychic capacities "will doubtless succeed in time in moving small, light objects — that is, if he is at all gifted in this phase of mediumship."[3] Reports of various contacts with UFO's elaborate these things. The symptoms are the same, whether they be associated with spiritual seances, UFO's, or other forms of occult manifestation.

TAKING ADVANTAGE OF "INNOCENT ACTIVITIES"

These spiritual beings are likely to take advantage of seemingly "innocent" activities, and there are many well-attested stories where deep involvement has been traced to what was considered a harmless diversion. That "harmless activity" has led to a bondage that proved terrifying and has on many occasions led to suicide.

We are not exaggerating. The facts are there for any who will investigate. They can be rejected, but ignoring the truth does not make it go away. UFO's and spiritism stem from the one source, and dabbling with either of them involves the same deadly risks, both spiritually and physically.

Kurt Koch wrote *Between Christ and Satan.*[4] He has become recognized as one of the most authoritative modern writers on the occult, having counselled over 20,000 people, thousands of them subjected to occult bondage. He states, "I would like to point out that in my own experience numerous cases of suicides, fatal accidents, strokes, and insanity are to be observed among occult practitioners."[5] He tells the story of a farmer's wife who had a persistent pain in her right forehead. She found this was relieved by writing, and she would therefore write letters when she had this pain. Eventually she developed an automatic writing compulsion and found after some time that she was writing some sort of religious treatise. She took the writings to her minister, and he was surprised at the intellectual content of the messages.

This is a common practice with those who become contactees — they are given information in language beyond what would be expected of them. The name of Felix appeared in the notes, and the woman was led to believe that she was to pass on some special revelation to the world. The entity claimed that his message was "in the Name of the Lord Jesus, our blessed and exalted Lord and Savior."[6] Remember, demons can use Scripture also, as Satan did, and do know Christ is Lord. Kurt Koch urges Christians against being involved with the materialization of spirit entities. He states that if a person has frequently taken part in spiritists' seances, there is a certain immunizing effect against the Holy Spirit and toward the things of God.[7] In that same context he tells us, "Contact with the spiritistic world blunts the personality against the power that flows from the Word of God."

THE DEVIL IS THE MIMIC OF GOD

In a later book, Kurt Koch recognizes the problem of hoaxes, but also puts a convincing case for the reality of Satan's activities as he imitates the works of God. As Koch says, "The Devil is the ape of God."[8] It is a tragic fact that many Christians do not recognize the Satanic basis of so much associated with the occult. For example, much that is practiced in the name of parapsychology isn't science, but is occultism. It has as its basis the essence of occult magic.[9] Satan's tactic of disguising himself as an angel of light is still effective, and many people are deceived by his wiles. This is especially true with many young people who have not had elaborate experience of his devices. Some others regard advice from an older generation as irrelevant. However, it is not really a matter of one generation opposing another. Satan doesn't discriminate. Dr. Koch, with his 40 years of counselling experience, states:

> The devil is a skillful strategist. He is a master of every tactic of the battlefield. He befogs the front. He hides behind a camouflage of empty religious talk. He operates through the use of the latest scientific method. He successfully fires and launches his arguments on the social and humane plane. And his sole aim is to deceive, to entice, and to ensnare his victims.[10]

Dr. J.W. Montgomery says:

> The problem involved in determining whether demon possession

occurs and whether witchcraft works is absurdly simple. The documentation is overwhelming. Even if 99 percent of all witchcraft cases are thrown out (and that would be very difficult to do) the remainder would easily establish the reality of the phenomenon.[11]

Montgomery further reminds us, "The tragedy of most sorcery, invocation of demons, and related practices, is that those who carry on these activities refuse to face the fact that they *always* turn out for the *worst*."[12]

The young person is urgently warned to keep away from all practices that have any bearing on the occult. If he wants to find satisfaction in the spiritual realm, he *can* find it, in the Person of Jesus Christ Who is revealed as Savior in the Bible. That will involve self-discipline and "the way of the cross," but the ultimate rewards are infinitely greater than the temporary excitement of Satanism and a spiritual experience that is likely to lead to eternal suicide.

THE CORRELATION BETWEEN NEGATIVE OCCULT ACTIVITY AND MADNESS

As Dr. Montgomery tells us:

There is a definite correlation between negative occult activity and madness. European psychiatrist

L. Szondi has shown a high correlation between involvement in spiritualism and occultism (and the related theosophical blind alleys) on the one hand and the schizophrenia on the other. Kurt Koch's detailed case studies have confirmed this judgment."[13]

The quotation further on states that "the members of the sorcerer's family can likewise be affected — even if they do not practice the vile activity themselves."[14] Montgomery reminds us that even members of a family in later generations are subject to various mental illnesses and "possession." He makes the point that a Christian can be affected by the consequences of sorcery and black magic that were in his background in previous generations of the family.

Professor Hans Bender is one of the world's leading parapsychologists, being a member of the Psychology Department of the University of Freiburg in Germany. He is director of its Institute for Border Areas of Psychology and Psychohygiene.[15] In *"Psychosis in the Seance Room"* he discusses some of the dangers involved. In one case, a woman began attending seances but would not follow the instructions of the spirit and was subsequently asked to leave. She then attempted to become a medium herself. Before long she was writing automatically and hearing voices which demanded that she take her own life. She was barely prevented from throwing herself off a balcony, because she felt "it was a force I had to obey."[16] He refers to another woman and tells us "at the bequest of one spirit, the patient once tried to cut her wrist with a piece of glass."[17] In a third case, another woman, believing she was in contact with "God," was urged to sacrifice her life and was rescued from drowning "much against her will."[18]

CONFUSION BETWEEN "MEDIUMISTIC PSYCHOSES" AND SCHIZOPHRENIA

Professor Bender discusses the fact that many psychiatrists tend to confuse "mediumistic psychoses" with schizophrenic psychoses and gives case histories to show that the two conditions are not the same. (This is not to say that mediumistic psychoses are not serious, or that we agree totally with Bender.) He elaborates with examples of patients having suicide tendencies that are induced by outside spirits. He tells how some cases were considered at first to be schizophrenic, but with the proper treatment, recognizing the factors at their true worth, they were eventually successful in dealing with the problem. He tells of wrong information given by spirit beings to those

whom they contact. This wrong information is sometimes written off as merely disturbances by interfering low entities, but
often the contactees find themselves led
astray by the suggestions of "allegedly
high level discarnate entities."[19] These beings are deceivers. If they are giving true
information it is merely to accomplish
their purpose of gaining the confidence of
contactees. They have no interest in the
well being of humans. Their whole design
is evil, for they are the servants of that one
whom Jesus referred to as a murderer and
the father of lies, even the Devil himself.
(John 8:44)

Other highly respected writers have
emphasized that the entire purpose of
these spirit powers is to deceive and to gain
subservience to themselves. Professor
Merrill Unger states:

> If demon powers heal, they also
> cause diseases. Their object is not
> to liberate the victim but to
> deceive and enslave him. They
> either heal or cause sicknesses that
> further their nefarious plans.[20]

As Unger points out, "Even if demons do
help in the healing of physical diseases
they themselves exact a price of whereby
the victim either is oppressed by the occult
or has some sort of psychic disturbance, or
falls prey to error and false doctrine."

MEDIUMS ARE TAKEN OVER BY OUTSIDE INTELLIGENCES

We have referred to Raymond Buckland and H. Carrington who wrote *Amazing Secrets of the Psychic World*. They write at considerable length about what takes place as the medium is taken over by an outside intelligence. We are not anxious to elaborate the steps, but we want to show the end result. They tell us, "When the student has progressed thus far, the final step must be taken, namely the transferring of this power to the control of a spirit, or outside intelligence. This is a very delicate and subtle process which is understood very little, even by mediums."[21] They further tell us that the most striking evidence of transference is seen in physical phenomena at a seance "when the medium is in a deep trance. The deeper the trance, the better the phenomena! In other words, the more the medium's will is in abeyance, the more opportunity there is given to the external will of the spirit to become active and bring about the required results. This fact is very strikingly proved by nearly all the best physical mediums in the history of spiritualism."[22]

The significance of this for the Christian is obvious. The quotations above are not taken from those who are writing from a Christian point of view, but are telling how one can be in touch with these spiritual phenomena. Nevertheless, they point to the very real danger which we who are Christian writers recognize and urge young people to avoid. Read the above quotation again, and undoubtedly there is a handing over of one's will, intellect, and personality to an outside being. It is no wonder that as those authors say, this process is understood very little even by mediums.

This is one of the subtleties of the Devil, for it is in the realm of parapsychology, and therefore on the surface to many people it would seem legitimate. Many psychologists would tell us that these things are associated with the deep subconscious of the individual, that the human mind has all sorts of powers beyond what we understand, and that we are but on the threshold of new and exciting developments in the "new consciousness" movement, transpersonal psychology, etc. In reality, much of this is just a cover for covert demonic activity. It is also true that the person who opens his mind to these phenomena is on dangerous ground. The battleground of spiritual realities is through the mind, and when a person makes himself available in these ways, there are beings all too ready to take over. Tragedy follows, witnessed to by millions of cases all around the world. There is no escape except by the power of the Lord Jesus Christ.

DEMONS SEARCHING FOR HUMAN BODIES

Buckland and Carrington even say that you cannot be sure that you will be taken over, but you can only hope that it will be so when you have passed into a trance. Therefore, they reason you should pass into a trance first. This is an open invitation to demon powers, allowing them to do as they will with the medium through whom they will work. They are limited in that they do not have physical bodies, and they are searching for human bodies that will be made available to them.

Those two authors go on to say that if one cannot do such things as moving material objects alone, he might be able to do it by gathering strength from others. They tell us that in this way a vital magnetic current is established which may gradually add to one's powers, making it possible to move objects and produce phenomena which would be impossible otherwise.[23] Various UFO writers suggest that some special power is available through electromagnetism. They point to both physical injuries and healings associated with rays from the weapons carried by UFO entities and conjecture that there is some "advanced" use of electromagnetism. These two authors (Buckland and Carrington) also refer to it in relation to spiritism. Those who are familiar with the UFO literature, with the constant stories of electromagnetic power, will recognize the great similarity in the two fields. They are clearly related. The UFO phenomenon is but another manifestation of the power of these spiritual beings who are so clearly opposed to the true God and to His Christ.

MATERIALIZATION . . . BAFFLING AND MYSTERIOUS

Buckland and Carrington make a further interesting statement as they emphasize that the phenomena of materialization is baffling and mysterious.

Ideally, one minute nothing exists in the cabinet except the entranced medium; the next minute there is a solid, tangible form, possessing all the properties and appearances of matter — often seeming to have solid flesh and bones just as a human being would, and being apparently composed of cells and tissues such as any material body would be! How to account for this? It is surely a most bewildering and incredible fact.[24]

Here we see an occult parallel to the more solid and complete manifestations of UFO entities. They can be just as real as they choose to be, at least temporarily.

The great tragedy is when people reason that since the numerous manifestations in the UFO and occult worlds are real, they are therefore "good." They fall prey to one of the oldest methods of deception — that of camouflaging one's true intents and nature. (How different it is to personally know the one true God, who is Himself Truth, and who never lies or deceives. If you want to know Him, read the next chapter, and be honest in examining your own life, your motives, and the desires of your heart. Those who truly come to know Him never regret it. All their sins are forgiven, and they find *real* peace and joy and meaning in life, now, and inherit eternal life in the future. You have nothing to lose and everything to gain by giving your life to Jesus Christ and becoming "born again." We honestly pray you will. Both the authors' lives have been radically changed by Christ, and He will do the same for you.)

Footnotes: Chapter Twelve

1. Parker Pub. Co., West Nyack, New York, 1975.
2. Ibid., p. 31.
3. Ibid., p. 35.
4. Kregel, 1962.
5. Ibid., p. 102 cf. *Occult Bondage and Deliverance* p. 30.
6. Ibid., p. 102.
7. Ibid., p. 106, 120-25.
8. Koch, *Christian Counseling and Occultism,* p. 170.
9. Koch, *Between Christ and Satan,* p. 62; *Occult Bondage and Deliverance,* p. 22.
10. *The Devil's Alphabet,* p. 7.
11. *Principalities and Powers,* p. 146.
12. Ibid., p. 149.
13. *Christian Counseling and Occultism* (Kregel, 1972).
14. Montgomery, p. 149.
15. Ebon, Martin, (ed.) *The Satan Trap: Dangers of the Occult,* chap. 21.
16. Ibid., p. 232.
17. Ibid., p. 236.
18. Ibid., p. 235.
19. Ibid., p. 237.
20. *Demons in the World Today,* chapter 7.

21. Note 1, p. 36.
22. Ibid.
23. Ibid., p. 36-7.
24. Ibid., p. 107-8.

---

*"Greater is He who is in you, than he who is in the
world."*
I John 4:4

Chapter 13
CRIES FOR HELP

Both the authors of this book have received cries for help. To the contactee, it seemed so innocent at first, and then it even seemed beneficial. But later it was sheer terror. So what advice should be given to that one so urgently in need?

BE A CHRISTIAN

This first piece of counsel is the most important. It is: be a Christian. That is not as unnecessary as it might seem to some people who think that being "born in a Christian country" automatically makes one a Christian. Being a Christian is a personal rather than a national matter. The New Testament teaches that "the gift of God is eternal life through Jesus Christ our Lord" (Romans 6:23). That gift is available to all who will accept it, but they *must* accept it: "To as many as *received* Him, *to them* He gave the power to become the sons of God" (John 1:12).

Jesus died on a cross to give man forgiveness of sins, and all men need that forgiveness, "For all have sinned and come short of God's glory" (Romans 3:23). Because "the wages of sin is death" (Romans 6:23) no man could pay the price of his own sin. Jesus is sinless, and He is infinite, and His death can atone for as many finite persons as will put their trust in Him. "He is able to save to the uttermost *all* who come to God by Him, seeing He ever lives to make intercession for them" (Hebrews 7:25).

It is not a matter of how good or bad I am — for "come short" applies to everybody. One person can swim 10 miles, and another only one, but neither can span the ocean. One person jumps up to within an inch of a rope across the top of a well filled with mud, whereas another person can only get to within a foot of that rope. Both will fail, no matter how hard they try. They will fall back — neither made it, and they equally "come short." God's perfect standards of holiness cannot be reached by any human, no matter how morally upright. Such a person must take the same way to God as that other person who is so obviously imperfect. That way is "the way of the Cross."

It is a matter of personally accepting Jesus Christ into one's own life, by praying a prayer such as this:

Lord Jesus, I'm a sinner. You died for sinners, and that means me. I ask You to be my Savior. Come into my life and give me the

power to live for You, from this day
on.

To say, "I'm a sinner," does not mean
you are a murderer, or some "really bad"
character. It simply means you recognize
you do not measure up to God's holy standards, and nothing less than that will do.

Nor is that the end of the matter. The
penalty for sins was met by Jesus Christ,
and we by faith accept His death as the
substitute for our own. The good works
come later, but they *do* come. In the New
Testament Book of James we read that
faith without works is dead. We prove our
faith by our works. There is a relevant explanation that goes like this:

By *grace* you are saved, through
faith, and that *not of yourselves,* it
is the gift of God. [It is] *not of
works,* lest any man should boast.
For we are His workmanship,
created in Christ Jesus *unto good
works* which God has ordained that
we should walk in them (Ephesians
2:8-10).

We are saved only by Christ's death. We
accept Him into our lives, and the good
works follow. That is the pattern — it is
not a matter of working our way to heaven,
or hoping we are good enough. *He* was
good enough: we could never be, but God
accepts us in Christ. The condition is that
we personally accept Christ, *now* — for
"*Now* is the accepted time, *now* is the day

of salvation" (II Cor. 6:12).

That is what we mean by, "Be a Christian." According to the Bible, such a person is indwelt by the Holy Spirit of God. While he "abides in Christ," no demonic being has any power against him.

ABIDE IN CHRIST

Some people believe that demons cannot attack true Christians. We have already commented on this, but shall emphasize it at this point, to have the subject matter in this one chapter.

Jesus Himself was offered the kingdoms of the world and more, on the condition that he worshipped Satan, with the bondage that would entail. Paul the Apostle said he had a thorn in the flesh which was a messenger from Satan. Paul was abiding in Christ, and so the "messenger" was not effective. It was to Christians that John the Apostle wrote, "Test the spirits." They could resist the spirits, but they needed to test them sometimes. Satan CAN be disguised as an angel of light.

The fact is, Christians can be attacked by Satan, and they are likely to be so menaced unless they are abiding in Christ. The Christian who is involved in sinful practices is not abiding and cannot effectively claim the power of Christ against opposing evil powers.

The New Testament teaching is that if a demon leaves a person who is merely "reformed" (not regenerated, born again), it is likely to come back with seven other beings even worse than itself. Thus, the last state is worse than the first (Matt. 12:45). There are many cases in exorcism where an evil spirit has appeared to submit to the command of the exorcist, but soon returns, for the individual has no personal power of himself. They may even brutally attack the exorcist if he is not a Christian (Acts 19:13-19). Only the "abiding" Christian can effectively resist the forces of evil. Others are merely laughed at by these beings who have dared to oppose God Himself.

The abiding Christian has the right to claim that power of Jesus Who said, "All power is given to Me, in heaven and earth. Go *you* therefore. . . ." (Matt. 28:18 ff). "Resist the Devil and he will flee from you," we are told (James 4:7). Abide and resist in the name of Jesus Christ and in the power of the Holy Spirit. When those conditions are observed, no demonic being has any power against the Christian.

"BUT I'M A PSYCHIC"

If you are in that significant minority of the human race that is involved with things psychic and occult, you need to be especially aware of the evils of Satan as he attempts to deceive you. Christ's promises and protection can be especially precious to you as you claim your right not to be afraid "of the terror by night" (Psalm 91:5). It is your privilege, by faith, to appropriate His perfect provision for your need. Hebrews 13:5 assures you that He Himself will never leave you nor forsake you. If demonic attacks are real, so also is His availability. Accept the contest only in thankfulness for His victory. You can actually laugh at the attacks, for "greater is He Who is in you than He Who is in the world" (I John 4:4). No weapon formed against you will prosper (Isaiah 54:17).

Do not be surprised that there *will* be attacks. Satan and his forces hate you, and you are engaged in a spiritual battle, not wrestling against flesh and blood but against spiritual rulers and powers (Ephesians 6:12). It should not be a surprise to find you are so engaged: beings who would rebel against God, who would challenge the authority of Jesus in His earthly ministry, and would continue a relentless warfare through long centuries, are certainly likely to tackle you, especially at a point of weakness.

The very fact that you are psychic immediately makes you especially liable to attention. Be aware of it, but be even more aware of the supernatural power that is instantly available to you. Your Captain is the leader of a great host of heavenly beings, and no temptation can come to you beyond what you are able to endure (I Corinthians 10:13). Christ Himself will fight through you *provided* you abide in Him, living a life that is honorable to Him. You should set your affection on things above, where Christ sits at the right hand of God, and have your mind transformed (Colossians 3:1-4, Romans 12:2).

DO NOT SEEK INVOLVEMENT

This applies in two major areas. All people, and especially those with psychic tendencies, should be aware of the dangers involved in dabbling with the occult and with parapsychology. This has been stressed through this book: seemingly "innocent" pastimes that allow intrusion from external forces are giving an invitation to these beings to take over.

Secondly, do not over estimate your own power to resist evil forces. While it is true that total victory is constantly available to the abiding Christian, he has no right to meddle foolishly in the areas of demonic activities.

In Our Lord's model prayer for His disciples, one expression was "Lead us not into temptation" (Matthew 6:13). This can be translated, "Lead us not into testings." The Christian who openly courts a contest is asking for more trouble than he anticipates. If a testing comes, Christ's power is available and will prove sufficient for the man who has the right to use that power. If we deliberately seek testing we are (metaphorically) casting ourselves over the Temple Wall, one of the temptations put to Jesus by the Devil, quoting scripture that supposedly supported such an action. However, Satan omitted the words, "In all thy ways," from the Old Testament verse he quoted (Matthew 4:6, cf Psalms 91:11-12). The fullest possible protection is available as we are in God's will, "In all our ways." Casting ourselves over a Temple would not be in that category. It would be putting ourselves out of the will of God. Those who deliberately play with serpents are doing the same thing, and it is not surprising to hear of deaths from time to time.

So if you boast to yourself of your strength, your courage, and even your faith, be careful. Rather be thankful when attacks are *not* taking place. Under no circumstances should you enter into such folly as tormenting demons or seeking a contest so that you can prove your superiority as you demonstrate your power over those Satanic beings.

"BUT I'M ALREADY INVOLVED!"

If you are already involved, you need help. That help will not be effective UNLESS you yourself become a true Christian and know the power of Jesus Christ in your life.

As we have already pointed out, demons will pretend to leave a victim at the time of an "exorcism," but they soon come back. Much of so-called exorcism is a mockery anyway, with rituals that are close to magic, and they have no real power over these Satanic messengers. Only the true power of Jesus is effective with them.

Thus, your first essential step is to repent and accept Jesus into your life. Read Part I of this chapter again. Having become a Christian, resist the demonic powers when they attempt to influence you. "Resist the Devil and he will flee from you," is the New Testament teaching (James 4:7).

Even as a Christian, be aware of his devices. He will come as an angel of light (II Corinthians 11:14), seeking to deceive you with a message of love and concern. Remember, "test the spirits" (I John 4:1). He must acknowledge that Jesus is Lord, and that salvation is available only through the blood of Jesus Who died to give us forgiveness of sins. Any spirit denying these doctrines is of the Devil. A message of love and concern, or urging "Trust me," is not sufficient. Satan has many fiery darts, and if one does not work, he will try another.

If you are psychic, you know you have a real problem in this area, and to some extent you will need to be careful all the days of your life. The alcoholic who comes to Jesus can find deliverance, but there are many cases of truly born-again persons having a real problem, and "breaking out" from time to time. Psychics have their problems too, and they, as well as others, should have nothing to do with such areas as parapsychology. Strict avoidance is the right way for the wise man who would know deliverance.

At the practical level, there are other more positive aspects. Not only should you avoid "psychic" areas but (more positively) you should develop the daily habits of prayer and Bible reading. These should be practiced as often as possible, and especially at a definite time. For most people first thing in the morning and last thing at night are best.

Also cultivate Bible-believing Christian friends, and regularly attend a Bible-teaching, Christ-centered Church. "Forsake not the assembling of yourselves together" is the injunction at Hebrews 10:25. You *need* Christian help, counseling, and fellowship.

Above all, crown Christ the Lord of your life. When you fail, recognize His forgiveness, thank Him for it, and mean it. Keep short accounts with God, and believe that Jesus really is ready to forgive. Failure is likely from time to time, but that does not really excuse it. Failure must be confessed, and the forgiveness appropriated (I

John 1:9). As the New Testament puts it, keep "looking unto Jesus, the Author and completer of our faith" (Hebrews 12:2). He Himself is our victory. He Himself is our Life, and He seeks continuing fellowship with you.

Special note: For new Christians we would like to recommend they read Hal Lindsey's *The Liberation of Planet Earth.* For those involved in occult matters, we recommend Dr. Kurt Koch's *Occult Bondage and Deliverance.* Both will be of great help.

"In the last eight months I have learned of more than a dozen alleged 'abductee' cases in Southern California, with many others already reported. I suspect strongly that there are thousands of closet CE-III's in the United States alone. If ufologists nationwide working with hypnotists, psychologists, or other students of human consciousness could confirm this suspicion, we might sooner expect professional funding of long-range studies to answer some of these questions, and to develop means of interpreting paranormal aspects of narratives, as well as determining the social implications of such a vast body of underground occult experience . . . . For too long we have dismissed the 'contactee' and his bizarre narrative of paranormal events."

Dr. A. H. Lawson
California State University Long Beach
Flying Saucer Review, *Vol. 22, No. 3*
(Oct. 1976) p. 24-5

Chapter 14
CASE HISTORIES

The following three cases are representative of both the subtlety of spiritual warfare and the victory in Christ. All three incidents involved correspondence with coauthor Weldon. They include a business executive, policeman, and Canadian Indian and housewife. In the two close-contact cases, the individuals told Mr. Weldon that literally almost everything written in his book, *UFO's: What on Earth Is Happening?*, had happened to them personally.

CASE ONE

Mr. Robert Prentiss served eight years as a police officer in southern California. He is presently employed by the State of Minnesota, working with adolescent behavioral problems and emotional disturbances. He holds degrees in sociology and nursing and the M.S. in educational psychology and counseling. The UFO's appeared ONLY to him and his wife, and he became convinced they would usher in the

"New Age," only to be seriously disappointed. This incident is a good lesson on the subtlety of spiritual warfare in the life of a Christian.

STATEMENT

I had my first encounter with two UFO's at fairly close range while working as a veteran police officer in southern California in June, 1966. Only a few months prior to this, in the late autumn of 1965, I had accepted Jesus Christ as my personal Savior and had also resolved to read through the entire Bible. During the weeks that followed the initial UFO encounter, I personally experienced a variety of remarkable sightings and illusions. In addition to several of the "routine" UFO's, there was a "mothership" (that discharged a number of smaller lights which later returned and entered the "craft" at incredible speeds from improbable angles), a nearby UFO which divested itself of a great ball of multicolored light, a parade of slow-moving fireballs that sailed down to the same general area, to be followed by smaller UFO's ascending from the "landing" site moments later, etc. There was a time when I would have been content to think I had merely been hallucinating were it not for the fact that Phyllis, my very practical wife, was with me on many of these occasions over this period of several weeks and witnessed these same spectacular manifestations. Except for two, all of these sightings occurred at night. One evening we observed what appeared to be a landing by an unusual type of UFO. Interestingly enough, we personalized this "craft" even as we watched, giving the object a nickname and referring to it as "he" and "him." On the following day we climbed to the site and found very convincing evidence that something strange had indeed taken place. A deep red circular patch on the angled mountain ledge gave the appearance that the ground had been scorched. At the edge of this circle, in decomposed granite nearly as hard as concrete, we found a cleanly cut depression or void more than 4 inches deep and 6 inches long, concave/convex at the ends as if it had been made by a landing pad, or as if a plug had been removed for a soil sample.

During these weeks of tantalizing sightings, I became totally obsessed with the UFO's, convinced that something *great* was about to happen. I abandoned my daily Bible reading and turned my back on God as I began reading every UFO book I could lay my hands on, each book being more trashy and occult-oriented than the preceding one. Many nights I watched in vain, trying to mentally communicate with what I then thought were extraterrestrial beings, almost praying to them to appear and establish some sort of contact with me. My final sighting was that of a "craft" perhaps 80 feet in diameter, with rotating white, red, and green lights around the perimeter, which approached from a great distance to descend and move slowly overhead, so close that I could have hit it with a thrown object. This particular entity emitted an audible humming-buzzing noise and, having passed my immediate location, swung around to gain altitude and depart at an unbelievable speed in the direction from which it had come. More than a decade has now passed and I have never seen another UFO since that time.

Having skillfully seduced me into believing something truly great was about to unfold, the manifestations came to an abrupt halt, leaving me frustrated, angry, empty, and feeling betrayed. I quickly plunged into grievous sin, began using alcohol to excess, dreadfully hurt others, almost lost my family, and entered a prolonged period of acute depression during which I nearly lost the will to live and even contemplated suicide. My Christian testimony was reduced to a shambles as the depression persisted for many months. I can be thankful for the experience now, in that God allowed me to choose in stepping outside His perfect will to experience firsthand the near devastating consequences. I believe that all things work for good as He allows us to learn from our

failure experiences, as well as our suc-
cesses. As I chased after the UFO gods, my
thought processes were influenced and
developed step by step to embrace the concept of extraterrestrial beings with its con-
comitant theory of naturalistic evolution
which would, of course, serve to negate the
Biblical truth that Christ died *once for all*.
Since then, however, as I have allowed
Jesus Christ to become Lord of my life, certain inner convictions have been reinforced
through study of the scriptures, as well as
the preponderance of scientific evidence
supporting the Biblical account of Creation. There is no doubt whatsoever in my
mind but that the current havoc-wreaking
UFO's are demonic manifestations
originating with Satan, whom the Bible
refers to as "the god of this world" and
"the prince of the power of the air." I am
thoroughly convinced that we can expect
increasing UFO activity as this age draws
to a close, including more reports of human
interaction with the so-called occupants of
UFO's, and perhaps reported cases of abduction with increasing frequency.

I have much to be grateful for. Had I
been merely holding the Lord's hand when
I turned away from Him, I would not be
writing this today. But He who never turns
away was holding *my* hand and drew me
back slowly and steadily from the brink of
total disaster. As a Christian police officer
told me when I first came to Jesus: "He'll

never let you go." *Amen*.

Robert B. Prentiss
December 25, 1976

CASE TWO

In Spring of 1974, executive R. L. was in a state of occult meditation, and two entities became prominent in his consciousness. In July of 1974, he picked up a copy of *The Interrupted Journey,* a story of the famous Betty and Barney Hill abduction, and saw the same entities in his meditation which the Hills had encountered during their abduction. This incident caused him to think he too may have been abducted during his UFO experience. Hypnotic regression confirmed the "abduction." Today he is convinced the experience was not real, but implanted in his mind. Here is his story in brief form in his own words.

STATEMENT

I am an executive, currently based in the state of Ohio. My occupational demands are both analytical and interpersonal in nature. The level of my performance has adequately satisfied those demands since the 1960's. This information is important to develop some semblance of credibility. The following summation of events in my life will undoubtedly provoke a rather diverse reaction.

Before reaching the age of 18, I had twice observed what could be considered UFO's and had been the subject of a psychic experience. Prior to 1973 the psychic experiences had steadily increased both their frequency and intensity. The third UFO sighting in my life occurred in 1972, setting the stage for the ominous trials that were to follow. I was considered a good man, although not a religious one. The basis for this consideration was my tremendous regard for human life and the willingness to freely help people in need. Progressive liberalism highlighted my social attitudes, while intellectualism served the foundation of my mentality. The objectives of my life would have been considered both personal and humanitarian. With this background, I decided to exercise the full potential of my mind. Unfortunately, I viewed psychic phenomena as a human potential.

I met with almost immediate success in areas of consciousness control, telepathy, psychokinesis, and conscious clairvoyance. These appeared to be voluntary experiences controlled by myself. This notion was soon to be shaken at its foundation. Without warning I came under a tremendous psychic attack. These attacks included voices, visions, unusual dreams, compulsions, poltergeist experiences, doubles, forced out-of-the-body experiences, materializations, etc.

The only effective defense I had was to seek God's help at the first conscious indication of attack. This battle raged throughout 1973.

In October of that year, while traveling Interstate Highway 71, a UFO proceeded to pace my car. After observing the object for a short duration, it increased its velocity and disappeared from view. At this point I lost complete consciousness, only to have occasional conscious awareness. I was still driving my car, but something other than myself was controlling my body. I drove to a desolate area and stopped the car. There were entities on the road who approached the car, two in front and one which appeared to be materializing by the driver-side window. The two entities in front of the car projected their eyes into my brain and out again. The next memory I had was that of approaching a landed UFO. At this point a tremendous terror overtook me, abating only on entering the UFO. Inside the UFO, I perceived myself lying on a table and being examined by these entities. A bright light was brought to my head, hurting my eyes. Apparently some sort of communication took place, but its nature and content have not been discernible. The next memory I had was watching the UFO lift off. I did not regain full consciousness until the next day. This entire incident probably lasted over one hour and represented a missing time portion in my life.

It wasn't until 1975, under hypnotic regression by a psychologist, that the entire story was revealed.

After the UFO incident, there were occasions when I seemed to be under partial control. As if my reason had given way to an indwelling alien intelligence. A miraculous religious experience followed, which appeared to give me control of my reason.

I continued to resist this invading intelligence. It attempted to gain my acceptance in a variety of ways. Having rejected all these manipulations, it turned to force. There were direct attempts to kill, possess, or mentally destroy me. As I persevered, my love for God grew. God had helped me every time I called, and prayed to Him. In 1976, after 3½ year's of struggle, I have surrendered my life to our Lord and Savior, Jesus, and have found peace.

It has been reduced to an encounter between the forces of God and the forces of Satan. I have had to work for the good while the evil attempted to take me by manipulation and force. In the wake of all this, a new and ever broadening reality has taken place. My life confirms the Bible passage of Ephesians 6:11-12 which stated:

Put on the armor of God so that you may be able to stand firm against the tactics of the devil. Our

battle is not against human forces,
but against the principalities and
powers, the rulers of this world of
darkness, the evil spirits in regions
above.

One unalterable fact, an undeniable
reality, that man outside the light of God is
morally, intellectually, and spiritually im-
potent. Literally, without God he is
nothing and with God he is everything. No
force, regardless of how seemingly powerful
it appears, can overcome a human who has
surrendered his or her life to our Lord and
Savior, Jesus Christ.

Mine is a faith in God, constructed on
the trials and tribulations of my life. Mine
is a love of God, born in exposure of God's
awesome love and patience, demonstrated
toward me. As He is my God, He is also
your God. If God could give love to a fool
like myself, there has to be hope for
everyone.

Praise to my Lord and Savior, Jesus
Christ, to the heavenly Father, Host of
Hosts, and to His Holy Spirit.

CASE THREE

Mrs. Peggy Waltham is a Canadian Indian with a strong Roman Catholic
background. After a UFO appeared to her
one evening, she became a contactee. She
saw numerous UFO's, communicated with
UFO entities via telepathy, and they appeared visibly in her house. They were very

religious entities, claiming to believe in Jesus Christ as Savior and that the Father had sent them to her. Their theology was partly very Biblical and partly non-Biblical. They said it didn't matter what religion a person belonged to. Numerous occult manifestations occurred during the period of contact (e.g., poltergeist phenomena, necromantic contacts, etc.), and Mrs. Waltham firmly believed she was communicating with God's messengers. They attempted to deceive her into believing I was making contact with them by telling her they had been in my home three times, had shined a beam of light on me, etc. She says today, "It really scares me to think how Satan can deceive even those who are very religious. It proves one thing, a person doesn't dare stray very far away from God." These entities caused her a great deal of suffering, but after she gave her life wholly to Jesus Christ, they eventually bothered her no more. Here is her story.

STATEMENT

A few years back I became involved with UFO's and their occupants. They contacted me first and had told me they were here to help the earth people. They claimed to be in direct contact with Christ and all those who had passed on. With the help of these beings, I was able to contact my late grandparents and an Indian girl I never knew. Since I am Indian, they told me how the Indian will rise out of the depths of despair into a place of honor. The white man would have to learn to depend on the Indians in order to survive the great famine. I was to be used as a mediator between them and us. They taught me their explanation of the Bible. It was this that made me start to question if they were good or evil. They came into our home during the nights, frightening the children, took control of our minds and played tricks on us. We would at times see their shadows running about the house. Food disappeared or had growths on it.

Later I was given a book called *The Late Great Planet Earth* by Hal Lindsey. After reading it, I really began to wonder about these beings. I wrote Hal Lindsey and asked him his thoughts about UFO's. John Weldon was given my letter and wrote to me on the subject. We conversed back and forth concerning the UFO's. John Weldon's references came directly from the Bible. He also sent a book of his called *UFO's: What On Earth Is Happening?* After reading this, I then really came to realize that the UFO's were evil and how they had deceived us. I then devoted my time to Christ and the Bible. The more I came to Christ, the more the UFO beings tried to get me back on their side. But

Christ won out. Even now when I think back, I say "What a fool, what a fool you were." Then I think and say, "Praise the Lord" for he didn't forsake me. To this day, the UFO's put on a display in the sky for me at night. So I turn my head and say a little prayer, and all is forgotten. Life now has changed for the better, since my husband and I have turned completely to Christ. We know now that only Christ can give us peace of mind, heart, and soul.

UFO Report:
How many abduction cases might there be that we
don't even know about yet?
Harder:
You mean in the United States? At least hundreds,
may be thousands. . . .
UFO Report:
What kinds of people get abducted? Are there
similarities between them?
Harder:
In my experience, these people seem to be at least
slightly more psychic than most of their fellow
citizens. Aside from that, all I can say is that at one
time I evaluated about 20 cases and found five
college graduates and one Ph.D. Most of the 20
were women.
Dr. James Harder
U.C. Berkeley Professor of Engineering
and authority on hypnotic regression
of UFO close encounter-abductions cases
UFO Report interview December, 1977, p. 39

Appendix A
THE UNITY OF ALL OCCULT AND UFO PHENOMENA

To the reader with a technical interest in UFO's, this might well be the most relevant section of this book. From the Biblical viewpoint, the contactee phenomena is clearly demonic, since the messages are without exception anti-Biblical and conveyed through occult supernatural means. If there is a unity flowing between all categories of the UFO phenomena — Close Encounters of the first, second, and third types,* abductions, and contactees — it is logical to accept that their source is the same. Until now nearly all researchers have tried to say the contactee phenomena was not to be placed in the same category as UFO sightings and close encounters. The latter was the hard data, the signal, the true UFO phenomena. The former was the unreliable, the hoaxes, the unbelievable, the noise, the unreal. With the great increase in abduction cases, and with researchers being a little more willing to report the stranger aspects of the close encounter cases, a unity in the UFO phenomena has emerged. *The non-contactee UFO phenomena has forced a re-evaluation of the validity of the contactee phenomena, because there is a definite connection between them.* The

---

*Close encounters I and II are the same, except that in the latter environmental effects occur. Close encounter III involves occupants. See Preface for complete explanation.

following statement by Dr. Vallee shows the transition that is occurring. After referring to a large scale revision in attitudes taking place in the scientific community regarding UFO's, he says:

> I find myself now looking at data in a very different way from how I was looking at it five years ago. I've had to reconsider many of the things I said earlier about the contactees. Some of the contactees may be telling the truth. Ten years ago, I said, "Well, these people obviously are lying." I wouldn't even have stopped ten minutes to listen to them.[1]

Contactee episodes usually contain elements of the supernatural, very disturbing to rational, materialistic investigators. Yet Dr. Vallee notes: "In recent years, too, the report of paranormal events in connection with close encounters with UFO's seems to have become the rule rather than the exception."[2] And he states: "But once the connection [i.e. between UFO's and the psychic] was established, there could not be any more doubt that we had to deal with one, not with two subjects; not with two sets of phenomena but with a single universe of events in which a single set of laws was in force."[3]

It is clear there is a unity of relationship between UFO categories and the occult: (Refer to chart on next page.)

On what basis does the UFO researcher make arbitrary distinctions when similar phenomena are involved in all the categories in both fields? The parallel is not exact, but it would not be expected to be so. For example, whereas contactees are not normally abducted against their will (they do not need to be) or examined, they do have the same trip on a spaceship that some abductees have. Whereas mediums do not generally go on a spaceship, they do go on astral flights, sometimes to other planets. We have to keep in mind that the intent of demons is simply to *deceive* and *subjugate*. This is done in many different ways and by many different means. In some cases they "abduct" people. In other cases when people *want* to be contacted, they do not need to "abduct" them. In most cases, they accomplish their goals — increased public exposure to UFO's, contacts and revelation given, people's views changed. There does not have to be exact parallels in all UFO categories to show they are all demonic manifestations. In some cases they present "religious" (but generally non-Biblical) revelations; in other cases they give anti-religious "revelations." It all depends on their purposes and with whom they are dealing. So even though there are some differences in the phenomena and manifestations, there is a clear underlying unity of purpose, of *basic* phenomena and of impact. However, even though the relationship is not exact, there are always exceptions, so that

	CE I	CE II	CE III	Abductions/Examinations	Contactees
UFO WORLD	X_o	Environmental Effects Animate & Inanimate — A	Entities: human, humanoid Monster/Anthropoid — B	Trips on Spaceship Physical exams, messages/ Communication from entities — C	Supernatural Contact via occult Means:Messages — D
OCCULT WORLD	No Parallel — X_1	Teleportation, Telekinesis Poltergeists, Animal Fear — 1	Entities human (Yogananda's Master), Monster/Anthropoid, Humanoid — 2	Same things in Astral Flight Eckankar, the I AM Group, Hare Krishna, etc. and Shaman initiation — 3	Mediumism — Same Thing — 4

nearly every category has some common elements with the others. (Refer to comparative chart on previous page.)

D has elements in common with C,E,A and 4,3,2,1 and X_0
C has elements in common with D,B,A and 4,3,2,1 and X_0
B has elements in common with D,C,A and 4,3,2,1 and X_0
A has elements in common with B,C,D and 4,3,2,1 and X_0
4 has elements in common with 3,2,1 and A,B,C,D and X_0
3 has elements in common with 4,2,1 and A,B,C,D and X_0
2 has elements in common with 4,3,1 and A,B,C,D and X_0
1 has elements in common with 2,3,4 and A,B,C,D and X_0

On Categories of LTS (lights in the sky) and CE-I, we should note the presence of blobs of light in seances and on astral flights.

Simply because the entities communicate or have their impact in a different manner (i.e. abductions, contactees, mediums) is no reason to say they have a different nature or source. Their methods are numerous. They accomplish their goals by deceiving some people through "occult illumination" or mediumship, or others through contactees, abductions, and other UFO phenomena. Some are deceived in both areas. Communication with the entities also has parallels in the physical/psychological/philosophical impact on humans, particularly in the sense of altering a person's metaphysical view in line with that of occultism, in their psychic-occult aspects, and in the fostering of a belief in the plurality of inhabited worlds or spheres of existence.* Both UFO and occult phenomena, it should be remembered, encompass physical, non-physical, and quasi-physical elements. With the ability to manipulate sensory input in the brain, there is no way of distinguishing between them. A particularly good discussion of this and numerous parallels between UFO and occult phenomena is found in Luis Schonherr's "The Question Of Reality," (*Flying Saucer Review*, Vol. 17, No. 2), and Pierre Guerin's (Principal Research Officer in the French National Center for Scientific Research) "Concerning the Profound Unity of Paranormal Phenomena," (*Flying Saucer Review*, Vol. 21, No. 5). The article by Guerin is a key article for seeing the unity between UFO-occult phenomena. He brings out numerous parallels between them and ties in the contactee-CE-III cases by noting parallels.

In CE-III cases, the entities do not give long philosophical-type discourses, but there are numerous cases where they have given contactee-type messages. Since it has been determined that the average time

---

*One interesting possible dissimilarity is that abductions usually involve semi-humanoids, whereas CE-III are mostly human, and contactees are all human entities. However, even here there is considerable overlap except in the contactee category, e.g. in the Cisco Grove and Sutton cases.

of a UFO's duration on the ground is 5-10 minutes, we would not expect to see the entities giving long discourses in the landing-occupant cases. They may want merely both to document the contactee message, and/or provide a basis for the extraterrestrial theory, i.e., mankind would expect things like the Close Encounters of the third kind (CE-III) phenomena. However, at the same time, in both abductions and landing-occupant cases, contactee-messages are sometimes given, even in short form. It follows that they are of the same source. Dr. Guerin concludes:

> And so, it seems, the situation still remains. And we can now sum up what we have said above: namely that, beneath diverse forms, one same, single paranormal phenomenon executes incursions from time to time into this physical world which we hold to be rational, while always carefully refraining from leaving behind any absolutely indisputable direct proofs of its reality. Consequently we are unable to form any judgment as to its reality except through an individual study of the best eyewitness accounts and a careful comparison of them (so long as they are independent of one another and not influenced the one by another). Such a comparison brings to light these concordances and similarities which I have set forth above and is an argument in favor of the reality and, above all, of the single and undivided nature of the phenomenon, but still without telling us what it is, nor who it is that manipulates us through it. God, the Devil, the Dead, the Extraterrestrials, etc., etc., all these are but the successive names given by the Entities, or the Entity, responsible for the phenomenon.[4]

Continued experimentation is just what the demons want — to make people think there really is something worth studying, yet always eluding their grasp. This equals *control* on their part. Aime Michel, after a study of Guerin's law (basically, that any UFO law is subsequently falsified by further sightings, as soon as it is formulated) concludes "they" deliberately keep researchers involved by selective control of the quality and content of UFO information: "This is why 'they' or 'somebody,' or 'something' is showing us just enough for us to have no possible doubt that (a) there *is* something; and (b) that it is very important. This is precisely what the mouse in the maze knows."[5]

ABDUCTION EXPERIMENTS

We would like to give one example of parallels between several categories of UFO and occult phenomena.

Often in abduction experiences, people report being medically examined by aliens with medical instruments, i.e. having blood samples taken, stomach fluid withdrawn by syringe, etc. The following case was investigated by Dr. J. Allen Hynek and reported in brief in the *Flying Saucer Review*. Reportedly, on August 26, 1976, Mrs. Sandy Larson, her daughter, and her daughter's boyfriend, were taken on board a UFO and given complete medicals. Mrs. Larson underwent hypnotic regression by Dr. Leo Sprinkle of the University of Wyoming. According to a news report, she stated under hypnosis:

> A creature with elastic bandages for a head, or elastic
> bandages around its head subjected her and her daughter's
> boyfriend to a complete medical examination, stripped
> naked, and all parts of the body examined . . . even our
> heads were opened and all parts of our brains looked at . . .
> we were dissected like frogs.[6]

TRUE EVIDENCE OF AN
ABDUCTION BY ALIENS ON A
PHYSICAL SPACECRAFT?

Consider the following accounts of Shaman initiation of the medicine man of the Unmatjera tribe of Central Australia. (Shaman initiations are hallucinatory experiences of a supernatural nature that qualify a person to become a shaman and involve numerous experiences with spirits and periods of temporary insanity.) "In the majority of instances, the initiation consists of an ecstatic experience, during which the candidate undergoes certain operations performed by mythical Beings, and undertakes ascents to Heaven or descents to the subterranean world."[7] Not much different from a UFO abduction!

Shaman initiation has numerous parallels to all types of UFO encounters, from sightings, to close encounters, to abductions, and contactees. These include: (1) the percipient is selected for the experience by the spirits; (2) aerial flights and visits to other realms that can be described in intricate detail; (3) apparitions and hallucinations of beings with various functions; (4) teleportations; (5) the production of psychic substances on the physical plane, e.g. ectoplasmic substances; (6) trance and dream states; (7) mysterious lights; (8) succubae phenomena with female spirits (they even marry the spirits); (9) possession; (10) poltergeist phenomena; (11) physical and psychological illnesses to the percipient; (12) control over animals; (13) psychic healing; (14) prophecy given by the entities; (15) and, finally, the entities are at times responsible for the death of people.[8] Hence we see that it is hardly necessary to posit "extraterrestrial intervention" to explain the UFO phenomena. Very similar things have been going on for millennia in the world of the occult.

Further documentation for the unity of CE-I, II, III and contactee and abduction categories is provided in abundance by a close analysis of the UFO literature. The following in particular are representative. All references are from fifty articles of the *Flying Saucer Review*, which is, according to Dr. Hynek, "The best UFO magazine in the world."

CE-I + Contactees[9]
Abductee + Contactee[10]
CE-I, CE-III + Mediumism[11]
CE-III + Contactee[12]
Abduction + Mediumism[13]
CE-I + Entities[14]
CE-III + Mediumism[15]
CE-I, CE-II, CE-III, Abductions, Contactee + Poltergeist[16]
CE-II + Abduction + LTS[17]
CE-I, CE-II, CE-III, Mediumism, Contactees[18]
Contactees; Mediumism, CE-I[19]
CE-II, CE-III, Contactee[20]
CE-I, CE-II, CE-III, Contactee, Mediumism[21]
CE-I, CE-II, CE-III (Abduction probable)[22]
CE-II, CE-III, Occult & Poltergeist, Psychic Witness[23]
CE-II, Abduction, Mediumism[24]
CE-I, CE-II, Abduction, Occultism, Contactee[25]

These are simply 17 cases: we have listed the general category and not specific details. Many cases involved things like teleportation, mediumism, telepathic contact, paralysis, etc., but we have simply listed the topic designation such as CE-II, abduction, etc.

Further documentation can be found in numerous other cases.[26] These cases (found in footnote No. 26) are only a few more of all the available articles that show the unity of all UFO and occult phenomena. *To an unbiased researcher these fifty articles clearly document that unity.* Hence, for the Christian, since contactee phenomena is clearly demonic, so is all the rest.

We could provide examples of a hundred or so particulars of correlation. However, only a few will be noted: nighttime occurrence; telepathic contact; messages; percipient an excellent hypnotic subject; entities have difficulty with extremities; paralysis (temporary); no visible facial features; marks or symbols left on body; mechanical voices, EM effects, etc. John Keel has even noted the similar appearance of entities of both the CE-III-contactee phenomena and "the men-in-black" phenomena.[27]

Some of the best articles for indicating the overall correlations and overlap between all categories of UFO and occult phenomena are listed in reference twenty-eight.[28]

Footnotes: Appendix A

1. *The Edge of Reality*, p. 202.
2. *The Invisible College*, p. 17.
3. Ibid., p. 186.
4. FSR, Vol. 21, No. 5, p. 17.
5. FSR, Vol. 20, No. 3, p. 9.
6. FSR, Vol. 22, No. 1, p. iii.
7. Eliade, Mircea, *From Medicine Men to Muhammad* (Harper and Row, 1974) p. 8, 7 of p. 3-25.
8. Harner, M.J., (ed.) *Hallucinogens and Shamanism* (New York: Oxford, 1973) esp. p. 21-6, 169-73 and Ibid.
9. FSR, Special Issue No. 2, "Canada's UFO Poltergeist," p. 63-66.
10-11. FSR, Special Issue No. 5, p. 21 "Itaperuna: 1970-71," "Stella Lansing's Movies; Four Entities and a Possible UFO." (Lansing is a medium: Both mediums and contactees are excellent hypnotic subjects.)
12-13. FSR, Special Issue No. 3, "Gary Wilcox and the Ufonauts," p. 20, "UFO's and Parapsychology," p. 33.
14. FSR, Vol. 22, No. 1, "Diving UFO with Occupants."
15. Ibid., "Benacazon Landing and Two Humanoids," and postscript.
16. FSR, Vol. 22, No. 2, p. 11-22, "The Main Encounter" parts 1-3.
17. FSR, Vol. 22, No. 2, "The Cyrus Case."
18. FSR, Case Histories, supplements 12, 15, 16, "The Investigations of General Uchoa in Brazil," parts 1-3.
19. FSR, Vol. 20, No. 4, "The mysterious Ummo Affair" and parts 2-5.
20. FSR, Vol. 4 and 5, "The Extraordinary Case of Rejuvenation," p. 16 (of parts 1-3).
21. FSR, Vol. 17, No. 1, "Muzios Contacts" (Muzio is a medium).
22. FSR, Vol. 21, Nos. 3 and 4, "The Anthropomorphic Phenomena at Santa Isabel, part 2."
23. FSR, Vol. 20, No. 2; 20:3; 21:3 and 4, "The New Berlin Case."
24. FSR, Vol. 21, Nos. 3 and 4, "The Case of the 'Greenmen'."
25. FSR, Vol. 21, No. 2, "Escorted By UFO's From Umvuma to Beit Bridge," "Investigation under Hypnosis: Contact Revealed."
26. FSR, Vol. 21, No. 1, p. 3, 14, 26 (three articles); Vol. 20, No. 1, p. 3; Vol. 19, No. 6, p. 6, 16 (two articles); Vol. 16, No. 6, p. 12, 14, 18, 23 (four articles); Vol. 16, No. 4, p. 8, 15, 27 (three articles); Vol. 19, No. 1, p. 3, 7, 18, 28 (four articles); Vol. 19, No. 2, p. 6, 10, 18, 26 (four articles); Vol. 16, No. 3, p. 16, 25 (two articles); Vol. 17, No. 3, p. 11, 14, 21 (three articles).
27. *The Mothman Prophecies*, p. 20.
28. a. FSR, Vol. 19, No. 2, E.A.I. MacKay "UFO Entities: Occult and Physical."
    b. FSR, Vol. 21, No. 2, p. 3-11, The Peter and Frances Case.

c. FSR, Vol. 22, No. 2, p. 7-23, The Main Encounter.

d. FSR, Vol. 19, No. 4, p. 10, The Ventura Maceiras Case.

e. FSR, Vol. 20, No. 4, The Ummo Case.

f. FSR, Special Issue 3, The Case of Dr. "X".

g. FSR, Case Histories, Nos. 12, 15, 16, The Investigations of General Uchoa.

h. FSR, Vol. 16, No. 4, "UFO's and the Occult" — 1.

i. FSR, Vol. 20, No. 2, (3 parts: Vol. 21, Nos. 3 & 4, p. 22; Vol. 20, No. 2, p. 21; Vol. 20, No. 3, p. 24), The New Berlin Case.

j. FSR, Vol. 19, No. 6, The Bebedouro Case (c.f. FSR Vol. 21, No. 3 & 4).

k. FSR., Vol. 20., No. 1, "Berserk: A UFO Creature Encounter."

l. FSR, Vol. 21, No. 1, The Stella Lansing Case (of Special Issue No. 5, FSR).

m. FSR, Vol. 20, No. 3, " 'Parallelism' as a Terminology and Classification for concepts in Ufology."

n. FSR, Vol. 17, No. 3, The Trancas Case.

o. FSR, Vol. 15, No. 5, "UFO's and Signs of the Times."

p. The Brian Scott Case (personally investigated) of FSR, Vol. 22, No. 3, p. 18.

q. FSR, Vol. 16, No. 3, "On Unipeds and Asparagus."

r. FSR, Vol. 21, No. 5, The Santa Isabel Case.

s. FSR, Vol. 16, No. 5, "A weird Encounter in Utah."

t. FSR, Vol. 22, No. 3, "Hypnotic Regression of Alleged Close Encounter III cases."

u. (Further refs; *The Humanoids*, pp. 84-130, 143-177; Mufon 1976 Symp. Proceedings p. 30; *The Edge of Reality*, p. 202, 250.

Appendix B
LIFE BY CHANCE IN OUTER SPACE: POSSIBLE OR IMPOSSIBLE

It is rapidly becoming almost a dogma among some scientists that since life started by chance on earth and evolved into what we now have, the same must have happened elsewhere. But the chances of this are so remote that they are beyond possibility. Unfortunately, though scientific calculations show more clearly than ever that life could not start *any* time or *any* place by chance, scientists are generally unwilling to accept the conclusions these calculations present.

In the October, 1969, issue of *Nature* magazine, Dr. Frank Salisbury of Utah State University, currently on leave at the Division of Biomedical and Environment Research at the U.S. Atomic Energy Commission, examined the chance of one of the most basic chemical reactions for the continuation of life taking place. This reaction involves the formation of a specific DNA molecule. It is important to realize that Dr. Salisbury was assuming that life *already* existed. His calculations do not refer to the chance of the *origin* of life from dead matter — something infinitely more improbable — but to the continuance of life already existing.

He calculated the chance of this molecule evolving on 10^{20} hospitable planets, or one hundred, thousand, million, billion planets. This is a figure with twenty zeros after it and is at least 1,000 times *more* hospitable planets than the number many scientists have estimated could exist. Dr. Salisbury allows four billion years for the chance coming into existence of this molecule on all these planets.

But remember he is not speaking here of life as we know it — developed, intelligent living beings, or even of *one* single cell for that matter. He is only calculating the chance of this one appropriate DNA molecule.

He concluded that the chances of just this one tiny DNA molecule coming into existence over four billion years, with conditions just right, on just one of these almost infinite number of hospitable planets, including the earth, as *one chance* in 10^{415}. This is a number with 415 zeros after it. Such a large number is unimaginable, as we will see. Here is how 10^{415} looks in print: 10,000 (thousand) 000 (million) 000 (billion) 000 (trillion) 000 (quadrillion), 000. Even if we packed the entire universe with hospitable planets, so no space was left between them, the chance of this molecule forming on all these planets would still be *one* chance in a figure with 377 zeros after it.[1] This shows that life simply could not originate in outer space, period. But, you ask, isn't there still *one* chance in a number this size, even if it is so large? Given enough time, wouldn't eventually *anything* happen?

Dr. Emile Borel, one of the world's great experts on mathematical probability, formulated a basic law of probability. It states that the occurrence of any event where the chances are beyond one in 10^{50} — a much smaller figure than what we have been dealing with — is an event which we can state with certainty will *never* happen — no matter how much time is alloted, no matter how many conceivable opportunities could exist for the event to take place.[2] In other words, life by chance is mathematically impossible on earth or any place else.*

A rather humorous example will help us to understand the size of very large numbers. Suppose that an amoeba, that microscopic little creature, were given the job of moving the entire universe — the earth, the solar system, all the stars, all the galaxies etc., *one atom* at a time. He had to carry each atom across the entire universe, a distance of thirty billion light years (A light year is the distance light travels in a year going at the speed of 186,000 miles per second). To top it off, he had to carry these atoms at the incredibly slow traveling speed of one *inch* every 15 *billion* years. If this amoeba, traveling one inch in 15 billion years over such a vast distance, moved atom by atom not just one universe, but six hundred thousand trillion trillion trillion trillion universes the size of ours, the number of years it would take him would be "only" 10^{171} years.[3] This is almost infinitely smaller than 10^{415}, the chance that for all practical purposes the universe could evolve one appropriate DNA molecule necessary for a certain chemical reaction!

If you want a *really* big number, try calculating the chance of life *itself* evolving on just *one* planet, i.e., the earth. Dr. Carl Sagan of Cornell University estimated this to be roughly one chance in ten followed by two *billion* zeros.[4] A number this large would fill over 6,000 books this size just to write it out. A number this size is so infinitely beyond 10^{50} (Borel's upper limit for an event to occur) it is simply mind-boggling.

As scientists have faced the logical conclusions of their own research and theories, they have been slow to accept the implications. Dr. George Wald, Nobel prize-winning biologist of Harvard University, stated several years ago: "One only has to contemplate the magnitude of this task to concede that the spontaneous generation of a living organism is impossible. Yet here we are — as a result I believe, of spontaneous generation."[5] This statement might cause us to wonder about the rational thinking of so great a scientist. But a year earlier Dr. Wald stated what evidently was the real problem: "The reasonable view was to believe in spontaneous generation; the only alternative, to believe in a single, primary act of supernatural creation. There is no third position. For this reason many scientists a century ago chose to regard the belief in spontaneous generation as a philosophical necessity. . . . Most modern biologists, having viewed with satisfaction the downfall of the spontaneous generation hypothesis, yet unwilling to accept the alternative belief in special creation, are left with nothing."[6] And the outstanding biologist D.H. Watson once stated, "If so, it will present a parallel to the theory of evolution itself, a theory universally accepted not because that it can be proved by logically coherent evidence to be true, but because the only alternative, special creation, is clearly incredible."[7] In other words, if I face the alternative of believing a scientific impossibility or believing in the more sensible alternative of a supernatural creator, as a good, rational scientist, I choose to believe in a scientific impossibility! Dr. Coppedge has an interesting summation for us: "The margin by which chance fails is so vast that no conceivable amount of new discovery along this line could change the basic conclusion that complicated working systems do not arise by chance."[8]

The scientific community has, apparently, never adequately answered Salisbury's article, even though he issued a call for them to solve the dilemma he encountered. In fact, in the five years since the article appeared, there has even been little discussion of it; apparently because its conclusions and implicatons are too unsettling or embarassing.

It is interesting to note, however, that Salisbury himself has an interest in UFO's and may be willing to concede that extraterrestrials might exist.[9] This does not mean his calculations are wrong. Dr. James G. Coppedge, Director, Probability Research In Biology, was kind enough to check them for me and he declared them quite sound. That Dr. Salisbury shows an interest in the whole extraterrestrial idea is a good example of the attitude expressed by Dr. Wald when he agreed the spontaneous generation of life was impossible, but believed it, because, after all, "here we are." Since man does exist, spontaneous generation must have occurred. And after all, since the UFO's are here, life must exist in outer space. We see that even though Dr. Salisbury's calculations show that life could not exist in outer space, he still thinks UFO's might be real — because after all, here they are! That even some scientists will believe in the impossible only goes to show they are setting up themselves, as well as others, for what might ultimately be the greatest mass deception ever.

Recently, the eminent Nobel prize winner, Dr. Francis Crick, theorized that life on earth might have originated from a spore of life planted long ago by some outer space civilization. This type of reasoning is due mostly to the fact that some scientists are having increasing difficulties believing that life could arise by chance. If however, life was planted here, this supposedly solves the problem. In reality it doesn't solve anything — it just pushes the question back a notch. Where did the life that created us then come from? At some point in the past life had to have originated by chance, and then we are back where we started with our original question — where did life come from? There is one question, however that is answered by this type of reasoning. It shows how far even brilliant men will go to escape the idea of God being their Creator. It is a sad commentary on the human condition when we find a belief in the obvious replaced by a belief in the impossible. Clearly, God Himself had no second thoughts:

"It is I who made the earth, and created man upon it. I
stretched out the heavens with my hands, and I ordained
all their host" (Isaiah 45:2).

Footnotes: Appendix B

1. 10^{58} planets would pack the universe with earth-size planets. *Elsewhere, Borel uses a figure of 10^{200} in calculations relating to the sciences, however 10^{200} is very *extreme* concession. The figure of 10^{50}, which Borel himself uses, is more reasonable. Even if we used the 10^{200} figure, however, this would change nothing.

2. Borel, Emile, *Probabilities and Life* (New York: Dover, 1962), chapters one and three.

3. Coppedge, James, *Evolution: Possible or Impossible* (Grand Rapids: Zondervan, 1974), pp. 118-120.

4. Sagan, Carl, ed., *Communication With Extra-Terrestrial Intelligence* (MIT Press, 1973), p. 46.

5. Taken from Henry Morris and John Whitcomb in *The Genesis Flood* (Nutley: Presbyterian and Reformed, 1971), p. 234.

6. Taken from R. Clyde McCone, "Three Levels of Anthropological Objection to Evolution" in the *Creation Research Society Quarterly*, March 1973, p. 208. Used by permission.

7. Taken from Henry Morris, ed., *Scientific Creationism* (San Diego: Institute for Creation Research, 1974), p. 8.

8. Coppedge, p. 113.

9. *Proceedings of the 5th APRO UFO Symposium*, p. 22.

Appendix C
THE BIBLE AND FLYING SAUCERS

This appendix will deal primarily with the theory that all the supernatural elements in the Bible are a result of flying saucers or their inhabitants. There are many books written on the subject (at least 15), a few by respectable men. The following three examples can be considered representative of many who have attempted to correlate events in the Bible with flying saucers. R.L. Dione "a practicing Catholic teacher" who has the B.S. and M.A. degree is the author of *God Drives a Flying Saucer*. Barry Downing has his B.D. degree from Princeton Theological Seminary and his Ph.D. from the University of Edinburgh. He is the pastor of Northminster Presbyterian Church, Endwell, New York. He wrote *The Bible and Flying Saucers*. Joseph F. Blumrich, author of *Spaceships of Ezekiel* is a NASA engineer who "spent 18 months scientifically analyzing the first chapter of the Book of the Prophet Ezekiel and believes that Ezekiel had indisputable contact with a UFO."[1]

BOOK ONE: GOD DRIVES A FLYING SAUCER

The first book *God Drives a Flying Saucer*[2] begins with this statement by the author:

> I present the material in this book, not as a theory based on some sort of mystical revelation [perhaps a reference to contactee revelations] or metaphysical hunch, but rather as a collection of pure, hard facts — facts based on statistical evidence — which, along with some elementary logic, leads to the following startling conclusions:

1. Flying saucers are not only real, but closely associated with the Christian religion . . . .

6. Flying saucer occupants are responsible for the scriptures, prophecies, and miracles of the Christian religion.

7. God is not supernatural, but rather supertechnological and is capable of all acts and all characteristics hitherto attributed to miraculous powers. That he created man in his image is not a myth or a parable; for God, while humanoid, is nevertheless immortal through technology.

    All of these conclusions will be documented, explained, and proved in the pages that follow."[3]

Remember his assertions: "pure, hard facts," "conclusions will be . . . proved."

One of the major biases of this book is the author's set of presuppositions: The miraculous simply does not occur. Everything that seems supernatural is explained as resulting from advanced technology. To Dione reason is the measure of all things. Technology can explain everything. Unfortunately, he uses Biblical material when it fits his theories, but he ignores anything which would contradict them.

This is Dione's definition of God:

    "The leader of the master technologists"[4] who (1) knows our thoughts and answers prayers by computers,[5] (2) perhaps heals blinded eyes by laser beams,[6] (3) perhaps used hypnotism causing hallucinations to produce the star of Bethlehem,[7] (4) is limited and dishonest, "something other than a perfect spiritual being,"[8] and (5) "By the use of hypnotism He created the twisted, blinded, and insane subjects whom Jesus was to cure at a later date."[9]

Some of his other statements claim (1) Adam and Eve were three or four feet tall;[10] (2) practically all of Jesus' miracles are explainable in terms of flying saucer devices (which Dione has never seen).[11] Dione notes that the virgin birth of Christ is one of the exceptions, but "We can be reasonably certain, however, that a biological specialist, the angel Gabriel, used the hypnotizing device [the Holy Spirit[12]] prior to and during the artificial insemination of Mary; and to insure that she retained her virginity, Gabriel undoubtedly used a hypodermic needle." "This explanation is not heresy . . . ;"[13] (3) There is "no doubt" that the Holy Spirit is God's brain-manipulating device;[14,15] (4) "A hypnotically induced paralytic condition resembling death" accounts for Jesus' ability to raise the dead;[16] (5) What sets God apart from man is his technological superiority;[17] (6) Dione strongly implies that the God of the Bible is insecure, a psychopath, and a braggart;[18] (7) Heaven is only a supertechnological society — and pitiable at that;[19] (8) God is basically playing a game with man. "As part of the game, God has told us . . . ." "God obviously gets carried away with His games;"[20] (9) The star of Bethlehem was a hovering luminous flying saucer;[21] (10) Jesus was in continual contact with a UFO, usually hidden in the clouds. This UFO made it seem as if he was doing the following miracles — feeding the 5,000; Saul's blindness; walking on the water; also the crucifixion and resurrection "indicated that a UFO was involved."[22]

Dione also refers to the Fatima miracle which he believes was a "revelation" from "God." This miracle was obviously not from God, because it involved elements of the Roman Catholic Church which are opposed to the Bible. The Bible teaches that Satan can easily do great miracles (Exodus 7:22, Job 1, II Thess. 2:9, etc.). The mother of Christ was a very blessed woman, but nothing more. She cannot intercede for the saints (I Tim. 2:5), is not to be worshipped (Luke 4:8), was not sinless (Romans 3:10-12), is not to be prayed to, and has no power over Jesus. Dione reports that at La Salette "Mary" stated, "If my people will not obey, I shall be compelled to loose my son's arm."[23]

Dione's approach has several aspects in common with others who use the Bible to substantiate their own non-Biblical theories or presuppositions:

1. The theory interprets Scripture; Scripture does not interpret itself.

2. Those aspects of Scripture which are clearly contrary to the theory are either ignored or, in opposition to accepted rules of interpretation, reinterpreted to fit the theory (the Urantia Book is a classic example).

3. Poor scholarship in general.

In Dione's case, his presupposition is pure rationalism:

Miracles can never occur once all the laws of nature are understood.[24]

Such a view (i.e., of a soul) is inconsistent with reason.[25]

Finally, with the following question, I direct one last fatal blow at the authenticity of Jesus' power as a supernatural healer. Why did he not, with one all-inclusive announcement, heal all the faithful afflicted of his time? There is no reasonable answer to this question except the admission that indeed he was not supernatural.[26] [i.e., because God does not do something means he is incapable of it!]

The occult rules supreme . . . as long as we admit and submit to the myth of miracles.[27]

In heaven we will not be spiritual or supernatural beings.[28]

Obviously, he doesn't like true miracles. Note Dione's views on inspiration:[29]

From all the evidence, it is apparent that God never

lies to his "divinely inspired" writers. Of course, this
doesn't mean that He tells all; but what He does tell is essentially true. . . .[30]

We can be reasonably certain that all historical elements in it are true and accurate.

I will show that the Bible, though divinely inspired,
was not supernaturally inspired. I will show and explain
how divine inspiration is a fact always imposed by a technological device on board a nearby UFO. And we shall see
that God always refers to this device as the Holy Spirit.[32]
[Elsewhere, the Holy Spirit is referred to as "the electromagnetic signal beamed from a UFO by God to His subjects"[33] and "the brain manipulating device."[34]]

Scripture denies this flatly — the Holy Spirit is the Third Person
of the Trinity and a Personal Being — He has an *intellect* (I Cor.
2:10, 11; Isaiah 11:2); *emotion* (Eph. 4:30, Romans 15:30); *will*
(I Cor. 12:11, Acts 16:6, 7, 10); He *teaches* (John 14:26); *guides*
(Romans 8:14); *commands* (Acts 8:29); *calls* (Acts 13:4); *sends* (Acts
10:19, 20); *intercedes* (Romans 8:26-27); can be *lied to* (Acts 5:3);
resisted (Acts 7:51); *blasphemed* (Matthew 12:31); *outraged* (Hebrews
10:29); He *comforts* (John 14:16); and *convinces* (John 16:8). Scripture declares Him to be God unequivocably: Acts 5:3, 4; John 15:26;
Acts 10:19, 28, 33 and 11:17, 18; Acts 28:26-27 plus Isaiah 6:9-10;
Hebrews 10:15-17 plus Jeremiah 31:31-4; I Cor. 3:16; Hebrews 1:1
plus II Peter 1:21; Heb. 9:14; Psalm 139:7; I Cor. 2:10, 11. (In my
opinion, the best book out on the subject of the co-equal deity of the
Father, Son, and Spirit is *The Trinity* by Edward Bickerseth.)

Dione claims to accept the authority of Scripture literally,[35] so let's
compare the Bible and Dione's view.

DIONE

"...God, while humanoid...to admit God is physical should detract nothing from His image...."[36]

"...is impossible to foretell — even for God."[37] Later he seems to contradict himself.[38]

"Jesus never exhibited fleshly weakness."[39]

"There is no supernatural spirit or soul — it is only physical and/or electromagnetic and may or may not be eternal."[40]

"Jesus never resurrected genuine cadavers."[41]

THE BIBLE

God is Spirit — John 4:24.

God is omniscient — Psalm 139.

In His humanity, Jesus exhibited weakness. He got tired (John 4:6), was distressed (Matt. 26:38), and weak (Luke 22:43-44).

Jesus said there was a soul in man (Mark 8:36-7; I Thess. 5:23) and that man was eternal (Matt. 25:46).

Jesus resurrected the truly dead (Matt. 9:25; Luke 7:12-16).

At other times, Dione states the Bible is not to be trusted, perhaps so that difficult areas (for him) can be explained away: ". . . at any rate, we know that at least some of its passages are correct."[42] Unfortunately, Dione never gives us *any* reason for rejecting just what the Bible claims — miraculous supernatural events. He only says they are too hard to believe in. "It should be much easier for anyone to picture a UFO removing the slab from the tomb (i.e., at Christ's resurrection) than to imagine an invisible, supernatural being shouldering it out of the way."[43] The only reason he finds miracles hard to believe is because of his own rationalistic premise. If a supernatural God exists, they are to be expected, not explained away. His biases also creep in and circumvent key Biblical doctrines. "Jesus, we can be sure, was not meant to die on the cross that day at Calvary. . . . there is little to indicate that he expected to suffer any great physical pain."[44] However, Christ said He expressly *came* to die (John 12:27; Matthew 20:28) as part of a foreordained plan (Luke 22:22; Acts 2:23) to save those who place personal faith in Him (John 3:16). Why did Christ sweat blood in the garden (medically — hematratosis), and why did He say His soul was greatly troubled to the point of death (Luke 22:44; Matthew 26:38) if indeed He did not expect to suffer?

In concluding, it is unfortunate Dione does not apply his own recommendation of "carefully reading the Scripture."[45]

Near the end of his book he notes:

> Faulty and mystical interpretations of the Bible have
> beclouded God's real purpose.[46]

How true.

BOOK TWO: THE BIBLE AND FLYING SAUCERS

The next book we consider is *The Bible and Flying Saucers* by Dr. Barry Downing. In a *Christianity Today*[1] review of Wilson's *Crash Go the Chariots*, he says he is "basically troubled by Wilson's work. I agree with him that the Bible must be the authority for Christians in dealing with the issues von Däniken is raising, but I do not think Wilson has really faced the issues squarely."[2] Then he presents his belief in UFO phenomena and relates it to the Bible. In this article he questions if all the angels are supernatural beings and implies some may be from another planet, with no Biblical support given. He believes if von Däniken changed the title of his book to *Chariots of God's Angels*, "he might not be far from the Biblical view." That this is an entirely false assessment is clear from Wilson's first work, his *The Chariots Still Crash*, Thiering and Castle's *Some Trust in Chariots*, and Story's *The Space Gods Revealed*. Von Däniken's latest book, *Miracles of the Gods*, is composed of little more than poor scholarship and heresy.

In an article in the *Flying Saucer Review*, a respected journal in the area of UFO's (Vol. 18, #3), Downing implied that God's wrath and Shekinah glory are both manifestations of the electromagnetic radiation of a UFO! Let us examine Downing's book and see how consistently he believes "that the bible must be the authority for Christians." Thirteen examples will be listed. We must again face the anti-supernatural bias.

1. The parting of the Red Sea was caused by intelligent beings in a space vehicle.[3] This clearly opposes Exodus 14:21; 30; 15:6, 8, 10, which states that God directly parted the sea — not some creatures "in a space vehicle."

2. Jesus may have ascended in a space vehicle.[1] "Ordinary white, fluffy cumulous clouds do not carry people off into space." Obviously, they do not. This was a miracle.

3. When a "cloud" is referred to in the Bible it refers to a space vehicle that "seems to look and operate very much like modern flying saucers."[5] The Greek and Hebrew words for cloud lend no support for this idea.

4. "We have to admit immediately that there is much historical evidence to support the view that much of the Biblical material is mythological."[6,7] Serious, unbiased scholarship lends no support to this idea.

5. "Bishop [John A. T.] Robinson has the right to maintain that the ascension is highly improbable, but it is by no means impossible in the light of present scientific thinking, particularly if one provides Christ with an adequate space vehicle. One may not be pleased with the theological implications of the suggestion . . . but the implications fit the evidence better than the suggestion that there was no ascension at all."[8] May we ask, what is wrong with a real ascension, like the one found in the Bible? Why will some people not take the Bible at face value? Why impose a biased system of anti-supernatural interpretation upon it?

6. Downing says that the Biblical UFO is called by many names: the "Lord," "the angel of God," "My angel," "My presence," etc. "Because of its various names, it is certainly difficult to come to a definite conclusion about the shape and size of the UFO. . . ."[9] [no wonder!] Thus, for him, God is apparently, a UFO.

7. Referring to the miraculous Exodus delivery from Egypt he asks "Is this history, myth, or a combination of both?"[10]

8. Moses seems to have received the ten commandments at Mount Sinai, from the "being" inside the UFO. Moses entered the UFO to receive the stone tablets."

9. The burning bush was a UFO inside the thicket.[12]

10. It was customary for Elijah to disappear in some sort of UFO, and the Spirit of the Lord is equated with the UFO.[13]

11. Moses and Elijah, at the mount of Transfiguration, departed by means of a UFO.[14]

12. Christ was baptized and carried into the wilderness by a UFO.[15] Since the Holy Spirit referred to here (Luke 3:22) is also referred to as the one who caused Mary to conceive, are we to believe Mary conceived Jesus by a UFO? (Luke 1:28)

13. The same vehicle Jesus ascended in brought Him to Paul on the Damascus road.[16] Obviously his views of the Bible are both inconsistent, biased, and opposed to the views held by Jesus and the true church (cf. Wenham's *Christ and the Bible*).

Downing speaks of "proper Biblical exegesis,"[17] yet rarely follows it. In reference to the above statements, he remarks: "We have not *proved* this is the case, but it seems quite likely — it has a fair degree of *probability*."[18] Elsewhere, he says his personal belief that the parting of the Red Sea was caused by a UFO is at "about 80 percent."[19] Yet elsewhere, he doesn't seem so sure:

> If we keep these problems in mind, we can partially understand why even the suggestion of a relation between the Bible and flying saucers seems ridiculous — which it may be.[20]
> I am most anxious to underline that I consider most of the hypothesis in this book to be quite tenative. I do not doubt that in time my perspective will seem very limited.[21]

We wonder why he has taken the trouble. He certainly does not help make the Bible (God's own words) very respectable by interpreting them to absurdity. As pastor of a church, it is unfortunate he holds to such a low view of Scripture.

Yet elsewhere he implies he is correct and that he is being consistent with the Bible. "The UFO theory I have outlined is certainly consistent in explaining the Biblical data."[22] Barry Downing states his own real problem: "While a study of the Biblical idea of truth might be useful, most of us undoubtedly share Pilate's confusion, "What is truth?"[23] (John 18:38).

Three further examples of his exegesis will indicate his low view of the Bible.

The Bible argues that the wind caused the sea to part

. . . but we are not thereby compelled to conclude that the
wind caused the sea to part.[24]

Moses remained at the top of the mountain to talk with
the Angel of God for long intervals of time — the Bible
suggests forty days and nights (Exodus 24:18), which is
the Bible's way of saying a long time.[25]

The Holy Spirit seems to be an invisible power from
another universe which is right in the midst of our universe.[26] [This is a far cry from the third person of the
Trinity — personal, infinite, eternal God.]

Downing chides others for a low level of scholarship in their writings concerning the Bible and UFO's.[27] It is hard to understand how
he can say this and remain consistent with his statement "the Bible
must be the authority for Christians." It appears it is little more to
him than a twisted guidebook, and hardly an authority.

Scripture states: "Be diligent to present yourself approved to God
as a workman who does not need to be ashamed, handling accurately
the word of truth" (II Tim. 2:15), and "Let not many of you become
teachers my brethren, knowing that as such we shall incur a stricter
judgment" (James 3:1).

BOOK THREE: THE SPACESHIPS OF EZEKIEL

NASA engineer, Joseph Blumrich, author of *The Spaceships of
Ezekiel*, had his interest in UFO's sparked by reading von Däniken's
first book, *Chariots of the Gods?* His book has been claimed to be proof
that at least, in part, von Däniken is correct. Although Blumrich was
at first a skeptic, he became quite convinced as he pursued his study.
The covert jacket of the book claims there is "startling proof" and
"evidence that will overpower you" inside.

Actually, his whole theory rests on a faulty premise. He never sat-
isfactorily proves that what Ezekiel saw was truly part of the real, objective world. His argumentation is that because it is so unlikely you
could have a record that fits the technological description of a spaceship, it cannot have been just a vision. It must have been real:

To wish to negate this self-contained evidence by continuing to speak of vision, dream, hallucination, or poetic
invention means to accept a long series of coincidences
which would indeed be needed to substantiate all the con-
gruities we have proved here. A juxtaposition of this acceptance of chance with the analytical and structural
argumentation illustrates best how untenable the former
attitude is.[1]

At this point we can make several comments.

1. *Even if* Blumrich's UFO interpretation were correct (which it is not), how can he say Ezekiel didn't see just a *vision* of what looked like a spacecraft, i.e., it was not part of the real world. Blumrich unnecessarily and unconvincingly extrapolates from a true *vision* which he *interprets* to be a spaceship, to the real world. "What remains fantastic is that such a spacecraft was a tangible reality more than 2500 years ago."[2]

2. The Biblical text, from which Blumrich *derives* his theory, clearly states Ezekiel had a *vision*. Just because Blumrich's interpretation "fits" modern technology, it does not demand that Ezekiel (a) saw a spaceship, either visionary or real, or (b) that what he saw was real, in the sense of being a part of his objective, tangible world. The Text is clear: Ezekiel 1:1 — "I saw *visions* of God;" Ezekiel 8:3 — "brought me in the *visions* of God to Jerusalem;" Ezekiel 11:24, 25 — "And the Spirit lifted me up and brought me in a *vision* by the Spirit of God to the Exiles in Chaldea. So the *vision* that I had seen left me. Then I told the exiles all the things the Lord had shown me;" Ezekiel 40:2 — "In the *visions* of God He brought me into the land of Israel . . .;" Ezekiel 43:3 — "And it was like the appearance of the *vision* which I saw, like the *vision* which I saw when He came to destroy the city. And the *visions* were like the *vision* which I saw by the river Chebar; and I fell on my face."

If the author wanted to imply that what was happening was *not* part of the objective world, i.e., that it *was* a vision, could he have written it any clearer? Blumrich ignores this. He must or he has no basis for his theory that the spacecraft was real and we have been visited from outer space. Blumrich gave up the idea of inviting the cooperation of an expert in ancient languages,[3] however, the Brown-Driver Briggs Lexicon defines the word *hazon* (the word Ezekiel uses) as a *"vision,* as seen in the ecstatic state." It is a vision as seen in an oracle or prophecy given by God and comes from the unseen world. An "appearance" of some more normal physical phenomenon is not described by this word. Just as John saw visions of what was going to happen in the future, so did Ezekiel (12:11). The visions concern the fact that the people were going to be taken away into exile. God even warns the people about *false* visions (Ezekiel 13:1-9) implying again that we are not dealing here with anything other than a prophetic vision of God's judgment on a rebellious people. (Ezekiel 43:2 proves this was a vision and not part of the objective world. I doubt Blumrich would admit to a literal view of the earth shining with God's glory. It is even less improbable with Blumrich's view of God being the spaceship.)

Now let us proceed to a general analysis of the book. First of all, he arbitrarily assumes that the technical parts of Ezekiel are not visions and vice versa: "In the course of these investigations it was tacitly assumed that the non-technical parts of Ezekiel's reports are visions."[4] He has no sound hermeneutical basis for doing this.

Also, Blumrich has to take Ezekiel out of his historic, cultural Jewish setting to even have a basis for his theories. This cannot be done and is *not* sound exegesis. Ezekiel would never have admitted to involvement with "space creatures." He was involved with *Yaweh*, the majestic, sovereign judge and ruler of the universe. Ezekiel knew his God — he would never have "bowed down to other gods," which would have been idolatry and blasphemy (Ezekiel 43:3). This was what he was sent to warn the people *against*.

Once Blumrich establishes his theory, then everything else is interpreted to fit it. Things which don't fit his theory, he either changes or deletes. This, in effect, destroys the whole base for his theory, because if Scripture is taken at face value, it means his theory doesn't stand. Several examples follow:

1. "Therefore, the statement in Verse 12 [Chapter 10]: 'And their whole body, and their backs, and their hands, and their wings, and the wheels were full of eyes round about . . .' can be regarded with certainty as incorrect."[5] Blumrich incorrectly attempts to make the description fit technology and vice versa, when it was never meant to in the first place. When it doesn't, he throws it out. ("Both descriptions rule out any disruptions of surfaces by structural patterns. Therefore, the statement in Verse 12 . . . can be regarded with certainty as incorrect.") What he doesn't understand is that there never were any "surfaces."

2. "Throughout this chapter [10] the helicopters [his interpretation of 1:5-6] are called cherubim, which justifies our speaking of helicopters in the plural (Plural form — im). On the other hand the use of the term 'living creatures' is confusing when it relates to the vehicle, since Ezekiel used it earlier to identify the helicopters."[6] Here Blumrich is hopelessly mixed up — his interpretation does not fit the text at all.

3. "Verse 24 and also verse 25 [Chapter 1] do not really belong here, because they describe the still-running rotors and attending phenomena, while verse 23 already gave a description of the UFO position at rest. This information is part of the description of the hover flight and the subsequent landing and should, therefore, be inserted between verses 14 and 15."[7] Again, the text must change to fit the theory.

4. "A superficial assessment would show this passage [10:3] as

an unnecessary and misplaced repetition of Chapter 9, verse 3."[8] Again, the theory and presupposition interprets Scripture — Scripture does not interpret itself.

5. "At the place where it occurs in the text, this verse [10:1] was inserted out of context and in fact disrupts the description of the progress of the action. It seems that it would best belong to Chapter 9, verse 3."[9]

6. "Besides, this verse [10:2] appears too early in the text. To be consistent with the course of events [i.e., his extrapolation of theory to text], it would belong to verse 6."[10]

7. "Chapter 10 generally presents some difficulties in its structure."[11] "But the most extended confusion of the text is encountered in Chapter 10. Here not only the basic action becomes mixed with structural descriptions, but the technical descriptions themselves are again incoherent, uneven, and repetitive."[12] We must point out again, that the only reason for this, is because the text description does not and was never intended to fit his tecnological application. So, part of verse 8 and all of verse 9 are "undeniably at the wrong place here,"[13] and Blumrich has to mention four places where the text must be fragmentary (i.e., part of it is missing). Thus when the text doesn't fit the theory, part of it must be missing or in error: "The new identification used here [the Lord] can therefore only be regarded as an error."[14]

8. Here is his general conclusion of Ezekiel's book: "The traditional text is therefore unmistakably a fragment. A mention of the return flight is missing . . ."[15] And he seems to agree that "we are not in possession of Ezekiel's original writing, but we have a revised text before us."[15a]

What follows is even more difficult to accept. Because "these quite noticable discrepancies in the text" do not fit with Ezekiel's "exceptional lucidity of mind and powers of observation," therefore "we can with full assurance eliminate Ezekiel as the direct writer of the book which has come down to us."[16] Thus, what we have occurring here is this: Blumrich first imposes his 20th Century theory on a 6th Century B.C. book, throws out the "discrepancies" which don't agree with his theory, and says that the author of the text itself (see Chapter 1) undoubtedly was not the author because he would have really written it differently and agreed with Blumrich's theory more exactly!

Blumrich's theory cannot stand the honest study of Jewish history and the rest of the Old Testament. Let's look at some of his interpretations and ask ourselves if the Jew Ezekiel would have ever agreed with them.

1. The "glory of the Lord" is Ezekiel's description of "the majestic spectacle of the flying spaceship."[17]

2. "The hand of the Lord" which he (Ezekiel) feels is "strong upon me" could simply have been the pressure of the shoulder strap holding him to his seat.[18] Or a hypnotic influence.[18a](Ezekiel 8:1 presents some problems to this view: What was Ezekiel doing sitting in a rocket ship in his own living room?)

3. l:4 is an account of a spaceship's blasting engines, which gave the impression "the heavens were opened."[19] (Verse 1)

4. "The hand of the Lord . . ." always introduces "the words as a kind of leitmotif — the encounter with the spaceship and its commander,"[20] yet by this analysis we are forced to the conclusion that the spaceship appeared inside Ezekiel's house on one occasion (8:1). A 60' diameter spaceship (p. 174) in your house might be a little awkward.

5. "God" is the commander of the spacecraft (40:2).[21]

6. Verse 24: (Chapter 11) "At the beginning we encounter again two already well-known expressions ["the spirit" and "in the vision of God"] which tell us that Ezekiel boards a spaceship and flies in it."[22]

7. A "mechanical arm" is used in 8:3.[23] The Spirit referred to here is "a wind."

8. ". . . brought me in visions of God. . . . always means Ezekiel's flight in the spacecraft."[24]

If "saucer theologians" would take the time to culturally and contextually study these expressions, they would find they offer no support to their theories. It is clear Blumrich is not interested in the possibility of discrediting his theory: "The investigation of the actual meaning of this expression [i.e., the "hand of the Lord"] does not belong among the objectives of this book."[25] Should not a careful researcher always attempt to find the historical and cultural meaning of a term before he attempts to base his theories on them? Blumrich finds an answer to one of his questions "when we again take Ezekiel at his word,"[26] but often he does not take Ezekiel at his word.[27]

Blumrich has a particular problem with the "eyes" of 1:18 — the context clearly implies the rims were full of eyes. He cannot allow this however. His rendering of 1:18 is: "and their rims were full of eyes round about."[28] Two parallel passages also are the same (Ezekiel 10:12; Rev. 4:6, 8). But later he changes the meaning of the context: "These round protrusions on the rims required for a mobility in two directions look to him 'like eyes'. "[29] Ezekiel did *not* say "*like* eyes," he said "full of eyes." Later Blumrich says the eyes are "dark openings," which look like eyes from a distance,[30] which is no better. The faces of 1:10 are also explained away as structural features: "Such a

combination of structure features can assume a certain resemblance
to faces or can best be described by such a comparison."[31] What
Ezekiel really saw was a vision of creatures in heaven, not UFO's or
aliens from another planet.

Blumrich is aware of the problem between the usual definition of
visions and real spaceships. He states: "We have proved that it was a
very real spaceship [sic]. But this realization confronts us with a conflict resulting from the incompatibility of visions and physical
presence of spaceships. This conflict can be resolved in two very different ways."[32]

He admits that his first resolution is an assumption: First he accepts the truthfulness of Ezekiel's vision — but he separates them so
that the "visions took place at a point in time different from that of
the encounters with spaceships."[33a] This is his *assumption*: but it has to
be true, or his case does not stand. However, the distinction is arbitrary. By his own admission, he has a fatal problem here. In three
of the four cases of contact with the "spaceship" (i.e., glory of the
Lord, hand of the Lord, etc.), visions *are* mentioned, and the context
shows a connection. *Nothing* in the context implies even a remote
hint of a separation of time. (See Ezekiel 1:1 + 15 + 8:3 and 40:1, 2.)

His statement that "the Biblical texts suggest this"[33b] (a separation
of time) is not true and anyone can verify this by reading the text for
himself. When he says there is only one link between spaceship and
vision,[34] he is wrong as we have just pointed out. There are three
links out of the four. Then he comments, trying to explain the "one"
link: "With the above clarification of its background we have done
away with this link and can therefore accept the separation in time as
a credible solution."[35] In his second solution the visions turn into
"statements made by the Commander [i.e., of the ship] and thus lose
their character of visions."[36] (!)

At one point, using evolutionary theories (common to all saucer
theologians), he "deduces" the space creatures have a skeleton and
skin and thus they would be expected to look "like a man" as Ezekiel
reports.[37,38,39] This is guesswork. Elsewhere he contradicts himself by
first saying that the UFO visitors knew human inhabitants and cus-
toms quite well, then saying the opposite.[40,41,42]

In conclusion, there is one truth Blumrich mentions on which we
are in agreement: "Of course, these results are in sharp contrast to
text interpretations by many devout and learned men during all the
past centuries."[43]

Footnotes: Appendix C

Book One

1. *National Enquirer*, interview — Feb. 3, 1974.
2. Dione, R. L., Bantam 1973.
3. Ibid., p. vii-viii.
4. Note #1, pp. 15, 66-7, 96-7, 101.
5. Ibid., p. 47-8.
6. Ibid., p. 45.
7. Ibid., p. 44.
8. Ibid., p. 66-7, 96-7, 50.
9. Ibid., p. 101.
10. Ibid., p. 95.
11. Ibid., p. 100.
12. Ibid., p. ix, 103-105.
13. Ibid., p. 100.
14. Ibid., p. 103.
15. Ibid., p. 104.
16. Ibid., p. 107.
17. Ibid., p. 98.
18. Ibid., p. 123.
19. Ibid.
20. Ibid., p. 121-5, 127.
21. Ibid., p. 101.
22. Ibid., p. 109.
23. Ibid., p. 49.
24. Ibid., p. 44-5.
25. Ibid., p. 87.
26. Ibid., p. 108-9
27. Ibid., p. 117.
28. Ibid., p. 129.
29. Ibid., p. 118.
30. Ibid., p. 101.
31. Ibid., p. 78.
32. Ibid., p. ix.
33. Ibid., p. 77.
34. Ibid., p. 80.
35. Ibid., p. 3.
36. Ibid., p. viii, p. 47.
37. Ibid., p. 50.
38. Ibid., p. 114.
39. Ibid., p. 114.
40. Ibid., p. 87-8, 93.

41. Ibid., p. 107, 102.
42. Ibid., p. 78.
43. Ibid., p. 115.
44. Ibid., p. 112-3.
45. Ibid., p. 87.
46. Ibid., p. 119.

Book Two

1. *Christianity Today*, Aug. 31, 1973, p. 30-31.
2. Ibid., p. 30.
3. Downing, Barry, *The Bible and Flying Saucers*, Avon 1970, p. viii.
4. Ibid., p. 17, 58.
5. Ibid., p. 18.
6. Ibid., p. 26.
7. Ibid., p. 27.
8. Ibid., p. 47-8.
9. Ibid., p. 70.
10. Ibid., p. 71.
11. Ibid., p. 93.
12. Ibid., p. 78.
13. Ibid., p. 103, 119.
14. Ibid., p. 113.
15. Ibid., p. 117, 122-3.
16. Ibid., p. 134.
17. Ibid., p. 153.
18. Ibid., p. 137.
19. Ibid., p. 182.
20. Ibid., p. 38.
21. Ibid., p. 184.
22. Ibid., p. 135.
23. Ibid., p. 34.
24. Ibid., p. 72-3.
25. Ibid., p. 90.
26. Ibid., p. 154.
27. Note 1, p. 31.

Book Three

1. Blumrich, Josef, *The Spaceship of Ezekiel*, Bantam, 1974, p. 145-6.
2. Ibid., p. 3.
3. Ibid., p. 52.
4. Ibid., p. 119.
5. Ibid., p. 88.

6. Ibid., p. 89-90.
7. Ibid., p. 67-8.
8. Ibid., p. 80.
9. Ibid., p. 82.
10. Ibid., p. 111.
11. Ibid.
12. Ibid.
13. Ibid.
14. Ibid., p. 112-114, 117, 75, 67, 112, 38.
15. Ibid., p. 108.
15a. p. 119.
16. Ibid., p. 114-115.
17. Ibid., p. 98.
18. Ibid., p. 73.
18a. p. 102.
19. Ibid., p. 54.
20. Ibid., p. 54.
21. Ibid., p. 93.
22. Ibid., p. 91.
23. Ibid., p. 103.
24. Ibid., p. 104.
25. Ibid., p. 102.
26. Ibid., p. 115.
27. Ibid., p. 118-122.
28. Ibid., p. 12.
29. Ibid., p. 17.
30. Ibid., p. 39.
31. Ibid., p. 57.
32. Ibid., p. 120.
33a. Ibid., p. 120.
33b. Ibid.
34. Ibid., p. 120.
35. Ibid., p. 120
36. Ibid., p. 120.
37. Ibid., p. 144.
38. Ibid., p. 129.
39. Ibid., p. 123.
40. Ibid., p. 21.
41. Ibid., p. 3.

BIBLIOGRAPHY

GENERAL WORKS

1. Baker, Douglas, *The Occult Significance of UFO's,* (Privately Published).
2. Bergier, Jacques, *Extra-Terrestrial Visitations from Pre-Historic Times to the Present,* (N.Y. Signet, 1974).
3. Bergier, Jacques, *Extra-Terrestrial Intervention: The Evidence,* (N.Y., Signet, 1975).
4. Blum, Ralph, *Beyond Earth, Man's Contact With UFO's,* (N.Y., Bantam, 1974).
5. Blumrich, Joseph, *Spaceships of Ezekiel,* (N.Y., Bantam, 1974).
6. Bowen, Charles, ed., *The Humanoids: A Survey of World-wide Reports of Landings of Unconventional Aerial Objects and Their Occupants,* (Chicago, Henry Regnery Co., 1969).
7. Gracewell, Ronald, *The Galactic Club: Intelligent Life in Outer Space,* (Stanford Alumni Association, 1974).
8. Catoe, Lynn, *UFO's and Related Subjects: An Annotated Bibliography,* Washington, 1969, U.S. Government Printing Office (Prepared by the Library of Congress Science and Technology Division for the Air Force

Office of Scientific Research Office of Aerospace Research, USAF, Arlington, Virginia 22209, Under AFOSR Project Orders 67-0002 and 68-0003, Library of Congress Card Catalogue Number 68-62196).

9. Clark, Jerome, and Coleman, Loren, *The Unidentified: Notes Toward Solving the UFO Mystery,* (N.Y., Warner, 1975).

10. Condon, Edward, *Scientific Study of Identified Flying Objects,* (N.Y., Bantam, 1969).

11. Constance, Arthur, *The Inexplicable Sky,* (N.Y., Citadel, 1956).

12. Crabb, Riley, *Flying Saucers and the Coming Space Probes,* (Borderland Sciences Research Assoc., San Diego).

13. David, J., ed., *The Flying Saucer Reader,* (N.Y., Signet, 1967).

14. Dione, R.L., *God Drives a Flying Saucer,* (N.Y., Bantam, 1973).

15. Downing, Barry, *The Bible and Flying Saucers,* (N.Y., Avon, 1970).

16. Edwards, Frank, *Flying Saucers — Serious Business,* (N.Y., Bantam, 1966).

16a. Ellwood, Robert, *Religious and Spiritual Groups in Modern America,* (Prentice Hall, 1975).

17. Emenegger, Robert, *UFO's Past, Present and Future,* (N.Y., Ballantine, 1974).

18. Flindt, Max, & Binder, Otto,

Mankind — Child of the Stars, (Greenwich, Conn., Fawcett, 1974).

19. Fuller, John, *The Interrupted Journey,* (N.Y., Berkeley Medallion, 1974).

20. Fuller, John, *Incident at Exeter,* (N.Y., Berkeley Medallion, 1974).

21. Gaddis, Vincent, *Mysterious Fires and Lights,* (N.Y., Van Rees Press, 1967).

22. Hobana, Ion, & Weverbergh, Julien, *UFO's from Behind the Iron Curtain,* (N.Y., Bantam, 1975).

23. Holiday, F.W., *Creatures from the Inner Sphere,* (N.Y., Popular Library, 1973).

24. Holter, Hans, *The UFO-Nauts,* (Greenwich, Conn., Fawcett, 1976).

25. Hynek, J. & Vallee, Jacques, *The Edge of Reality,* (Chicago, Henry Regnery Co., 1975).

26. Hynek, J., *The UFO Experience: A Scientific Inquiry,* (N.Y., Ballantine, 1974).

27. Jessup, M.K., *The UFO Annual,* (N.Y., Citadel, 1956).

28. Jessup, M.K., *The Case for the UFO,* (N.Y., Citadel, 1955).

29. Jacobs, David, *The UFO Controversy in America,* (N.Y., Signet, 1975).

30. Jung, Carl, *Flying Saucers,* (N.Y., Signet, 1969).

31. Kehoe, Donald, *Aliens from Space,* (N.Y., Signet, 1974).

32. Kehoe, Donald, *The Flying Saucer Conspiracy*, (N.Y., Holt & Co., 1955).
33. Kehoe, Donald, *Flying Saucers from Outer Space*, (N.Y., Holt & Co., 1953).
34. Keel, John, *Strange Creatures from Time and Space*, (Greenwich, Conn., Fawcett, 1970).
35. Keel, John, *UFO's: Operation Trojan Horse*, (N.Y., P. Putmans Sons, 1970).
36. Keel, John, *Our Haunted Planet*, (Greenwich, Conn., Fawcett, 1971).
37. Keel, John, *The Eighth Tower*, (N.Y., Saturday Review Press/E.P. Dutton & Co., 1975).
38. Keel, John, *The Mothman Prophecies*, (N.Y., Saturday Review Press/E.P. Dutton & Co., 1975).
39. Klass, Phillip, *UFO's Explained*, (N.Y., Random House, 1974).
40. Lorenzen, Coral & Jim, *Flying Saucer Occupants*, (N.Y., Signet, 1967).
41. Lorenzen, Coral, *Flying Saucers: The Startling Evidence of the Invasion from Outer Space*, (N.Y., Signet, 1966).
42. Lorenzen, Coral & Jim, *Encounters with UFO Occupants*, (N.Y., Berkeley Medallion Books, 1976).
42a. Lunan, Duncan, *The Mysterious Signals From Outer Space* (N.Y., Bantam, 1977).
43. McCampbell, James, *UFOLOGY:*

New Insights from Science and Common Sense, (Bellmont, Ca., Jaymac, Co., 1973).

44. McWayne, Glenn & Graham, David, *The New UFO Sighting*, (N.Y., Warner, 1974).

45. Michel, Amie, *The Truth About Flying Saucers*, (N.Y., Pyramid Books, 1967).

46. Michell, John, *The Flying Saucer Vision*, (N.Y., Ace, 1967).

47. Norman, Eric, *Gods and Devils from Outer Space*, (N.Y., Lancer, 1973).

48. Norman, Eric, *God, Demons and UFO's*, (N.Y., Lancer, 1970).

49. Sanderson, Ivan, *Uninvited Visitors*, (N.Y., Cowles, 1967).

50. Sanderson, Ivan, *Invisible Residents*, (N.Y., Avon, 1970).

51. Sagan, Carl & Paige, Thornton, eds., *UFO's: A Scientific Debate*, (N.Y., W.W. Norton & Co., Inc., 1972).

52. Shklovskii, I. & Sagan, Carl, *Intelligent Life in the Universe*, (N.Y., Dell Publ. Co., 1966).

53. Sagan, Carl, ed., *Communication with Extra-Terrestrial Intelligence*, (Cambridge, Mass., M.I.T. Press, 1973).

54. Simpson, George, *This View of Life*, (Harcourt, Brace & World, 1964).

55. Smith, Warren, *UFO Trek*, (N.Y., Zebra, 1976).

56. Steiger, Brad & Whritenour, Joan,

Flying Saucers Are Hostile, (N.Y., Award Books, 1976).

57. Steiger, Brad & Whritenour, Joan, *The UFO Breakthrough*, (London, Universal Tandam Publ. Co., 1973).

58. Steiger, Brad & Whritenour, Joan, *Flying Saucer Invasion: Target Earth*, (N.Y., Award Books, 1969).

59. Steiger, Brad, *The Aquarian Revelations*, (N.Y., Dell, 1971).

60. Stoneley, Jack, & Lawton, A.T., *CETI (Communication with Extra-Terrestrial Intelligence)*, (N.Y., Warner, 1976).

61. Stoneley, Jack, *Is Anyone Out There?*, (N.Y., Warner, 1975).

62. Sullivan, Walter, *We Are Not Alone*, (N.Y., Signet, 1966).

63. Thomas, Paul, *Flying Saucers Through the Ages*, (London, Universal Tandem Publ. Co., 1973).

64. Trench, Brinsley, *Mysterious Visitors: The UFO Story*, (N.Y., Stein & Day, 1971).

65. Trench, Brinsley, *The Flying Saucer Story*, (N.Y., Ace, 1966).

66. Vallee, Jacques, & Janine, *Challenge to Science: The UFO Enigma*, (N.Y., Ballantine, 1974).

67. Vallee, Jacques, *Anatomy of a Phenomenon: UFO's In Space, Scientific Appraisal*, (N.Y., Ballantine, 1965).

68. Vallee, Jacques, *The Invisible*

College (N.Y., E. P. Dutton & Co., 1975).

69. Vallee, Jacques, *Passport to Magonia,* (Chicago, Henry Regnier Co., 1969).

70. Vesco, Renato, *Intercept UFO,* (N.Y., Zebra, 1971).

71. Weldon, John, *UFO's: What On Earth Is Happening?,* (N.Y., Bantam, 1976).

72. Wilkins, Harold, *Flying Saucers Uncensored,* (N.Y., Pyramid, 1974).

73. Wilkins, Harold, *Flying Saucers on the Attack,* (N.Y., Ace, 1954).

74. Wilson, Clifford, *UFO's and Their Mission Impossible,* (N.Y., Signet, 1975).

75. Wilson, Clifford, *Crash Go the Chariots,* (San Diego, Master Books, A Division of CLP, 1976).

Journals, Symposia, Technical Reports and Articles

1. Andrus, Walter, N.J. Gurney, *Mufon Symposium Proceedings* for the years 1973-1976, *Mutual UFO Network,* 103 Oldtowne Rd., Sequin, Texas, 78155.

2. Dickinson, Terence, "The Zeta Reticuli Incident," published by *Astronomy Magazine, 1976).*

3. Emerson, A.D. (ed.), "Hypotheses Concerning the Origins of UFO's" *Thesis — Antithesis, American Institute of Aeronautics and*

Astronautics Symposium Proceedings, Sept. 27, 1975.

4. Hall, Richard (ed.), *The UFO Evidence,* published by NICAP (National Investigations Committee on Aerial Phenomena) Washington, D.C. 1964.

5. Kehoe, D. and Lore, G., *UFO's: A New Look* published by NICAP (above) 1969.

6. Lorenzen, Coral (ed.), *Proceedings of the 5th APRO UFO Symposium, June 15, 1974,* published by the Aerial Phenomena Research Organization, Tucson, Arizona.

7. Olmos, Vicente-Juan Ballester, *A Catalogue of 200 Type-1 UFO Events in Spain and Portugal,* published by Center for UFO Studies, Evanston, Ill., April 1976.

8. Pearman, J.P.T., "Extraterrestrial Intelligent Life and Interstellar Communication: An Informal Discussion" AIAA Technical Information Service No. A64-10238.

9. Phillips, Ted, *Physical Traces Associated with UFO Sightings,* published by Center for UFO Studies, Evanston, Ill., 1975.

10. Sturrock, Peter A., "UFO Reports from AIAA Members," *Astronautics and Aeronautics,* May 1974.

11. Webb, David, *1973 — Year of the Humanoids:* An Analysis of the Fall,

1973 UFO/Humanoid Wave, 1974 Oby David Webb (available from CFUFOS).

12. *Proceedings of the 1976 CUFOS Conference.* Center For UFO Studies, Box 11, Northfield, Ill. 60093.

13. *Flying Saucer Review (FSR)*, Vol. No. 1-23, West Malling, Maidstone, Kent, England.

CONTACTEE BOOKS

1. Adamski, George, *Inside the Flying Saucers,* (N.Y., Paperback Library, 1967).

2. Adamski, George, *Behind the Flying Saucer Mystery,* (N.Y., Warner, 1967).

3. Allan, W. Gordon, *Spacecraft from Beyond Three Dimensions,* (N.Y., Exposition Press, 1959).

4. Allingham, Cedric, *Flying Saucer From Mars,* (N.Y., British Book Center, 1955).

5. Angelucci, Orfeo, *The Secret of the Saucers,* (Amherst Press, 1955).

6. Barker, Gray, *They Knew Too Much About Flying Saucers,* (N.Y., University Books, 1956).

7. Beane, John W., *Flying Saucers Close Up,* (Clarksburgh, W. Virginia, 9/69 Published by Grey Barker).

8. Dutta, Rex, *Flying Saucer Message,*

(London, Pelham Books, 1972).

9. Fry, Daniel, *The White Sands Incident*, (Louisville, Ky., Best Books, Inc., 1966).

10. Fry, Daniel, ed., *Understanding Yearbook, 1958*, (Demonte, CA).

11. Geller, Uri, *My Story*, (N.Y., Warner, 1976).

12. Girvin, Calvin, *The Night Has A Thousand Saucers*, (Delmonte, CA, Understanding Publ. Co., 1958).

13. Ibrahin, Yosip, *I Visited Ganynede . . . The Wonderful World of UFO's*, (Unpublished English Manuscript published in the Spanish language by Evaristo Alprecht del Alcazar, Garcia *Airlé*s 515 Guayaquil, Equador S.A.).

14. James, Trevor, *They Live In The Sky*, (Los Angeles, New Age Publ. Co., 1958).

15. King, George, *The Three Saviors Are Here*, (Los Angeles, The Aetherius Society, 1967).

16. Leslie, Desmond, & Adamski, George, *Flying Saucers Have Landed*, (N.Y., British Book Center, 1953).

17. Mathes, J.H., Heuett, Lenora, *The Amnesia Factor*, (Millbrae, Ca., Celestial Arts, 1975).

18. Menger, Howard, *From Outer Space*, (N.Y., Pyramid Books, 1967).

19. Michael X, *Flying Saucer Revelations*, (Clarksburgh, W. Virginia, Saucerian Books, 1969).

20. Mustapa, Margit, *Spaceship to the Unknown,* (N.Y., Vantage Press, 1960).
21. Noonan, Allan-Michael, *To The Youth of the World: The Everlasting Gospel,* (Berkeley, The Universal Industrial Church of the New World Comforter, 1973, Starmast Publ.).
22. Palmer, Ray & Arnold, Kenneth, *The Coming of the Saucers,* (Privately published, 1952).
23. Puharich, Andrija, *URI,* (N.Y., Bantam, 1975).
24. Reeve, Bryant & Helen *Flying Saucer Pilgrimage,* (Amherst, Wisconsin, Amherst Press, 1957).
25. Sanctilean, *Flying Saucers — Portents of These Last Days,* (Santa Barbara, I.F. Rowny, 1950).
26. Steiger, Brad & Hewes, Hayden, *UFO Missionaries Extraordinary,* (N.Y., Pocket Books, 1976).
27. Stranges, Frank, *The Stranger at the Pentagon,* (Van Nuys, Ca., IEC Inc., 1972).
28. Stranges, Frank, *Saucerama,* (Van Nuys, Ca., IEC Inc., 1963).
29. Stranges, Frank, *Your Paradise Inside This Planet,* (Van Nuys, Ca., IEC Inc.).
30. Williamson, George, *Other Tongues — Other Flesh,* (London, Neville Spireman Ltd., 1965).
31. Nada-Yolanda, *Visitors From Other*

Planets, (Miami, Fla., Markage Meta Center Inc., 1974).

32. Zarkon, *The Zarkon Principle,* (N.Y., Signet, 1976).
33. *How To Do All Things: Your Use Of Divine Power,* (Miami, Fla., Markage Meta Center Inc., 1970).

OCCULT LITERATURE

1. Brennan, J.H., *Astral Doorways,* (N.Y. Samuel Weiser Inc., 1971).
2. Brown, Slater, *The Heyday and Spiritualism,* (N.Y. Pocket, 1972).
3. Buckland, Raymond and Carrington, Hereward, *Amazing Secrets of the Psychic World,* (West Nyack, N.Y.: Parker Pub. Co., 1976).
4. Conway, David, *Magic: An Occult Primer,* (N.Y. Bantam, 1973).
5. Cooke, Grace, *The Jewel in the Lotus,* (Hampshire England: White Eagle Pub. Trust, 1973).
6. Ebon, Martin (ed.), *The Satan Trap: Dangers of the Occult,* (Gardon City, Doubleday, 1976).
7. Ernest, Victor, *I Talked with Spirits* (Wheaton: Tyndale, 1971).
8. Fodor, Nandor, *An Encyclopedia of Psychic Science* (Secaucus, N.J. Citadel, 1974).
9. Flammonde, Paris, *The Mystic Healers,* (N.Y. Stein and Day, 1975).

10. Gasson, Raphael, *The Challenging Counterfeit,* (Plainfield: Logos, 1966).

11. Greenhouse, Herbert, *The Astral Journey,* (N.Y.: Avon, 1976).

12. Gruss, Edmond, *The Ouija Board: Doorway to the Occult,* (Chicago: Moody, 1975).

13. Hodson, Geoffrey, *Fairies at Work and at Play* (Wheaton: Theosophical Pub. Co., 1976).

14. Jayne, Watter Addison, M.D., *The Healing Gods of Ancient Civilizations,* (New Hyde Park, N.Y. University Books, 1962).

15. Koch, Kurt, *Between Christ and Satan,* (Grand Rapids: Kregel, 1962).

16. Koch, Kurt, *Christian Counseling and Occultism,* (Grand Rapids: Kregel, 1972).

17. _____, *Demonology: Past and Present,* (Grand Rapids: Kregel, 1973).

18. _____, *Occult Bondage and Deliverance,* (Grand Rapids: Kregel, 1970).

19. Mishlove, Jeffrey, *Roots of Consciousness,* (N.Y.: Random House, 1975).

20. Montgomery, J.W., *Principalities and Powers,* (Minneapolis: Bethany, 1973).

21. Montgomery, J.W. (ed.), *Demon Possession,* (Minneapolis: Bethany, 1976).